Studies in Creation

A General Introduction to the Creation/Evolution Debate

John W. Klotz

Publishing House
St. Louis

Copyright © 1985 Concordia Publishing House
3558 S. Jefferson Avenue, St. Louis, MO 63118-3968
Manufactured in the United States of America

Library of Congress Cataloging in Publication Data

Klotz, John W. (John William), 1918-
      Studies in Creation.
      1. Creation. 2. Evolution. 3. Religion and science—1946-   . I. Title.
BS651.K58 1985   231.7'65   84-27440
ISBN: 0-570-03969-X

1 2 3 4 5 6 7 8 9 10 MAL 94 93 92 91 90 89 88 87 86 85

To Florence,
my wife, companion, and fellow traveler,
who with me has retraced the footsteps
of Charles Darwin.

Contents

Preface

The theory of evolution is once more a matter of intense public and scientific interest and controversy. For one thing, there is the ongoing debate between creationists and evolutionists resulting in a number of court cases in California, Texas, Indiana, Arkansas, and Louisiana. But the scientific community itself is also in ferment regarding the theory of evolution. While there continues to be general acceptance of evolution, Darwinism has come under increasing attack. If the ideas of Gould and Eldredge prevail, Darwinism may well become as much a museum piece as phlogiston, luminiferous ether, and body humors.

Why should the current controversy between the creationists and the evolutionists be such an emotional one, as is evident from discussion in the public press and in the court cases? Is it not a case of pitting faith against facts? No, it is not, for there is much faith in the acceptance of the theory of evolution. Because it deals only with those things that can be observed and measured, science excludes from its consideration what many regard as one aspect of reality, the supernatural. Morever, it is based on acceptance of a series of assumptions. It makes a number of these and accepts a chain of presuppositions; many of these are in agreement with Scripture and are part of our Judeo-Christian heritage. But being assumptions and presuppositions, they are as much matters of faith as is acceptance of the Biblical creation account.

It is significant that in many ways the evolutionist does indeed have a god, even though he seeks to exclude the supernatural from scientific discussions. That god is the god of chance. And in a real sense it requires more faith to believe that he could accomplish the vast changes that evolution demands than to believe they have been brought about by the wisdom and planning of a supernatural being.

The history of the so-called "warfare of science and theology" suggests that we will have to expect a great deal of emotion. It is not surprising that evolutionists frequently charge creationists with ignoring evidence in favor of an unsubstantiated Biblical account. Many creationists may indeed have reevaluated the facts because they have accepted the Scriptural account. Yet that they should have begun with

7

an acceptance of the Scriptural account is really irrelevant to the argument, since the facts should speak for themselves. But this is not really possible even for evolutionists. Because of the paucity of facts it is quite clear that there is as much faith and perhaps even more faith involved in accepting the theory of evolution than in accepting the Scriptural account.

In this controversy charges and countercharges of dishonesty are not helpful. In general, we must agree that the scientific community has developed high ethical standards. It may indeed be true that some members of that community have with revivalistic fervor sought to manipulate the facts and to deceive. But these are certainly the exception, and the scientific community has been eager to expose such frauds. Scientists are as much committed to the pursuit of truth as are churchmen.

The present book is an attempt to understand the nature of science and to explain some of the tensions which exist between the scientific community and the evangelical community. The theory of evolution is discussed in considerable detail. Evidences suggesting a great deal of change within living things are evaluated, as are the series of evidences which are difficult to reconcile with the idea of such a vast change as evolution demands.

The author hopes that this book will be a contribution to an understanding of the current controversy.

John W. Klotz
St. Louis, Mo.
July, 1984

1
Science and the Scientific Method

There is no doubt that many of the blessings that God has bestowed on those of us living at the end of the 20th century and the beginning of the 21st century have come as a result of science and the scientific method. The Lord has literally opened the windows of heaven to us and has showered His blessing upon us. He has enabled us to learn much of the ways in which He governs the universe. He has given us a measure of control over our environment. Tremendous progress has been made in medicine, so that in the western world the average life span is the proverbial three score and 10 or four score years of Psalm 90. Moreover, we are able to alleviate and ameliorate much of the pain and suffering that come from disease and disability.

The Lord has also permitted us to utilize the sources of energy which He created. At one time the only energy available came from the muscles of animals and the muscles of human beings, including slaves. Then God permitted us to discover the energy stored in coal. This was followed by our discovery of the energy stored in oil and natural gas. Now we have learned to use the energy stored in the atom. In one sense slavery is no longer necessary because we have discovered abundant sources of energy about us.

There is no doubt that there were brilliant men in past societies. It is quite possible that the I.Q. of Greek intellectuals exceeded the I.Q. of men today. We marvel at the engineering projects of past societies, the blocks of stone at Stone Henge, the pyramids of Egypt, the temples and astronomical observatories of the Incas and the Mayas.

The Greeks were geniuses at rationalization, but unfortunately they failed to appreciate the importance of manual manipulation involved in the experimental method, so much a part of the scientific method today. Indeed, they despised manual manipulation and regarded it as the work of a slave on a much lower level than the rationalization they themselves practiced. Consequently, they did not make the progress we have made.

Today the scientist works with two "things." He works with facts, and he works with explanations for those facts, the theories and hypotheses of modern science. The facts he gains through his sense organs. The sense organs are the tools God has given us to keep in touch with our environment. The scientist gathers his observations made with his eyes, ears, and chemical senses. It is here that he uses the experimental method.

The tool by which he constructs his explanations is his mind. He reasons inductively and deductively to explain the observations he makes with his sense organs.

Thus, it should be noted that there are two sorts of "things" that the scientist is working with. These dare not be confused. An explanation cannot become a "fact"; it always remains a mental construct.

This is not to suggest that theories and hypotheses are unimportant. They are extremely important because they guide practical activities. George Washington probably died because of the application of a wrong theory. In his day it was believed that disease was due to an imbalance in the body humors; specifically, that disease was frequently the result of "bad blood." It followed logically that if you believe disease was due to bad blood, you ought to remove some of the offending fluid. This led to the practice of bleeding, and there is little doubt that Washington's demise was at least hastened by the bleeding to which he was subjected when he became ill.

Our theories are equally important today. They mold and direct much of our thinking. It is for that reason that evolution cannot be dismissed with the judgment that it is "only a theory." It has a great many practical applications and has had these in the past century. One of these is secular humanism. There is good reason for the concern that continues to be expressed over the fact that it has become the teaching of the public schools, to the exclusion of crucial parts of our heritage.

Assumptions

It should also be pointed out that the scientist makes a great many common sense assumptions. There is nothing esoteric about these assumptions, nor is there anything esoteric about the scientific method. The scientist, for example, assumes the existence of other people. He assumes that space is three-dimensional even though the image that falls on his retina is two-dimensional. He assumes that the existence of objects is independent of the presence of the observer. And, most importantly, he assumes the orderliness and uniformity of the universe in which he lives—something which follows from the Biblical teaching that God is a God of order.

It should be very evident that modern science could only have developed in the environment of the Judeo-Christian emphasis on the orderliness of creation. The gods of many religions are erratic. They play "cat and mouse" games with man. They tantalize him and change the rules. Their actions are not predictable, and consequently the universe is not regular and predictable.

From time to time the scientist does make other assumptions, which may or may not be true. Assumptions are matters of faith; by their very nature they cannot be proven. If accepted, they may lead to wrong or meaningless conclusions. For that reason assumptions always deserve examination. Ernst Mayr is quoted as saying, "Two years ago I saw a paper in the *Proceedings of the National Academy of Sciences,* and the author wrote, 'Let's assume the gene has a constant selective value; let's assume there is no gene flow from any other population.' He made about five such assumptions, each of which was equally unrealistic, and then he went on to prove something very beautiful mathematically, but it was meaningless."[1]

Common Sense

At the same time it should be noted that modern science has tended to move away from "common sense" theories and assumptions. When they are carefully studied, things are not what they appear to be. The Ptolemaic theory is a common sense theory; the Copernican theory is an abstract theory. "Anyone can see that the earth does not move and that the sun, moon, and stars revolve around the earth." Yet today there is almost universal agreement among astronomers that the sun is the center of the solar system and that the earth moves around the sun.

Our modern theory of the nature of matter is an abstract one. Try to convince an aborigine who has not had the benefit of a modern scientific education that a table is mostly empty space and that it is made up of particles in constant motion. He will tell you that you are crazy.

In mathematics, non-euclidean geometry, with its concept of curved space, is an abstract theory. In physics, relativity is an abstract as opposed to a common sense theory. Quantum mechanics is highly abstract. It and relativity "lead to realities beyond our common experience that cannot be rejected."[2] The reality of the common experience in the classical world is believed by some to be "only a small part of what there is."[3] The tendency in science throughout its history has been to move from common sense to abstract explanations.

This has some relevance when it is argued that common sense tells you that fossils are related by descent, and that anyone can see that "substantial changes have occurred" over the period of the earth's history.

The scientist moves back and forth between the study of facts and the development of explanations for those observations that he makes. He may collect a great many data (facts) and proceed by mental processes to sort them out, to classify, and to correlate them. He then may develop an explanation for them and from his explanation deduce the consequences of his explanation. Both these latter procedures are mental processes. He very likely will then proceed to test the correctness of his explanation by making additional observations. Thus, he moves back and forth between facts and explanations.

It should also be noted that one of the criteria for a scientific theory is that it must be testable. It must be possible to deduce the consequences from a theory or hypothesis, to predict and thus test the consequences of the theory or hypothesis. In evolution, little testing is possible by virtue of the very nature of the problem. It is not possible to test the changes that should take place as a consequence of the theory of evolution.

The Scientific Method

There are many scientific methods. The scientist is helped a great deal when he has clear-cut theories and hypotheses, and therefore he has a real incentive to develop these. If he does not have a clear-cut operational definition expressed in an adequate theory or hypothesis, he must operate with fuzzy ideas. This is the situation in the infancy of any science. Trial and error are necessary but are certainly wasteful. Medicine is a good example of this type of trial and error procedure. We may shudder at the practices of the past and thank God that we have been called into time in the last part of the 20th century. Yet the fact of the matter is that this trial and error procedure was necessary for progress in medicine, the benefits of which we enjoy. In

1860 Oliver Wendall Holmes, the dean of American medicine, said, "I firmly believe that if the whole *materia medica* as now used could be sunk to the bottom of the sea it would be all the better for man— and all the worse for the fishes."

The whole purpose of science, then, is to develop more acceptable explanations which it is hoped will more adequately describe reality.

One question that arises is the reliability of our sense organs. Can we count on the data which they gain for us and which we regard as "facts"? We are all familiar with mirages and optical illusions. We also know that our senses can sometimes deceive us. For example, something that is very hot may momentarily appear cold, and that which is very cold may "burn." The fact of the matter is that our sense organs are reasonably reliable and that the data they gather for us is reasonably dependable. These sense organs are the gift of God intended by Him to enable us to keep in touch with our environment. As such, they are "good" (Gen. 1:31).

Mental processes are less dependable. As we have pointed out, things are not always what they appear to be. There are inadequacies in both the inductive and in the deductive methods. It is apparent that man's mental processes have been more affected by the fall than have been his sense organs. Explanations must be corrected and evaluated more often than observations, though, of course, it is quite possible to be in error in the observations one makes.

One very important consideration is the fact, as hard as it may be to accept, that the human mind is limited. We are an arrogant generation; we insist on building intellectual towers that will reach to the skies. God has indeed permitted us to learn much about the nature of the universe and how it operates. Yet there may be things which because of the limitations of the human mind we cannot understand. It is certainly in order to explore these and to seek to understand them, but we need to recognize that some may be beyond our comprehension. Moreover, we need to recognize that things may not be what they appear to be. Witness the movement of scientific theories from common sense to abstract theories and the current discussions of quantum mechanics. Einstein is often quoted as saying that the Lord may be subtle, but He is not malicious. There is a third possibility. Perhaps some of our problems are due to our inability to discover His subtleties. Fifty million scientists, unlike 50 million Frenchmen, *can* be wrong. Phlogiston and luminiferous ether, which once had universal scientific acceptance, are now only historical curiosities.

The Experimental Method

The genius of modern science is the use of the experimental method. It has been by using this method that much of the tremendous progress made by modern science has been possible. The Greeks probably inadvertently limited their scientific progress by despising the experimental and overemphasizing the importance of the rational. The emphasis on the inductive method and the development of principles of inductive reasoning, especially by Mill, has made possible much of the progress of modern science.

An experiment is simply an observation made under controlled conditions. What is often not realized is that there are many situations in which experimentation is not possible. To begin with—and this is critical for a consideration of creation—the experimental method can be used only to study phenomena on our time level. It cannot be used to study the phenomena of the past or phenomena of the future. Consider for a moment the various predictions that are made of life a decade, a half-century, or a century in the future. Compare the predictions that were made of life in 1980 10 years prior to that time, in 1970. You will find that life in 1980 was far different from that envisioned just a decade prior to that time, and it is already quite apparent that life in 1990 and in the year 2000 will be different from that which was anticipated and predicted in 1980. The reason for this inadequacy is quite simple: the genius of the scientific method, controlled experimentation, cannot be employed. An illustration of the problem is the conflict between *Global 2000* and *Global Future: A Time to Act*. Both seek to describe the world of the year 2000, now less than two decades away. The former presents a very pessimistic picture, with vastly increased populations, more pollution, and an increasing gap between the "haves" and the "have nots." The latter predicts a world that will be less crowded, less polluted, more stable ecologically, and less vulnerable to resource-supply disruption. The authors and contributors to both reports are competent, highly respected individuals, but the pictures they draw are sharply contrasting predictions.[4]

The same thing is true of the past. It is simply impossible to reconstruct the environment of the past and to determine what effect it would have on living things. We cannot use the experimental method to study the changes from one life form to another, which are reported to have occurred in the past. We cannot determine the cause of the extinction of various forms.

All this does not mean that speculation regarding the past or the future is useless. It has its place and its value. But scientific reconstructions of the past or scientific predictions of the future do not have the validity and reliability of scientific conclusions regarding phenomena on our time level. The explanation is quite simple: the scientist does not have access to his most effective tool—controlled experimentation—when he deals with the past or with the future.

There are other areas, too, where experimentation is difficult or impossible. This is certainly true of such fields as astronomy and astrophysics. Sometimes the multiplicity of causes creates problems. In physics and chemistry we usually have one or a few causes for the effect we are studying. In biology we have what one scientist has called "a whole hatful." This is true to some extent of such fields as ecology, where today the role of interspecific competition is being debated.[5, 6]

It is interesting that this debate should center on the role of competition, one of the cornerstones of Darwinism, and that one of the participants in the debate should charge that current ecological theory emphasizing the role of competition "has caused a generation of ecologists to waste a monumental amount of time."[7]

Indeed, there are problems even when the scientist seeks to apply the experimental method on our time level. To be valid an experiment must involve both the test and a control. These must be as similar as possible in order to eliminate differences and to establish that the difference in results is due to the difference in treatment of the test and the control. The ideal subjects for experimentation in man are identical twins. Their identical background eliminates genetic differences as the cause for the difference in the results.

Obviously, an adequate number of identical twins is rarely available, and the scientist usually solves this problem through a process of randomization. By choosing subjects at random and by using enough of them, he believes that he can eliminate differences which may result from causes other than the one he is testing.

But there are other problems as well. One of these is the possibility that members of the test group will react merely because they are part of a test. It is a sort of Hawthorne effect. The participants are the objects of special attention, and that attention may bias the results. The very fact that they are receiving a new medicine may reduce the likelihood of their contracting the disease it is supposed to prevent.

It is to overcome this bias that we not only administer the medicine to the test group, but we provide a placebo for the control group, a harmless substance which has no known medicinal value. If the benefit is due merely to being a part of the study, both those who receive the medicine and those who receive the placebo should show a reduced frequency of the disorder.

But there is also a very real possibility that the experimenter himself may inadvertently influence the results. If he is administering both the drug and the placebo, he may indicate to the control group without being aware of it that they are receiving the placebo, not the drug being tested. In order to overcome this bias, we frequently use a "double blind" approach. In this circumstance neither the subjects nor the experimenter knows who is receiving the drug and who is receiving the placebo.

There are times, too, when the use of a test and a control group cannot be morally justified. One such situation is that existing with the Pasteur treatment, which is generally regarded as an effective preventive of rabies. Yet the fact of the matter is that its effectiveness against this disorder has never been tested in the way in which the Salk vaccine was tested over against polio. The reason is quite simple. If our understanding of the nature of rabies is correct, it is 100 percent fatal. To demonstrate the efficacy of the Pasteur treatment, it would be necessary to administer the Pasteur treatment to a test group and withold it from a control group. Both groups would be inoculated with the rabies virus, possibly through contact with a group of rabid animals. The test groups would receive the Pasteur treatment, and, if our theory is correct, they would all recover. The control group would receive no treatment or a placebo, and, if our theory is correct, they would all die.

Obviously, such a procedure could not be morally justified. Indeed, there are some who question the propriety of the test and control technique that was used to demonstrate the effectiveness of the Salk vaccine, since a substantial number of individuals in the control group who did not receive the vaccine developed polio.

There are some interesting consequences of the lack of experimentation with the Pasteur treatment. There have been instances of individuals who have been bitten by a rabid animal, who have not received the Pasteur treatment, and who nevertheless have survived. To "save" our theory, we have assumed that in these cases the virus was not introduced by the saliva of the rabid animal into the wound. There have also been instances of individuals who have received the

Pasteur treatment and have succumbed. In these cases we have postulated the introduction of the virus directly into a nerve and have assumed that in this case the treatment is ineffective. In both these cases we have sought to save the theory. This is characteristic of scientific procedures. Scientists are conservative, and they are also emotionally involved with explanations they have come to accept. Their inclination is to seek to fit observations into the framework of the accepted explanation rather than develop a new explanation.

Coefficients of Correlation

It should be evident that there are many situations to which we cannot apply the experimental method because of difficulties in setting up test and control. One very common procedure then is to seek to establish cause and effect relationships through coefficients of correlation. We deal with large numbers of people and seek to determine whether we can establish cause and effect relationships through the correlations we find.

It is generally agreed that coefficients of correlation may indeed suggest cause and effect relationships, but it is also agreed that they do not establish cause and effect relationships. One way scientists amuse themselves in their spare time is to develop coefficients of correlation which suggest impossible or implausible cause and effect relationships.

Extrapolation

A similar method is that of extrapolation. We determine the direction of change and its rate and then proceed to predict the outcome years hence or years ago. While interpolation is valid, extrapolation is quite hazardous. Mark Twain described the process in his "Life on the Mississippi" as follows:

> In the space of one hundred and seventy-six years the lower Mississippi has shortened itself two hundred and forty-two miles. This is an average of a trifle over one mile and a third per year. Therefore, any calm person, who is not blind or idiotic, can see that in the Old Oolitic Silurian period just a million years ago next November, the lower Mississippi River was upward of one million three hundred thousand miles long and stuck out over the Gulf of Mexico like a fishing rod. And, by the same token, any person can see that seven hundred and forty-two years from now, the lower Mississippi will be only a mile and three-quarters long, and Cairo and New Orleans will have joined their streets together, and be plodding comfortably

along under a single mayor and a mutual Board of Aldermen. There is something fascinating about science. One gets such wholesale returns of conjecture out of such a trifle investment of fact.[8]

Notes

1. Roger Lewin, "Biology Is Not Postage Stamp Collecting," *Science* 216 (1982):718.
2. Fritz Rohrlich, "Facing Quantum Mechanical Reality," *Science* 221 (1983):1251.
3. Ibid., p. 1255.
4. Constance Holden, "Simon and Kahn versus *Global 2000*," *Science* 221 (1983):341—43.
5. Roger Lewin, "Santa Rosalia Was a Goat," *Science* 221 (1983):636—39.
6. Lewin, "Predators and Hurricanes Change Ecology," *Science* 221 (1983):737—40.
7. Lewin, "Santa Rosalia," p. 636.
8. Samuel L.Clemens, *Life on the Mississippi* (New York: Harper & Brothers, 1874), p. 156.

2
Science
and Religion

Traditionally, religion—theology and the church—have been pictured as the bitter opponents of science and scientific progress. Today most people believe that the creation/evolution controversy is a battle between religion trying to hold on to antiquated notions and science trying to move mankind forward. The church is regularly portrayed as an opponent of scientific progress.

Much of this picture, which is actually a caricature of the situation, is due to a book written by Andrew D. White, entitled *A History of the Warfare of Science with Theology in Christendom*. It was published in 1896 and purported to show the constant battle that has gone on between Christianity and science and, for that matter, between religion in general and science. White wrote his book in a pique. He was the founder and first president of Cornell University. He wished to found a science university. There were no basic objections to this, but he did have one radical idea, and that was that he wished to do away with all compulsory chapel services. In this respect he was going counter to the trend of the times. It was taken for granted that college students would be required to attend chapel, and his proposal was viewed as anti-church and anti-religion. White sought funding from the state of New York, and a substantial number of clergymen opposed his proposal primarily because he sought to eliminate the chapel exercises.

White succeeded in setting up his university, but his wrath at the clergymen who opposed him knew no bounds. He wrote his book to get revenge, because he was convinced that churchmen have regularly opposed science and its endeavors. In the light of its origin, one would hardly expect the book to be an unbiased account, and it certainly is not that. It is unfortunate that most discussions of the relation of science with the church and theology are based on White's account. It is also unfortunate that this same emotional approach continues. Moore, for instance, writes, "The argument between the scientists and the creationists is between those whose fundamental goal is to understand nature and those whose fundamental goal is to control thought."[1] Lewontin refers to creationists as "know-nothings."[2] It is the same "white hats vs. black hats" caricature today that White pictured.

Most individuals cite three classical instances of a clash between science and the church. The first of these is the purported clash between Copernicus and the church over the nature of the solar system, which was followed by the Galileo episode a century later. In the 19th century Darwin and Huxley were pitted against the church over the question of evolution, and in 1925 the United States got involved in the controversy through the Butler law and the Dayton, Tennessee, "Monkey Trial."

Scientific Revolutions

All three of these episodes involved major changes in scientific thinking. Most historians of science today are of the opinion that science moves forward by what Thomas S. Kuhn calls "scientific revolutions." He has developed his ideas in a 172-page volume called *The Structure of Scientific Revolutions*.[3]

Kuhn believes that science is not the steady cumulative acquisition of knowledge that is portrayed in the textbooks. Rather, it is a series of "peaceful interludes punctuated by intellectually-violent revolutions." During the interludes, scientists are guided by a set of conceptual schemes—theories and hypotheses—which Kuhn refers to as a "paradigm." Nature, Kuhn believes, is too complex to be explored at random. The paradigm is an exploration plan, which both points to problems to be solved and guarantees that they are solvable.

But this tranquil period does not last. Sooner or later scientists try to extend the paradigm and find that there are puzzles which cannot be solved. These problems of the paradigm may have been there from the beginning, but they could be ignored during the early process of the development and study of the paradigm. Yet as time goes on these contradictions stand out with increasing prominence, and the time comes when they can no longer be ignored. At first, an attempt is made to reevalute the observations and experiments. A great deal of mental gymnastics goes on as scientists attempt to "save the theory." A new paradigm may be proposed, usually by people who are either very young or very new to the field whose paradigm they attempt to change. But defenders of the old paradigm patch it up with a variety of "fixes," and the battle is joined for the allegiance of the scientific community by the supporters of each paradigm.

The common picture of scientists as open-minded individuals willing to explore all areas and willing to study problem data as well as supportive evidences is a caricature. As we have pointed out, the scientist is not quick to abandon a theory which he has espoused, even though he has contradictory evidence. He rather attempts to establish that counter-indications are due to special circumstances or can be accounted for by elaborating the theory. Only if these and other efforts fail and additional "stubborn facts" incompatible with the accepted theory are encountered will he begin to consider other explanations.

The awarding of the 1983 Nobel Prize for Physiology or Medicine to Barbara McClintock at age 81 is an example of this. The discovery which the Nobel prize recognized was made 30 years earlier, but "few wanted to hear what she had to say." Dr. McClintock "had the courage to insist that she was correct" so that "30 years after her incisive insights, everyone knows she was right."[4]

Kuhn believes that non-rational factors play an essential role in the replacement of the paradigm. He states that logic and experiment are not sufficient. The transfer of allegiance from one paradigm to another "is a conversion experience that cannot be forced." The grounds for "conversion" may include arguments that "appeal to the individual's sense of the appropriate or the esthetic" and faith that the new paradigm will be better able to resolve the anomalies that precipitated the crisis.

Why can the problem not be solved by logic and experimentation? Proponents of rival paradigms are not speaking exactly the same language; they are bound to talk past each other because their frames of reference are not comparable. They are looking at the data from different points of view.

Kuhn believes that a new paradigm cannot be built on the one it succeeds; it can only supplant it. He believes that science is not a cumulative process as it is so often portrayed in the textbooks; it is a succession of revolutions in each of which one conceptual world view is replaced by another.

Kuhn does not believe that new paradigms necessarliy represent scientific progress in the sense that they give a better understanding of the world. He insists that the idea of progress in science can be true only in the relative sense that new paradigms can be recognized as more highly developed than those that they replace. He does not believe that paradigms carry scientists closer and closer to the truth.

It is his conviction that textbooks present an entirely false picture of science and scientific progress. There is a simplification in the history of science in the interest of pedagogic efficiency so that the student does not have to master all of the "wrong" ideas of the past. The effect, however, is to create a spurious tradition of uninterrupted progress and of the cumulative acquisition of knowledge.

A real maverick in dealing with science and scientific progress is Paul Feyerabend of the University of California at Berkeley. He believes that working scientists break every principle in the rationalist's rule book and adopt the motto "anything goes." Like Kuhn, he attacks logical positivism, which suggests that when old theories fall, new ones are proposed and adopted because of their greater explanatory power. Logical positivists, therefore, suggest that science marches inexorably closer and closer to the truth. While Kuhn emphasizes the importance of non-rational factors, Feyerabend goes farther. He argues that even "normal science" is a fairy tale, that scientific decision-making is a political and propagandistic affair in which prestige, power, age, and polemic determine the outcome of the constant struggle between competing theories and theorists. This, he argues, is because no theory, however good, ever agrees with all the facts in its domain. For that reason facts that seem to contradict the theory must either be ignored, defused by mental gymnastics, or rhetorically nudged out of the picture. All creativity in science, he believes, is a revolution in which the standard rules of the rationalists and their so-called "normal science" do not apply. He believes that if Karl Popper's falsification theory of science—that theories cannot be confirmed, only refuted, and when refuted must be abandoned—is taken seriously, all theories must be abandoned, for there are always important facts that do not agree with the theory. Since all scientific procedures have their limits, Feyerabend believes that techniques of persuasion are the decisive factor in determining which theory will prevail.[5]

Popper's approach to scientific theorizing, to which Feyerabend refers, deserves consideration in connection with the theory of evolution. He believes that researchers should test hypotheses not by seeking data that are consistent with them but by examining alternative explanations to the one embodied in the hypothesis. He urges the setting up of "null models," identifying observations and experiments that would be totally inconsistent with the hypothesis, and examining the evidence for these. If these exist, the hypothesis must be rejected as an explanation. Many philosophers of science believe that to be a scientific theory an explanation must be falsifiable, and that if it is not falsifiable, it is not science. On that basis, for example, Tipler expresses skepticism regarding the search for extraterrestrial life. He says, "If scientific theories are characterized by their falsifiability, then the proposed radio search (for extraterrestrial life) is not a scientific experiment at all because it cannot falsify the hypothesis being tested."[6]

Thus, exceptions do not prove rules; they destroy them. Right now considerable concern in astronomy is focused on the appearance of superluminal motion, which has been observed in some quasars and galaxies. A study of the quasar 3C 279 in the constellation Virgo suggests that components of this quasar are moving apart at about 10 times the speed of light. By common agreement such rapid motion is impossible. It is basic to relativity that nothing moves faster than the speed of light. Some believe that this apparent speed is an illusion. Others, however, insist that what is being seen is real. In any case, it is agreed that some explanation must be forthcoming or the laws of physics will have to be rewritten.

One suggestion has been that objects displaying the illusion of superluminal expansion are actually much closer to earth than their apparent astronomical distances. If objects showing superluminal expansion are, let us say, only a 20th as far away as they seem, then the speed with which their components are moving apart would be only a 20th as great as calculated. However, this creates some problems of its own. It would require that the uniform standard used to measure astronomical distances—the red-shift-based constant—does not apply to some selected quasars and galaxies. Others explain this apparent discrepancy on the basis of what has been called "the relativistic cannonball," but this proposal has several difficulties as well. In any case, some explanation in keeping with the presently accepted theories will have to be developed, or the theories themselves will have to be revised.[7]

It has been stated that beliefs, not proofs, are the issue in the controversy over evolution. Both tenets of religion and widely accepted scientific theories, it is agreed, are beliefs. However, it is argued that scientific beliefs require evidence of some sort before they can claim to be convincing, whereas religious beliefs are frequently held without substantiating evidence. Indeed, that is one of the qualities that justified the term "faith." In science we must maintain that distinction, it is said, or we will have no reason beyond their direct emotional appeal for choosing among the multitude of ideas.

It is interesting to note that Feyerabend believes that today we are choosing our theories because of their emotional appeal, not because they have substantiating evidence. Whatever theories he had in mind certainly do not fit the criterion of "significant substantiating evidence." Most scientific creationists are probably motivated to some degree and even to a large degree by their religious beliefs (Heb. 11:3). The scientific creationist is, however, seeking to present substantiating evidence for beliefs even though they may indeed be his for religious reasons. One proper question regarding the theory of evolution is whether it can accommodate the negative evidence, that is, the evidence which does not substantiate the theory of gradual change but rather substantiates the idea of a sudden origin of a wide variety of living forms.

It has been argued that one of the values of science is its predictive or postdictive value. Raup quotes Root-Bernstein as saying, "Evolution postdicts certain immutable trends of progressive change that can be falsified." Raup goes on to say, "This is simply not the case. In the fossil record we are faced with many sequences of change. . . . Darwinian interpretation can often be made after seeing the sequence. But the predictive (or postdictive) power of theory in these cases is almost nil." He adds, "One of the ironies of the evolution-creation debate is that the creationists have accepted the mistaken notion that the fossil record shows a detailed and orderly progression, and they have gone to great lengths to accommodate this 'fact' in their flood geology."[8]

The Copernican Revolution

Let us look at the science-religion conflicts. The first of these occurred in astronomy. The Greeks made considerable progress in astronomy. Their observational work was the basis not only for the Ptolemaic theory but also for the Copernican theory. Copernicus worked with the same observational data as did those who supported the Ptolemaic theory. Hipparchus, who lived about 200 B.C., produced a star catalog which served as the basis for many of the subsequent theories. He viewed his observations against the Platonic idea of perfect circles and uniform speed. He could not conceive of elliptical orbits for the planets or of variations in their speed as they moved through their orbits. In order to preserve the concepts of perfect circular motion and uniform speed, he developed the idea of epicycles, which became an important part of the Ptolemaic theory and which were adopted also by Copernicus when he developed his theory.

It is interesting to note that Erastosthenes of Alexandria, who lived from 276 to 195 B.C., came very close to determining the circumference of the earth. He estimated it to be 24,662 miles, a figure that was wrong by only some 70 miles. His determination of the circumference of the earth is a classical example of the Greek use of rational processes. At the time of the summer solstice, Erastosthenes found that the sun was directly overhead at Syene, but at Alexandria it was 1/50th the circumference of a circle from the zenith. He therefore reasoned that the circumference of the earth is 50 times the distance from Syene to Alexandria.

This figure was later disputed by scientists, who believed that the circumference of the earth was less than one-half the figure which Erastosthenes determined. Fortunately or unfortunately, Columbus accepted the figure of the scientists of his day and estimated the distance to the Indies at about 2500 miles, whereas it was actually 12,000 miles. It is not true that most people of that day thought the earth was flat. Educated people since the 12th century had been aware that the earth was a sphere. Advisers to Ferdinand and Isabella objected to Columbus' proposal not because they believed the earth was flat, but because they were inclined to accept the figure of Erastosthenes or a figure for the circumference of the earth somewhat between his figure and that propounded by Columbus. But Columbus argued effectively, and Ferdinand and Isabella agreed to support his project. If he had recognized the actual circumference of the earth he probably would not have sought to sail to India by sailing west. It was only because he rejected the figure of Erastosthenes that he believed the project feasible.

In evaluating the Copernican theory we must recognize that a similar theory had been suggested by Aristarchus of Samos in 281 B.C. He suggested a heliocentric system and proposed that the distance from the earth to the sun was between 18 and 20 times the distance between the earth and the moon. He believed that the fixed stars and the sun were immovable, and that the earth was carried around the sun in a circle—he still was influenced by the Platonic idea of perfect circular motion.

It was only about 450 years later than Ptolemy, who lived from 100 to 170 A.D., suggested a geocentric theory. The earth, he believed, was a fixed sphere in the center of the universe. The sun and the moon traveled in eccentric circles around the earth. All motion in each order of the circles was uniform. He believed that the moon was the closest heavenly body to the earth, and that the moon was followed by Mercury, Venus, the sun, Mars, Jupiter, Saturn, the fixed stars, and the "primum mobile," a vast sphere which carried all the celestial bodies and rotated once a day. His system employed a great many epicycles, that is, circles within circles. He needed these to explain the observed backward (retrograde) motion of the planets.

It is interesting to note that our planetaria, which show us the sky and demonstrate the motion of the heavenly bodies, are based on epicycles. They project their stars on the basis of the Ptolemaic rather than on the basis of the Copernican system.

Nicholas Copernicus (1473—1543)

Copernicus was born in Poland, the son of a wealthy merchant, and was orphaned at a young age. He was adopted by his uncle Lucas, the Bishop of Ermland, who arranged for his early education at the University of Cracow. His uncle sought to secure for him a bishopric at Frauenburg; in this he was unsuccessful. He studied at Bologna and Padua, where he completed his advanced studies in canon law. However, he received his Doctor of Canon Law from the University of Ferrara, apparently for financial reasons. In 1501 he became canon of the Frauenburg Cathedral. To complete his studies in Italy he was granted a leave shortly after assuming this position. After receiving a degree in canon law, he resumed his earlier studies in medicine and finally assumed his duties as canon at Frauenburg in 1512. Copernicus was not a priest; he had a regular salary as canon which supported him comfortably.

Copernicus looked at the astronomical data from a point of view different from that of most of his contemporaries. The observational data which he had was identical with that possessed by proponents and apologists for the Ptolemaic theory. In this way he represents the concept of scientific revolution with a new paradigm suggested by Kuhn. He corresponded with a number of scientists of his day and discussed his ideas with visiting astronomers and with students.

His preference for the heliocentric theory was based on its simplicity. He believed that it was easier to calculate the observable position of the planets in their orbits on the assumption that the solar system was heliocentric rather than geocentric. His system still included 34 epicycles; he had not gotten rid of these.

Word of the new approach to astronomy reached Germany and also the University of Wittenberg. One of the faculty members there, George Rheticus, expressed an interest in this theory. He had been called to Wittenberg through the influence of Melanchthon in 1537. Subsequently, he requested a leave of absence to study with Copernicus in Frauenburg. His request was granted, and in 1539 he visited him. No one interfered with his going to Copernicus, whose views by this time were well known. Indeed, his position at Wittenberg was held open for him. In 1540 he publicized the views of Copernicus in the first printed summary of the heliocentric theory. His book was known as *Narratio Prima*, and it was the first statement of the views of Copernicus available to the general public.

In 1541 Rheticus returned to Wittenberg, resumed his work as a professor there, and was named dean of the arts faculty even though his espousal of the Copernican view was well known. At the end of the year we find him a member of the faculty at the University of Leipzig. We do not know why he left Wittenberg, but it should be noted that the University of Leipzig was also a Lutheran university. We do know that Rheticus spent quite a bit of time in Nuremberg overseeing the printing of Copernicus' works, which were printed by the Lutheran theologian Osiander in Lutheran Nuremberg. On his trip to Nuremberg he carried letters of introduction and recommendations from Melanchthon. While Copernicus' own book was published in Nuremberg, the shorter version of his views had been published under the supervision of Rheticus in Wittenberg by Hans Lufft, the publisher of Luther's Bible translation.[9]

Copernicus' own book was called *De Revolutionibus Orbium Coelestium*. It was published when Copernicus was dying. He feared to go into print earlier because he anticipated a great deal of opposition. He was almost paranoid in his desire to avoid controversy. Most of all he feared ridicule.

It is interesting to note that the preface to *De Revolutionibus Orbium Coelestium* was written by Osiander, a Lutheran theologian. He characterized the book as embodying an interesting point of view. It is true he did not give his wholehearted support to the heliocentric theory. Still, the theories of Copernicus were soon taught at the graduate level in many of the great Lutheran universities.

Another Copernican at Wittenberg was Erasmus Reinhold.[10] White reports opposition to his teaching at Wittenberg, but there is no evidence of such opposition. Reinhold left Wittenberg in 1546 because of the outbreak of the Smalcaldic War. At the beginning of 1547 he returned with Melanchthon and in the summer of that year was made dean of the arts faculty. In 1549—50 he was rector of the University. He left Wittenberg in 1553 because of the plague and returned to his native city, Saalfeld, where he died soon thereafter. While he was a member of the Wittenberg faculty in 1551 he published his *Tabulae Prutenicae*. These tables were certainly published with the knowledge of Melanchthon. They are the mathematical tables supporting the Copernican theory. Reinhold not only praises Copernicus but specifically his *De Revolutionibus*.

Luther is often cited as a critic of the Copernican theory. The criticisms attributed to him are found in his "Table Talk," by far the least authoritative of his works. The "Table Talk" consisted of a collection of his discussions which were subsequently set down by those who heard him. Luther in his "Table Talk" was certainly speaking "off the cuff." Moreover, it is quite possible that he was inaccurately quoted, since this particular section of the "Table Talk" was first published by Aurifaber in 1566, years after the time (1539) when Luther is said to have called Copernicus a fool. Indeed, the word "fool" does not occur in the Weimar edition, the most authoritative edition of Luther's works.

Luther himself had a high regard for science as such. In his "Table Talk" he distinguished carefully between astronomy and astrology. The latter he regarded as a pseudo-science of little value. Luther in his judgments depended on the scientists of his day. The vast majority of them accepted the Ptolemaic theory, and Luther was willing to defer to their scientific judgments.

John Calvin is also criticized for his support of the Ptolemaic theory. In his commentary on the Psalms, he assumes its correctness in commenting on Psalms 19 and 93. White quotes him as naming Copernicus by name, but Dillenberger reports that he has been unable to find such a passage in Calvin's works and "doubts that it exists."[11]

Tycho Brahe

Tycho Brahe (1546—1601) developed a star catalog to supplement that of Hipparchus. Brahe still worked without a telescope; this development was still in the future. Brahe was a Lutheran who rejected both the Ptolemaic and the Copernican theories. He tried for a compromise and proposed that the planets revolved around the sun, and that the sun, moon, and fixed stars revolved around the earth. His theory, known as the Tychonian theory, still has some advocates.

Kepler

Kepler, who lived from 1571 to 1630, developed three laws of planetary motion supporting the Copernican theory. He had been Tycho Brahe's assistant. His approach to astronomy was highly mystical. Like Brahe, Kepler was a Lutheran, although he did not accept the Book of Concord and left the University of Tuebingen for that reason.

Galileo

The real controversy came with the work of Galileo (1564—1642). It was Galileo's polemics that were responsible for putting Copernicus' book on the *Index of Prohibited Books* in 1616 "until suitably corrected." The Inquisition even spelled out the changes that it expected. Merely a few (about a dozen) cosmological passages that sounded too much like laws and descriptions were to be changed so that they seemed hypothetical.[12]

Galileo was one of the most brilliant men who ever lived. He studied medicine at Pisa but withdrew from the university there and went to the University of Padua. Galileo was the first individual to use a telescope extensively; it had been invented in 1608 by a Dutch spectacle-maker, Hans Lippershey. Galileo used it to describe the mountains and valleys of the moon. He also discovered the phases of Venus and trained his telescope on the sun, where he discovered the sunspots. These, he noted, moved, and therefore he concluded that the sun was not immutable. Galileo also discovered the four moons of Jupiter and a number of hitherto unknown stars in the Milky Way.

He published his *Sidereal Messenger* in 1610. Here he distinguished the stars and the planets. His ideas were regarded as heretical, and he was forced to recant in 1616.

Galileo first came under attack because of a statement by one of his students, Benedetto Castelli, who attacked Cosimo Boscaglia at a dinner in 1613. Boscaglia claimed that any motion of the earth was contrary to the Scriptures.

Galileo formalized his views in a letter to the Grand Duchess of Lorraine, who was the hostess at the dinner. Meanwhile, a Dominican friar, Caccini, preached a sermon on "Sun, Stand Thou Still," and another Dominican sent a copy of the Castelli letter to one of the Inquisitors-General in Rome in 1615.

The Congregation of the Holy Office held that the propositions that the sun is immovable at the center of the solar system and that the earth is movable and not the center of the solar system had to be condemned. They judged the new astronomy to contradict the Scriptures. Galileo was not directly involved; yet subsequently he was admonished by Cardinal Bellarmine not to hold or defend the Copernican system. Galileo was silent until his long-time friend Cardinal Barberini was elected Pope Urban VIII. In 1624 Galileo visited him in Rome, where he was cordially received and encouraged to continue his studies and his writings with the understanding that Galileo would stress the hypothetical nature of his ideas.

The real conflict between Galileo and the church came with the publication of his *Dialogue Concerning the Two Chief World Systems*, which was published in 1632. The *Dialogue* purported to be a discussion held by a proponent of the Copernican system and a proponent of the Ptolemaic system. The third individual in the party was a sort of mediator, Sagredo, an intelligent amateur who played a sort of "second fiddle" role. Salviati, defending the Copernican system, was Galileo's mouthpiece. The individual who defended the Ptolemaic theory was named Simplicio and proved to be a good-natured simpleton. At the end of the dialog, Simplicio quoted Pope Urban to the effect that an omnipotent God could make the universe a mystery even to rational men. It was this that was unacceptable, for in effect Galileo was sticking out his tongue at the pope, even though he considered him his good friend.

The result of Galileo's second conflict with the church was Urban's final judgment on the matter. Galileo was hauled before the Inquisition and once more required to recant. On the basis of a vehement suspicion of heresy, he was required to make public abjuration of his scientific opinions in the Dominican Convent of Maria Sopra Minerva on June 22, 1633 and committed to life imprisonment. His book was prohibited, and he himself was forbidden to treat in any manner questions as to the stability of the sun and the mobility of the earth. He was placed under house arrest at a small estate which he owned in Arcetri, a treatment much gentler than that usually dispensed by the Inquisition.

Galileo was the victim of machinations by a motley coalition of jealous Jesuits and domineering Dominicans, but he himself was not guiltless. He had given evasive answers and had failed to respect Bellarmine's admonitions. Galileo was a polemicist, good at debate, and quick witted.

It should be pointed out that when Galileo was dying, Pope Urban sent a special blessing to him. He was buried in consecrated ground within the church of Santa Croce at Florence, an honor given only to men viewed as faithful Catholics by the church. Santillana says, "It has been known for a long time that a major part of the church intellectuals were on the side of Galileo, while the clearest opposition to him came from secular ideas."[13]

Galileo is usually hailed as a scientific martyr whose research was forbidden by the church and brought to an end by the threats of a church-state. There is no doubt that the Galileo episode has been a real source of tension in the controversy between the church and the scientific community. It is rather interesting that some knowledgeable scientists believe the entire controversy was a bit of a tempest in a teapot. Fred Hoyle, the well-known British astronomer, writes, "Today we cannot say that the Copernican theory is 'right' and the Ptolemaic theory is 'wrong' in any meaningful sense."[14] Movement is relative, and it appears that all heavenly bodies move in space.

Newton (1642—1727)

The earliest controversy between science and the church was over the nature of the solar system. A second controversy is one which received little notice and which predated the controversy over creation, the controversy over preservation. Actually, it has had a tremendous impact on the thinking of the scientific world and also of the Christian church.

Like Galileo, Newton was one of the most brilliant men who ever lived. Some consider him the greatest scientific genius who has lived up until the present time. Newton was a posthumous and premature child whose entire life was spent in frail health. When his stepfather died, his mother tried to make a farmer of him. Newton was interested in mechanical toys and was sent back to school. He studied for the Anglican priesthood and was tutored at Cambridge by Isaac Barrow. Barrow was an able tutor, and Newton became his successor on his recommendation. Newton was a contemporary of Robert Boyle and of the first astronomer royal, Flamstead.

An outbreak of bubonic plague forced Newton to retire to Woolsthorpe, where he used his time for thinking and reflection. The first paper he presented to the Royal Society dealt with light and optics. Hooke claimed that the ideas presented there were really his and had been stolen, and there was animosity between the two as long as they lived.

Newton was involved in the politics of the day. In 1696 he was appointed Warden of the Mint and in 1699 Master of the Mint. His major work, *The Principia*, was published in 1687. It was written in Latin and presented Newton's three laws of motion. In 1703 he became president of the Royal Academy and was one of the early discoverers of calculus.

Newton was very pious. He believed in absolute time and absolute space, which he associated with God. Newton believed that the age of miracles was over. He developed the concept of the universe as a machine. He was a positivist who turned his back on metaphysics in favor of a small but growing body of exact knowledge. He believed that it was possible to acquire truth about things without presupposing any theory of their ultimate nature. Theologically, Newton seems to have been an Arian.

Newton's ideas of cause and effect led him to develop the concept of a watchmaker God. He accepted the miracles of the Old Testament and the New Testament, but he also believed the age of miracles was past. In effect, while he accepted creation he denied the doctrine of preservation. He believed that God had indeed created the universe and that He had established the laws by which it is governed. In our modern era Newton believed that God had withdrawn from the universe which He created, and that He operated solely through the laws which He had established at the time of creation.

This mechanistic approach reached its zenith in the work of Laplace, who believed that if there were a superhuman intelligence capable of knowing the position and momentum of every atom in the universe and capable of solving all mathematical equations, it could with precision state the minutest detail of every event "whether it be thousands of years in the future or remote in the past."

Newton's work and the work of Laplace led to a causal determinism in science. It made God philosophically unnecessary and irrelevant. There was no point in debating whether God existed. If He did exist and was the watchmaker God, He did not interfere with the affairs of the universe. The role of science was determining what these laws were, rather than seeking to debate the existence of the God who had given them.

Causal determinism was philosophically devastating to theology, but somehow or other it did not attract the attention or opposition of churchmen. It led to logical positivism, which until recently was embraced by the majority of scientists. The implications of causal determinism for orthodox Christianity were indeed profound. This was certainly as significant a philosophical attack on Christianity as any, yet its significance was largely overlooked. Logically it led to deism and made agnosticism a reasonable approach.

Today quantum mechanics has led to a questioning of determinism and of the idea that all phenomena may be explained on the basis of cause and effect relationships. To "save" determinism, the suggestion of "hidden variables" was developed by some. It was hypothesized that quantum mechanics—which suggests that the universe is probabilistic, not deterministic—is incomplete and presents us with averages that hide the detailed and deterministic reality. This led to the idea of "hidden variables," the idea that the universe is really deterministic and that quantum mechanics is a sort of average of these variables. But today it is believed that the local hidden variables theory is dead. "Our common language is utterly inadequate for the description of the quantum world . . . . mathematical language is much more suitable . . . . the reality of the common experience in the classical world is only a small part of what there is."[15]

Early Theories of Evolution

Evolution can hardly be called an idea originating among modern scientists. The early Greeks had their theories of evolution. Empedocles, who lived from 493 to 435 B.C., believed that plants and animals were not produced simultaneously. Plants, he postulated, originated first and animal life came into existence only much later. Empedocles also suggested a sort of "survival of the fittest" theory.

Aristotle (384—322 B.C.), certainly the greatest of the scientists of the ancient world, believed in a complete gradation in nature. He receives most attention for his work in astronomy, but his work in biology was much more far-reaching. Aristotle believed that there had to be a gradual transition from the imperfect to the perfect. He also believed that man stood at the highest point of one long, continuous evolutionary ascent.

It is particularly interesting that the ancients developed this as well as other "common sense" theories. The idea of gradual development as an explanation for the variety of living things was a very plausible one to them, as it is to many today.

However, just as modern science began with the Renaissance, so modern theories of evolution began at that time. Bacon (1561—1626) called attention to the variations in animals and the bearing of this variation upon the origin of new species. Leibniz (1646—1716) believed that all the different classes of animals were connected by transitional forms. Kant (1724—1804) believed that the higher organisms had developed from the simpler forms. He, however, doubted that any human investigation would come to an understanding of the laws governing this development.

Early speculation on evolution and the variety of living things was sparked by the work of Linnaeus (1707—1778), the "father" of modern taxonomy. His own father was a Lutheran clergyman and a collector of exotic plants. Linnaeus was trained as a physician. He was poor and suffered a great many hardships. His patron was Celsius, a well-known botanist and the inventor of the Celsius scale, which measures temperatures. Linnaeus became professor of botany at Upsala in 1741. He traveled widely and had representatives all over the world gathering specimens and data for him.

Linnaeus was responsible for the present classification system, which is applied to both plants and animals. He first published his *Systema Natura* in 1735; the 10th edition was published in 1758. Linnaeus established the system of classification and the categories we use today. His system was based on external and internal anatomy. In the case of plants he used the flower as the basis for classification. By and large, his system of classification on the lower levels—genera and species—has remained. The higher categories in his scheme of classification have been rearranged.

While any system of classification is arbitrary, we have found the system developed by Linnaeus and based on structure to be useful. The Scriptures use a different system of classification. They classify animals, for instance, on the basis of the habitat occupied. The Bible lumps together those organisms which live in the water, those which live on land, and those which live in the air. For that reason the Bible classifies together the whale, the fish, the shark, and the "sea monster" (Gen. 1:21). It classifies together the bat and the bird (Deut. 14:18), and the butterfly. There is nothing right or wrong about a system of classification, for, as noted above, any system is arbitrary. Linnaeus is also responsible for the "fixity of species" concept. He believed that the number of species was determined at creation and that these species do not change. Toward the end of his life he modified his statements a bit and suggested at least the possibility of some changes within the species category. At least some of the difficulty arose because of the confusion of the Latin word *species* (the Vulgate translation of the "min" of Genesis) and the biological term "species."

It is clear that Scripture teaches a "fixity of kinds" (Gen. 1:12, 24). As we shall see, it does not teach a "fixity of species."

Buffon (1707—88)

The first real theory of evolution was developed by Buffon, the outstanding biologist of the 18th century. Buffon belonged to the bureaucratic nobility. He became interested in natural history when he met a young Englishman, Lord Kingston, who was traveling on the continent with a tutor. Buffon went to England at his encouragement and studied there. In 1739 he became an associate of the French Academy and became Keeper of the Royal Botanical Garden.

Buffon had some difficulty with the church. He was a cynic so far as creation was concerned. While he managed to satisfy the theology faculty of the University of Paris that he was orthodox by using double-talk, in private Buffon was very skeptical of the creation account.

Buffon's book was entitled *Natural History*. It was a brilliant work, encyclopedic in breadth. Buffon believed that there were no absolute bounds between plants and animals. He rejected special creation and rejected Ussher's chronology. Buffon accepted the Aristotelian idea of a ladder of nature. He accepted the idea of spontaneous generation of life through minute life-units scattered throughout the universe. His *Natural History* is a carefully worked out explanation of the variety of living things based on the concept of their having developed from a common ancestor.

Lamark (1744—1829)

The first reasonably complete theory of evolution was enunciated by Jean Baptiste Pierre Antoine de Monet, the Chevalier de Lamarck, in 1809. He was sent to a Jesuit school to become a priest but was bored by the learning there. He enlisted in the army at age 16 and on the day after his enlistment was involved in a battle in which both the commissioned and non-commissioned officers were killed. Lamarck rallied the men and as a reward was made a lieutenant and put on safe garrison duty. This again bored him, and he resigned to become a literary hack in Paris.

Lamarck became interested in botany. He gained the support of Buffon and was admitted to the French Academy. During the French Revolution he was appointed professor of zoology by the National Convention of the French Revolution, primarily because he was self-educated, for in the anti-intellectual atmosphere of the French Revolution what could be a better recommendation for a professor than that he had never attended a university? As professor of zoology he lectured particularly on the invertebrates. His book in which he enunciated his ideas of evolution was known as *Philosophie Zoologique*, and it was published in 1809.

Lamarck suggested as a mechanism for evolution a use and disuse theory and an inheritance of acquired characteristics. He believed that organs developed or atrophied according to whether they were used or not used. He further believed that individuals inherited traits and characteristics which their forebears had acquired during their lifetime.

Perhaps a classical illustration of Lamarck's ideas was his explanation of the neck of a giraffe. He suggested that this long neck developed as a result of a prolonged drought on the plains of Africa. Because food was scarce, giraffes had to stretch their necks in order to secure the limited vegetation available. These long necks were inherited by their descendants until the giraffe acquired the neck which modern giraffes have.

The theories of Lamarck were challenged by August Weismann, a strong proponent of Darwin's explanation and of the genetics of Gregor Mendel, who cut off the tails of 22 generations of mice and found that the tails of subsequent generations were just as long as the tails of the first generation. He reasoned that if there was any validity to the idea of an inheritance of acquired characteristics, his experimental mice should have had shorter tails than their forebears. It is Weismann who developed the idea of the continuity of the germ plasm, the idea that there is a barrier between the germ cells (eggs and sperm) and the cells of the rest of the body (somatic cells). This barrier prevents any change in the somatic cells during the individual's lifetime from reaching the germ cells and thus being passed down to offspring.

Individuals unhappy with the Darwinian explanation of evolution have continued to search for evidence of a Lamarckian mechanism. Purported examples of Lamarckian inheritance were common in the 19th century, and they have continued to appear at regular intervals during this century. The idea that advantageous characteristics developing during the animal's lifetime can be passed on to its offspring is an attractive one that makes evolution easier to explain.

Recently Edward Steele, a young Australian immunologist, carried on research which he believes supports the Lamarckian theory.

He suggests that certain viruses, the retroviruses, can carry genetic material from somatic to germ line cells.

During the organism's early life, he believes, mutations occur in the somatic cells, some of which may be better suited to prevailing environmental conditions. These cells will proliferate relative to their non-mutant relatives and will eventually dominate the organ. The retroviruses will pick up some of the new genetic material, transport it to the germ cells and then insert it into the genome, whose role is to "make" the next generation.

Steele's experiments involved inducing a state of immune tolerance in one strain of mice by injecting into them cells of another strain and then determining if tolerant fathers would sire tolerant offspring. He reported that from 50 to 60 percent of the progeny from tolerant fathers were also tolerant to the test strain cells. In the second generation, the frequency of tolerance was still 20 to 40 percent. Steele's work has not been generally accepted because one requirement for acceptance of results such as this is independent repetition in a second laboratory, and other workers have not been able to duplicate his results. However, Steele criticizes their procedures, insisting they failed because they were not carried out properly. He also insists there are other reports in the scientific literature which support Lamarckian inheritance.[16]

Lamarck's theories have had an appeal in the Soviet Union, since the prevailing philosophy of Marxism has been "progress through a manipulation of the environment." Russian genetics during the Stalin era was dominated by Lamarckianism under the leadership of Lysenko. There is little doubt that his theories and the procedures followed in agriculture because of them contributed to the food shortages and crop failures of that era. In sum, the entire Soviet ideology is definitely Lamarckian.

If there is no inheritance of acquired characteristics, it is probably the provision of an all-wise and gracious Creator. We might well be a race of the handicapped if we inherited the defects acquired by our ancestors during their lifetimes.

Erasmus Darwin (1731—1802)

Erasmus Darwin, the grandfather of Charles Darwin, was an early evolutionist. He developed his evolutionary ideas in prose and poetry in his *Zoonomia*, which he first published in 1794. Subsequently, two other editions were published so that there were three editions of the work in seven years. The book was translated into

French, Italian, and German. Generally it was regarded as a textbook on disease rather than as an explanation of the origin of living things. The work was published in two volumes. One section of Volume I, entitled "Of Generation," dealt with evolution. *Zoonomia* was encyclopedic, providing practical suggestions for the diagnosis and treatment of all known diseases. Volume I concerned itself with the physiology of the different human systems. Volume II was a catalog of 474 diseases. Today scientists are most interested in the ideas of Erasmus Darwin on the origin of life and the development of living things.

Erasmus Darwin does not seem to have had too much influence on his grandson Charles. He was dead when Charles was born. It does, however, appear that Charles was familiar with his grandfather's work. Scientists probably would pay little attention to the work were it not for the influence of his more famous grandson.

Charles Darwin (1809—82)

Robert Waring Darwin, the father of Charles Darwin, was born in 1766. He married Susannah Wedgwood, the daughter of Josiah Wedgwood, the founder of the famous Wedgwood pottery works. The Wedgwood pottery works were known as the Etruria Works, a name suggested by Erasmus Darwin. Robert had attended school with Susannah at Etruria Hall. The school itself was known as the Etruscan School. Robert and Susannah were married in 1796. Charles Robert was their fifth child. He was born February 12, 1809, the exact date on which Abraham Lincoln was born. About the only thing the two men had in common was the birthdate. Darwin was born a wealthy man in a country that regarded itself as highly civilized. Lincoln was born in deep poverty on the frontier in a developing country.

Charles' father Robert was 6'2" tall and weighed well over 300 pounds. He was a physician, and when he went into the homes of poor patients he was accustomed to sending his coachman ahead to test the stairs.

Darwin was born at Shrewsbury and attended the Shrewsbury Grammar School as a boarding student. The curriculum there was rigidly classical. The school had been founded by Edward VI 250 years earlier. The master at Darwin's time was the Reverend Doctor Samuel Butler. Subsequently, the Darwin family moved to Plas Edwards, a Welsh seacoast resort.

Robert Darwin was displeased by Charles' slow progress at school. "You care for nothing but shooting dogs and rat catching. You will be a disgrace to yourself and all your family." Such was the judgment of his father.

It was determined that Charles should study medicine at Edinburgh, since this was one of the few professions open to a gentleman. At 16, prior to going to Edinburgh, Darwin took care of some of his father's charity patients. At this time he had about a dozen patients of his own. He would examine them and then confer with his father, who suggested medicine which Charles then prescribed and employed.

Darwin was sent off to Edinburgh to study medicine, but he was very unhappy with his studies there. He attended the clinical wards at Edinburgh and went twice to the operating theater. On the second occasion a child was being operated on. Since there were no anesthetics, it was a rather traumatic experience. For Darwin the sight was almost unbearable. He fled, never to return. The memory of that operation haunted him for years.

Darwin was bored by the lectures on *materia medica*. He was very much interested in the natural sciences. By the end of his second year at Edinburgh it was abundantly clear that medicine was not for him. From his father's standpoint the two years had been wasted.

Now it remained to choose another profession. The only ones open to a gentleman were law, medicine, and the ministry. Darwin had disgraced his father by his failures at Edinburgh. Now it was proposed that he attend Cambridge and study for the priesthood of the Church of England. Darwin found he could accept that church's creed and agreed to become a country clergyman. He himself reports in his *Recollections of the Development of My Mind and Character* (page 25) that he "liked the thought of being a country clergyman." It was planned that he should receive a sort of sinecure in some obscure parish, where he would be able to support himself through inherited wealth. From 1828 until 1831 he studied at Cambridge, where he attended Christ College. He stood 10th among those who did not go on for honors. In general, he was considered to be a member of the sporting crowd. He showed a passion for hunting, shooting, and cross-country riding. He was also known as a beetle collector.

Darwin and his family were Unitarians; they attended the Unitarian Church in Shrewsbury, though Darwin was baptized in St. Chad's Anglican Church. His wife, Emma, was also a Unitarian, though, like Darwin, their children were baptized in the Anglican Church. Darwin reports (*Recollections*, p. 610): "Whilst on board the *Beagle* I was quite orthodox and I remember being heartily laughed at by several of the officers (though themselves orthodox) for quoting

the Bible as an unanswerable authority on some point of morality."
In his *Autobiography,* which his son developed from the *Recollections,*
Darwin says that prior to going to Cambridge "as I did not then in
the least doubt the strict and literal truth of every word in the Bible,
I soon persuaded myself that our Creed must be fully accepted."[17]

In a letter to Asa Gray dated September 5, 1857, Darwin wrote:
"I think that generally (and more and more as I grow older) but not
always, that an Agnostic would be the more correct description of my
state of mind."[18] We are told that he "came to see that the Old Testament was no more to be trusted than the sacred books of the Hin-
doos."[19] And Darwin himself says, "I gradually came to disbelieve in
Christianity as a divine revelation."[20] He goes on to say, "The old
argument from design in Nature, as given by Paley, which formerly
seemed to me so conclusive, fails now that the law of natural selection
has been discovered."[21] ". . . I deserve to be called a Theist . . . But
then arises the doubt . . . Can the mind of man, which has as I fully
believe, been developed from a mind so low as that possessed by the
lowest animals be trusted when it draws such grand conclusions?"[22]

At Cambridge he became the friend of the Reverend John Steven
Henslow, the professor of botany. Darwin had entered Cambridge
after Christmas and had to remain for two terms after passing the
examinations in January 1831. Henslow persuaded him to study geology. He participated in a study tour of the rocks of Wales, led by
Professor Adam Sedgwick. Henslow, who had such a marked influence
on Darwin, is described as a deeply religious man "so orthodox" that
Darwin says, "he told me one day he should be grieved if a single
word of the Thirty-nine Articles were altered."[23]

But again Darwin let his father down. While he completed the
program at Cambridge, he did not seek ordination and did not accept
an assignment as an Anglican parish priest.

Then came his great opportunity. He was offered the position of
naturalist on *H. M. S. Beagle,* a refitted 10-gun, 242-ton brig which
was to make an extensive study tour and travel around the world.
He had been recommended for this position, a non-paying position,
by Henslow to Captain Robert FitzRoy.

But Robert Darwin would have none of it. Charles had let him
down at Edinburgh and at Cambridge, and he was sure that Charles
would let him down again if he were permitted to go on the *Beagle.*
Charles, however, was anxious to make the trip. He planned to visit
his uncle and aunt and cousins at Maer, the home of the Wedgwoods.
Robert told him, "If you can find anyone who thinks this is a sensible

idea, I'll give my consent." Robert had eight objections. Uncle Josiah answered these in writing point by point, and Robert reluctantly gave his consent.

The *Beagle* was to sail November 4, 1831. It actually sailed December 27. There were 72 men aboard, seven officers, five under-officers, two surgeons, a purser, a squad of 10 marines, 34 seamen, six boys, two servants, three Fuegians, a missionary, and Charles Darwin, the naturalist.

Darwin took along Lyell's *Principles of Geology* on the recommendation of Henslow. The book had just been published. The three Fuegians were York Minster, Fuegi Basket, and Jemmy Button. These were being returned to their home at the tip of South America. Three Fuegians had been seized as hostages on an earlier voyage. In addition, Jemmy Button had been purchased for a pearl button. One of the Fuegians had died of smallpox while in England; the three were now being returned to their native land. The missionary was aboard in order to go to Tierra del Fuego to conduct a mission program there.

Darwin was seasick during most of the voyage, yet he worked incessantly gathering notes, collecting materials, and making observations. Perhaps his most significant observations were carried out on the Galapagos Islands off the coast of Ecuador. Here he became convinced that he could demonstrate the development of new species. Much of his work was done with finches, rather drab birds, of which it is believed there are 14 species on the Galapagos which may be divided into three major groups. They are thought to have developed as a result of an adaptive radiation from a single ancestral species. The most marked distinctions are in the size and the shape of the bill, which presumably is related to the birds' food habits. These food habits vary from seed eating, through plant and insect eating, to blood drinking.

After his return from the voyage of the *Beagle*, October 2, 1836, Darwin worked and reworked his notes. He became convinced that species were not fixed and that one species developed from another. Particularly important in this connection were the observations he had carried out on finches on the Galapagos Islands. There is no doubt that Darwin's theological training at Cambridge played a part in the development of his theology and of his science. He had learned at Cambridge that Scripture taught fixity of species. There the theological professors followed the scientific judgment of the day that species were immutable. They believed that this agreed with the Genesis account and taught that the correctness of the Genesis account was supported by the science of the day. When Darwin became convinced that new species developed, he was forced to the conclusion that the Bible was wrong, and this conviction led to an undermining of his faith.

Darwin not only began to work and rework his notes, but he took to himself a wife. His sister Caroline had married Josiah Wedgwood III. Charles courted his cousin Emma and married her January 29, 1839. His wife was eight months older than he. There is no doubt that Charles felt very close to the Wedgwoods, and that he was especially grateful to his uncle who had interceded for him when he was offered the position of naturalist on the *Beagle*. Emma was growing toward spinsterhood, and Charles may well have felt that he ought to express gratitude toward his uncle by taking off his hands a spinster daughter.

In any case, Emma was a very good wife to Charles and a very good mother to their eight children. Darwin was ill most of his life, and it is generally agreed that he was a hypochondriac. Emma mothered not only her children but also her husband. They moved originally to London, but Darwin was unhappy with the hustle and bustle of the city. In 1842, they moved to Downe in Kent, where Darwin spent most of his life at Down House on Luxted Road, an 18-acre estate.

The original plan was to publish two volumes of journals of the voyage of the *Beagle* by FitzRoy and one volume by Darwin. The materials were published in 1839. Darwin's was so popular that it was published later as *Journal of Researches into the Geology and Natural History of Various Countries Visited by H. M. S. Beagle under the Command of Captain FitzRoy, R. N. from 1832 to 1836*. Later this same volume was published in the United States as *The Voyage of the Beagle*. FritzRoy was present at the famous Oxford meeting and opposed Darwin's ideas there. Subsequently, in 1865, he committed suicide.

Meanwhile, Darwin studied, worked, and reworked his notes. He was influenced in his thinking a great deal by Malthus, who suggested that populations increased geometrically while food supplies increase only arithmetically. It was this suggestion which led Darwin to the idea of a struggle for existence. He was also influenced by the geological ideas of Lyell, who suggested a uniformitarian approach to the study of geological phenomena instead of the generally accepted catastrophism.

Darwin confided in Hooker and corresponded extensively with him as well as with others. He first developed a 37-page abstract of his theory in June 1842 with the title "First Pencil Sketch of Species Theory Written at Maer and Shrewsbury During May and June 1842." In the summer of 1844 he enlarged the summary to 230 pages. In September 1854 his diary indicates that he "began sorting notes for species theory."

Most of the Darwin children were born at Downe. Two died in infancy, and Ann, who was born in 1841, died at the age of 10. Emma's life was fitted entirely to Charles. Her time was arranged so that she could be with him in all his free hours. In sickness she was constantly at his side, sitting by the hour in darkened rooms as he lay prostrate with severe headaches, always solicitous, never impatient, guarding his health and peace with unending tender care. Nursing was her forte. One writer has said, "the perfect nurse had married the perfect patient." Charles' love for her grew deeper with the years, and discord was almost unknown among them.

Early in 1858 Darwin received a letter from Alfred Russel Wallace (1822—1913), which brought Darwin close to collapse, for in this letter Wallace outlined a theory almost identical with the theory being developed by Darwin. The dilemma was this: if Darwin now proceeded, it might appear as if he were stealing Wallace's idea and developing it. However, if he did not proceed the work that he had done since his return from the voyage of the *Beagle* would be totally lost.

Brackman suggests that Darwin was unable to develop completely his theory until he had read and annotated Wallace's Sarawak Law in 1855 and Wallace's complete theory of the origin of species, the Ternate paper, in June 1858. The Sarawak Law was part of a 7,000 word essay entitled "On the Law Which Has Regulated the Introduction of New Species." Wallace's thesis was that "every species has come into existence coincident both in time and space with pre-existing closely allied species." The Ternate paper, entitled, "On the Tendency of Varieties to Depart Indefinitely from the Original Type," was slightly shorter—about 5,000 words. It dealt with overproduction in animal numbers, the struggle for existence, adaptation to the environment, and replacement of species by superior varieties, key principles of Darwinism. Wallace rejected completely Lamarckianism, which Darwin found a possible evolutionary mechanism.

While Brackman believes that Darwin was "a man of integrity and character," he also believes that he suffered "the fixation of priority." Brackman believes that Wallace, not Darwin, first wrote out the complete theory, the theory of natural selection commonly attributed to Darwin. He believes that Wallace was the victim of a conspiracy by the scientific aristocracy of the day and was "robbed" of his priority in proclaiming the theory. He also believes that the snobbery of the Victorian era deprived Wallace, with his relatively low social status, of credit for the theory. Finally, he believes that Wallace himself was a very mild person and turned the other cheek rather than protesting.[24] In his *Recollections* (page 56), Darwin himself says, "But I was also ambitious to take a fair place amongst scientific men—whether more ambitious or less so than most of my fellow workers I can form no opinion."

Darwin corresponded with Lyell and Hooker who now proposed to J. J. Bennett, secretary of the Linnean Society of London, that presentations prepared by both Wallace and Darwin "be laid before the Linnean Society." This was done July 1, 1858. The presentation consisted of the reading of Wallace's Ternate paper buttressed by a series of extracts from Darwin's 1844 sketch and a letter written to Asa Gray in 1857. The bulk of the presentation was really Wallace's work. Neither Darwin nor Wallace were present; Wallace was not even in England.

The idea of an origin of new species by natural selection became a topic of widespread conversation and discussion. Darwin's original idea of producing a monograph, his "big book," in which he would marshal all of the evidence for his theory, had to be abandoned, for the production of such a manuscript might well have required an additional 10 years of work. There was no time for this, and the idea of a monograph more than half of which had been completed when Wallace's letter arrived, was abandoned in favor of a shorter semi-popular book known as *The Origin of Species by Natural Selection*, which was published November 24, 1859. It was a volume of some 155,000 words without footnotes. The "big book" would have been three times as long with copious footnotes; the extant portions cite almost 750 books and articles. The book sold out on the day of its publication. For all practical purposes Wallace had been forgotten.

Darwin postulated a struggle for existence, a survival of the fittest, and the development of new species and evolution through the selection of these favorable traits.

The British Association Meeting, Oxford, 1860

Darwin's ideas as presented in the *Origin* were widely discussed and widely debated. Most scientists disagreed with Darwin. Even Lyell could not accept the ultimate conclusion that all life, including man, had descended from one beginning.[25] Evolution by natural selection was a new idea, a paradigm in the sense defined by Thomas Kuhn which would replace the idea of creation, and it is clear that it had the support of only a minority of the scientists. It was generally agreed that this new theory would be the major topic of discussion at the meeting of the British Association for the Advancement of Science to be held at Oxford in 1860.

Darwin did not like controversy, and he insisted that his frail health would not tolerate the type of controversy that he anticipated at Oxford. For that reason he did not attend the meeting. However, his point of view was ably presented by Thomas Huxley, an outspoken atheist of the day. Huxley was opposed by the Anglican bishop of Oxford, Bishop Samuel Wilberforce, the third son of the great English abolitionist, irreverently known as "Soapy Sam" because of his skill in the use of words. Wilberforce, a professor of mathematics as well as a clergyman, was himself an amateur scientist and was certainly at home in the natural sciences. He was fed information by Robert Owen, who was a bitter opponent of Huxley.

The rumbling began at a meeting of Section D on Thursday, June 28. Two papers attacking Darwin were presented. Huxley kept silent at first, but when the second speaker, his rival Robert Owen, declared that the brain of the gorilla differed from that of man more than from that of the lowest animal, Huxley flatly denied Owen's statements and promised to produce more evidence later. On Friday there was a lull, but on Saturday a meeting had been scheduled at which John W. Draper, president of New York University, was to speak on "The Intellectual Development of Europe, Considered with Reference to the Views of Mr. Darwin and Others." The rumor spread that Wilberforce would take the platform to attack Darwin. Darwin's old teacher, Professor Henslow, was in the chair.

Long before the meeting was to open the room was so overcrowded that a shift had to be made to a larger room, which itself was soon crowded with more than 700 men and women. Draper held forth for more than an hour while the crowd waited impatiently. When he finished, Henslow, who was presiding, announced that only those who had valid scientific arguments to present would be permitted to address the meeting. The crowd began to call for the bishop, who had come in late. For a half hour he spoke, savagely ridiculing Darwin and Huxley. Then he turned to Huxley, who was sitting with him on the platform. It was at this point that he put his famous question, whether it was through his grandfather or his grandmother that Huxley claimed descent from an ape. At the bishop's question Huxley is said to have clasped the knee of the individual next to him and whispered, "The Lord has delivered him into my hands." Working up to a climax, Huxley shouted that he would feel no shame in having an ape as an ancestor but that he would be ashamed of a brilliant man who plunged into scientific questions of which he knew nothing.

No one present took down what was said. The only reports of this famous meeting have come from the later recollections of those who were present. Hooker told of his feelings in a letter written to Darwin the next day. Huxley described his own reaction in a letter to Sir Francis Darwin written in 1891, and it confirmed previous reports of what he and others had said.

The room dissolved into an uproar after Huxley's statement. There were those who shouted that this was a direct insult to the clergy. Admiral FitzRoy, the former captain of the *Beagle*, waved a Bible aloft shouting over the tumult that it, rather than the viper he had harbored on his ship, was the true and unimpeachable authority.

In any case, the battle was now joined, and there was general sympathy for Huxley because it was felt that Wilberforce had taken improper advantage of him by ridiculing him, a reversal of the earlier situation in which most scientists disagreed with Darwin.

When Bishop Wilberforce was thrown from his horse and killed in 1873, Huxley commented that "reality and his brains came into contact and the result was fatal," a comment that was hardly kinder than the bishop's disgraceful attack on him in 1860.[26]

The outcome of this encounter, however, was unfortunate, for once more the church was represented as using its power and authority to stop the progress of science and to interfere with proper scientific research.

The Dayton, Tennessee, Monkey Trial

The controversy over the theory of evolution continued in England, on the continent, and in the United States. There was a great deal of anti-intellectualism and anti-scientism in the United States, especially in the years following Word War I. The war was a disillusioning experience. It put an end to the idea of progress. It was not true that "every day in every way we're getting better and better." It became very clear that there was evil in the world, as Scripture declared (Gen. 8:21), and that evil men could use scientific developments for evil purposes.

Considerable concern was felt over the rise of atheistic communism after the victory of Lenin in Russia and the spread of communism in many parts of the world. The universities also became the target of suspicion. It was felt that faculty members were interested not only in spreading communism but, as a corollary, in undermining the Christian faith of students who came into their classes.

There were those who believed that the solution to this problem was the typical American solution—"pass a law." Associated with communism and the undermining of Christianity was the teaching of evolution. It was very evident that this scientific theory undermined the Biblical account of creation and affected the Christian faith. One of the Tennessee legislators, John W. Butler, was disconcerted to find that his daughters had left the church when they returned from the university. They had enrolled as pious Christians; they returned totally uninterested in the church. Butler's conversations with them led him to believe that they had been especially influenced by the teaching of evolution at the university.

His suggestion was that the legislature adopt a law forbidding the teaching of evolution in the schools of Tennessee. He and others conferred with William Jennings Bryan, "Mr. Protestant" of the day. Bryan, a Presbyterian, was fully sympathetic to their concerns and to their desire for a solution. He cautioned, however, against the inclusion of any penalty in the proposed law. Rather, he suggested that the law be adopted as "the sense of the legislature." Instead, as the law was drawn up it provided a fine or imprisonment as the penalty for infringement on the law.

The Butler law was immediately challenged by the American Civil Liberties Union, and it was generally understood that the ACLU would proceed to test the law in the courts in one of the larger cities of Tennessee, either Nashville or Chattanooga. However, the businessmen of Dayton, Tennessee, at that time a backwater county seat, decided that it might be good for business to arrange to conduct the trial in Dayton. The plan was hatched May 5, 1925. The chairman of the Rhea County School Board, Fred E. Robinson, was the owner of Robinson's Drug Store, the social center for Dayton. Present at the meeting that day were Robinson; Brady, who ran the town's other drug store; Sue Hicks, the town's leading lawyer, who supported the Butler law; another attorney; a store clerk; and George Rappelyea, a vigorous opponent of the Butler law. John Scopes was invited to join the group and was asked whether it was indeed true that he was teaching evolution. He had filled in for the high school principal during the latter's illness. The high school principal was the regular biology teacher.

Meanwhile, the ACLU had advertised in the *Chattanooga News* offering to pay the expenses of anyone willing to test the constitutionality of the Butler law. When Scopes agreed to test the law, Rappelyea swore out a warrant which was promptly served. Robinson phoned the *Chattanooga News* saying, "This is F. E. Robinson in Dayton. I am chairman of the school board here. We've just arrested a man for teaching evolution." Subsequently, Rappelyea wired the American Civil Liberties Union and got a promise from them to assist in the defense of Scopes.

Since this action in Dayton took precedence over any action in Nashville or Chattanooga, the trial was conducted in Dayton. The local prosecutor felt inadequate to prosecute the case, and William Jennings Bryan reluctantly agreed to serve as prosecutor. The American Civil Liberties Union was represented by Dudley Field Malone and Clarence Darrow. The latter had just concluded the Leopold and Loeb trial in Chicago, in which he defended two young University of Chicago students who had been involved in a "thrill" murder. Bryan was reluctant to serve as prosecutor because he had not tried any cases in 25 years. He had been active in the U. S. Senate and had been the unsuccessful Democratic candidate for the presidency on three separate occasions.

The trial began July 10, 1925. Darrow very cleverly called Bryan to the witness stand as a witness for the defense. Bryan was disconcerted by this move, but the judge, somewhat amused by the discomfiture of such a prominent person as Bryan, reserved his decision. Darrow questioned Bryan regarding his understanding of Genesis. Bryan weakened and admitted that he believed the days of Genesis might well represent periods of time. With this admission he was very much on the defensive, and Darrow continued to press him as to why he insisted on accepting the historicity of other parts of the account but was willing to agree that the days of Genesis might be long periods of time.

The entire atmosphere of the trial was that of a circus. The seventh day of the trial, the day on which Darrow called Bryan to the witness stand, was held on the courthouse lawn because the overcrowding of the courthouse threatened the structure itself. Cracks appeared in the ceiling of the first floor under the second floor courtroom in which the case was being tried. There was a carnival and holiday air throughout the city.

The day after Bryan was put on the stand, Darrow suddenly moved to conclude the defense. The case went to the jury, which convicted Scopes. There was some lack of clarity in the law itself; it was not clear whether the penalty on conviction was to be assigned by the judge or by the jury. Scopes was fined $100 by the judge, and he appealed. The appeals court ruled that the penalty should have been determined by the jury. By this time Bryan had died; he was critically ill at the time of the trial and died five days after it ended. For that reason the case was never retried.

But once more it appeared as if the church in the form of Bryan, the leading Protestant layman of the country, was persecuting a helpless and inarticulate high school biology teacher. Thus, as in the Galileo case and the Oxford encounter, it was made to appear as if for the third time the church was using its power to interfere with scientific progress and scientific research.

Notes

1. John A. Moore, "Evolution and Public Education," *BioScience* 32 (1982):606.
2. R. C. Lewontin, "Evolution/Creation Debate: A Time for Truth," *BioScience* 31 (1981):559.
3. Thomas S. Kuhn, *The Structure of Scientific Revolutions,* Foundations of the Unity of Science Series, vol. 2, no. 2, 2d ed. (Chicago: University of Chicago Press, 1970).
4. Roger Lewin, "A Naturalist of the Genome," *Science* 222 (1983):402.
5. William J. Broad, "Paul Feyerabend: Science and the Anarchist," *Science* 206 (1979):534—37.
6. Frank J. Tipler, "Extraterrestrial Intelligence: A Skeptical View of Radio Searches," *Science* 219 (1983):110—12.
7. Edward Edelson, "Faster Than the Speed of Light?" *Mosaic* July/August (1982):25—29.
8. David M. Raup, "Evolution and the Fossil Record," *Science* 213 (1981):289.
9. William J. Broad, "A Bibliophile's Quest for Copernicus," *Science* 218 (1982):662.
10. Martin Luther, *Table Talk,* trans. and ed. Theodore G. Tappert, Vol. 54 in the American Edition of *Luther's Works,* gen. ed. Helmut T. Lehmann (Philadelphia: Fortress, 1967), pp. 358ff.
11. John Dillenberger, *Protestant Thought and Natural Science* (New York: Doubleday, 1960), p. 38.

12. Broad, "Bibliophile's Quest," p. 664.
13. Griorgia de Santillana, *The Crime of Galileo* (Chicago: University of Chicago Press, 1955) p. xii.
14. Fred Hoyle, *Nicholaus Copernicus: An Essay On His Life and Work* (New York: Harper & Row, 1973), p. 88.
15. Fritz Rohrlich, "Facing Quantum Reality," *Science* 221 (1983):1251—55.
16. Roger Lewin, "Lamarck Will Not Lie Down," *Science* 213 (1981):316—21.
17. Charles Darwin, *Autobiography of Charles Darwin* (London: Watts and Co., 1929), p. 20.
18. Ibid., p. 139.
19. Ibid., p. 143.
20. Ibid., p. 144.
21. Ibid., p. 144f.
22. Ibid., p. 149.
23. Ibid., p. 27.
24. Arnold C. Brackman, *A Delicate Arrangement* (New York: Quadrangle, 1980), pp. xi, 45.
25. Ruth Moore, *Charles Darwin* (New York: Knopf, 1958), p. 124.
26. Ronald W. Clark, *The Huxleys* (New York: McGraw-Hill, 1968), p. 117.

3
Creation in Scripture and Confessional Statements

The doctrine of creation is not an obscure doctrine in Scripture. There are many Biblical doctrines that are based on just a few Scriptural references, but there are at least 75 references to creation in the Old and New Testaments. The Bible assumes that God made heaven and earth, that man stands in a creature-Creator relationship to God, and that man owes obedience to Yahweh because He made him and all things.

Most of the references to creation simply state that God is the creator of heaven and earth. They are the basis for the general, all-inclusive statement of the Apostles' Creed, "I believe in God the Father almighty, maker of heaven and earth." However, there are a number of sections in Scripture which deal in considerable detail with the creation of heaven and earth, the plants, the animals, and man.

The most complete statement on creation is at the beginning of the Bible, in Genesis 1 and 2. This section is followed almost immediately by the account of the fall into sin. Later references to creation either serve to interpret the Genesis account or add details to it.

Explaining Genesis

In the light of the basic principle of interpretation that Scripture interprets Scripture, it is worth noting references in the Bible which throw light on the meaning of the Genesis account or focus on particular details of it. The Bible makes clear that creation is the work of the Triune God.

In Job 26:13 there is a reference to the activity of the Holy Spirit, the Third Person of the Trinity, in the work of creation. There is a similar reference to the activity of the Second and Third Persons of the Trinity in Psalm 33:6-9. In Psalm 104:30 there is another reference to the activity of the Third Person of the Trinity and in Proverbs 8:25-30 a reference to the Second Person of the Trinity, Wisdom personified. Psalm 148:5 refers to creation by the power of God's Word.

The New Testament clearly teaches that Jesus Christ, the Second Person of the Trinity, was involved in the work of creation. St. John in the introduction to his gospel makes that very plain. He says (John 1:3, 10), "All things were made through Him, and without Him was not anything made that was made. . . . the world was made through Him." St. Paul says the same thing in 1 Corinthians 8:6, where he speaks of "one Lord, Jesus Christ, through whom are all things and through whom we exist." He repeats this teaching in Colossians 1:16-17, where he writes, "for in Him all things were created, in heaven and on earth, visible and invisible, whether thrones or dominions or principalities or authorities—all things were created through and for Him. He is before all things, and in Him all things hold together." The author of the Epistle to the Hebrews makes the same point when he refers to our Lord (Heb. 2:10), as Him "for whom and by whom all things exist."

References such as these support the traditional understanding of the Genesis account as assigning the work of creation not only to God the Father but also to the Second and Third Persons of the Trinity.

Other sections of Scripture throw light on some of the disputed sections of Genesis. One of these is the much-disputed question of the length of the creation day. In Exodus 20:11 we are told, "for in six days the Lord made heaven and earth, the sea, and all that is in them, and rested on the seventh day." This is a clear reference to the length of the creation days and makes it evident that they are to be understood as ordinary days. This particular reference is associated with the sabbath commandment by which the Hebrews were limited to a six-day work week and were commanded to rest on the seventh day. God drew a clear parallel between the Jewish work week and the creation week. Just as He worked for six days in creating heaven and earth and then rested on the seventh day, so His people were to limit their employment to six days and were to rest and worship on the seventh day. It is this same parallel between the Jewish work week and the creation week that is drawn in Exodus 31:12-17. God commands His people to keep the sabbath and tells them that anyone working on the sabbath shall be cut off from among His people. In support of this command He tells them (v. 17), "in six days the Lord made heaven and earth, and on the seventh day He rested, and was refreshed."

In Isaiah 40:22 there is a significiant poetical reference which counters the oft-raised charge that the Bible teaches a flat earth. There Isaiah tells us, "It is He who sits above the circle of the earth." A similar reference in Job 26:7 tells us "He stretches out the north over the void, and hangs the earth upon nothing." While we must recognize the poetic literary genre, these references certainly do not support the picture of a flat earth which critics so often tell us is a part of Biblical cosmology.

Details of Creation

There are a number of references, some poetical, to details of creation. In Job 28:24-26 there is a rather detailed reference to the creation of the elements. The heavens attracted considerable attention from the Hebrews, and, as might be expected, there are a number of references to the creation of the heavenly bodies. In Job 37:16, 18 we are told, "Do you know the balancing of the clouds?. . . Can you, like Him, spread out the skies?" God is said to have laid the foundation of the earth in Job 38:4. In Job 38:7-10 there is a further reference to the natural elements of our environment. Psalm 74:16 refers to the creation of the heavenly bodies. Amos 5:8 speaks of the creation of the constellations.

There is a reference to the detail of the creation of the sun and moon and their purpose (cf. Gen. 1:16-18) in Psalm 104:19. A similar reference is found in Psalm 136:7-9. Jeremiah 31:35 is a further reference to the creation of the sun, moon, and stars.

In Isaiah 45:7-12 God emphasizes the Creator-creature relationship of man over against his God.

There are also details given elsewhere in Scripture which add to and supplement the Genesis account. The Genesis account does not have a clear reference to *creatio ex nihilo*, a creation out of nothing. But that this was the case is made quite clear by the New Testament. In Romans 4:17 St. Paul speaks of God who "calls into existence the things that do not exist." The author of the Epistle to the Hebrews is very clear in saying, in Hebrews 11:3, "by faith we understand that the world was created by the Word of God, so that what is seen was made out of things which do not appear."

The Heavens an Iron Vault?

In Jeremiah 10:12 we are told that by His understanding God "stretched out the heavens," a reference to what the King James Version translates as the "firmament" and which many people have understood in the sense of a solid iron dome. But Jeremiah describes it as something that is "stretched out," a better reference to the root meaning of the word used in Genesis 1:7 and one which suggests that the Biblical writers did not share in the Babylonian idea of a three-storied universe.

It is interesting to note in Jeremiah 51:15 that once more there is a reference to the "stretching out" of the heavens. Still another passage which talks about the heavens as stretched out is Psalm 104:2. There are further references to the heavens as stretched out in Isaiah 42:5; 44:24; 48:13; and 51:13, 16. It is a caricature of Scripture to picture it as representing the "firmament" as a solid iron vault separating earth and heaven. The Hebrews pictured it as something stretched out, not as something solid.

Creation and Preservation

The Bible clearly associates creation and preservation, although it does distinguish between the two doctrines. Preservation has been called *creatio continua*, a reference to the fact that at creation God established the laws through which He ordinarily governs the universe. In Nehemiah 9:6 we are told that Ezra in addressing the children of Israel spoke of God and said, "Thou art the Lord, Thou alone; Thou hast made heaven, the heaven of heavens, with all their host, the earth and all that is on it, the seas and all that is in them; and Thou preservest all of them." In Jeremiah 51:15-16 we are told, "It is He who made the earth by His power, who established the world by His wisdom, and by His understanding stretched out the heavens. When He utters His voice there is a tumult of waters in the heavens, and He makes the mist rise from the ends of earth. He makes lightnings for the rain, and He brings forth the wind from His storehouses."

In speaking at Athens St. Paul said, "the God who made the world and everything in it, being Lord of heaven and earth, does not live in shrines made by man, nor is He served by human hands, as though He needed anything, since He himself gives to all men life and breath and everything" (Acts 17:24-26). In Revelation 4:11 we are told, "Thou didst create all things, and by Thy will they existed and were created." Again, these are references to both creation and preservation.

New Testament References to Genesis

Our Lord referred to both Genesis 1 and Genesis 2 in His encounter with the Pharisees regarding divorce. He quotes Genesis 1:27 and goes on to quote Genesis 2:24. Both Matthew and Mark record this episode (cf. Matt. 19:4f; Mark 10:6-8).

St. Paul refers to the natural knowledge of man and to the clear evidence of His creative activity in Romans 1:20 and argues that for this reason there is no excuse for the atheist.

2 Corinthians 4:6 is a clear reference to Genesis 1:3.

2 Peter 3:5 is a clear reference to Genesis 1:9ff.

Certainly creation is not an obscure biblical doctrine. God has given us many details from what only He could know, details which He expects us to accept in faith.

The Historicity of Adam

A further question in connection with Genesis 1 and 2 is the question of the historicity of Adam. Was he a particular historical individual or does Adam represent mankind, the German *Mensch*? It is, of course, true that the Hebrew uses the word *Adam* as the word for "man" as well as for a particular individual. Yet is is also true that Adam occurs in the various genealogical records where he is named as an individual along with other individuals (1 Chron. 1:1; Luke 3:38). Jude 14 also refers to our first parent as an individual in a genealogical line. Job refers to Adam as an individual (31:33).

Particularly significant are the many references to Adam as an individual in the writings of St. Paul, references which require that Adam be identified as an individual, not as a representative of mankind; otherwise, St. Paul's whole argument in these particular references falls. St. Paul refers to Adam as an individual in Romans 5:14 (where there are two references to him); in 1 Corinthians 15:22 and 15:45 (where again there are two references which imply he was an individual); and in 1 Timothy 2:13, 14.

It is clear that while the word *Adam* is sometimes used for "man," it also refers to an individual, and that this is the case in the early chapters of Genesis. There is indeed a question as to where the word should first be used as a proper noun, and this is reflected in the various Bible translations. In the King James Version Adam as an individual is first named in Genesis 2:19. The New International Version first names Adam in Genesis 2:20. The Roman Catholic Douay Version first mentions Adam in Genesis 2:19, and the New American Catholic edition of 1961 first names him in Genesis 3:17. The Living Bible first uses the name "Adam" in Genesis 2:23. The Revised Standard Version first names Adam in Genesis 3:17, as does the New American Standard Bible. The Good News Bible reserves this name until Genesis 3:20. The Beck Bible and the Jerusalem Bible first use "Adam" in Genesis 4:25.

It is probably immaterial where the name "Adam" is first used to designate a given idividual; this is an arbitrary decision on the part of the translator. However, it is quite clear from St. Paul's references that Adam was an individual and that references in the early chapters of Genesis, whether translated "the man" or "Adam," are to a single individual who is the father of the human race.

The Bible on "Creation"

What conclusions can we reach from a review of what Scripture says about creation? It is quite clear that the doctrine of creation is by no means an obscure one in the Bible. It is referred to again and again from Genesis through Revelation. The assumption of the holy writers is that God is indeed the creator of heaven and earth.

It is also apparent that the Scriptures regard the creation account in Genesis as historical. There is no indication whatsoever that any of the sacred writers regard it as myth or saga or pre-history. The most complete account of creation is an account found in the first book of the Bible, which purports to be history. It is quite evident that our Lord regarded the Genesis account as historical, for His whole argument in the controversy with the Pharisees concerning divorce hinges on the historicity of the account of the creation of the two sexes. It is also very clear that St. Paul regards this account as historical, since a whole series of arguments of his depend upon the historicity of Adam and the historicity of the fall narrative.

Many of the references to creation outside Genesis are general in nature. They simply assume that God is the creator of heaven and earth, and they add no detail. However, there are a number of citations involving details of the creation account. There are references to the creation of light, to the creation of the sky, to the creation of the heavenly bodies, and to the creation of man himself.

There are some aspects of creation that are expanded in other parts of the Scripture. While there are references to the work of the Trinity in creation in the Genesis account, there are even clearer references elsewhere in the Scriptures. Thus, these references elaborate on and explain the role of the Second and Third Persons of the Trinity in creation.

The reference in Exodus to the days of Genesis makes it quite clear that the creation days were ordinary days; thus, this reference is a good illustration of the principle that Scripture interprets Scripture.

One aspect of creation that is assumed in Genesis but not explicitly taught is *creatio ex nihilo*. This teaching is clearly developed elsewhere in Scripture.

Interpretations of the Creation Account

There has been a wide variety of interpretations of the creation account among Christians. We shall have occasion to refer to some of these and to some aspects of them later. We may disregard commentators outside the Christian church who are not interested in Scripture and give it no credence. Those who accept the Bible as God's Word fall into three general categories: theistic evolutionists, progressive creationists, and fiat creationists.

Theistic evolutionists believe that God was behind the process of creation. Most of them believe that He created the matter/energy which constitutes the universe, and that He established the natural laws through which the universe is governed. They insist that God is behind the process of creation and that He guided the development of the universe, the earth, and the living things that it contains. But they are willing to accept the idea of development of life and of living things from an original life form. Most of them deny the historicity of Adam and believe that Adam represents an evolutionary population that had attained the status of *Homo sapiens*. They have no problem with modern scientific theories of evolution. They find it possible to accept limitless development so long as it is acknowledged that God has been guiding that development.

Progressive creationists believe that creation was accomplished by God's almighty power through a series of creative acts separated by vast periods of time. The days of Genesis are usually regarded as ordinary days, but progressive creationists believe that there may have been long periods of development by natural processes between the individual creative acts of God. They believe that the six days of

creation represent at least six separate supernatural creative inter-
ventions by God. The progressive creationist also accepts the historicity of Adam and his special creation. He differs from the fiat
creationist in that he does not believe that the days of Genesis represent a creation week.

Fiat creationists accept the Genesis account as an historical account. They believe that creation was accomplished by God's almighty
power in six ordinary days. They recognize that at creation God established the natural laws through which He ordinarily operates the
universe. But they believe that God can also intervene supernaturally
in the affairs of this earth and that He did so during the creation
week.

Defining Creation and Evolution

What is it that separates evolution and creation? Both evolution
and creation are attempting to account for the wide variety of living
things which we observe on our time level. The evolutionist believes
that matter evolved, possibly from an original mass of hydrogen, to
the 92 naturally-occurring elements which we know. He further believes that this process was a natural one, and by natural processes
non-living matter became alive. From this non-living matter that had
become alive, all the life forms that we know developed in a process
of branching. He believes that man himself is the product of a long
line of evolutionary development. All of this came about through
strictly natural processes.

The creationist believes that matter/energy came into existence
by God's almighty power. He denies that it is eternal; it had a beginning. He believes that God by His almighty power organized matter
into the form which we know today. He further believes that by God's
almighty power non-living matter became alive, and that from the
beginning living things existed in a wide variety of forms. He believes
that man was specially created, that he did not develop from lower
organisms.

The creationist recognizes—as does the theistic evolutionist—
that God at the beginning established the natural laws through which
He ordinarily governs the universe. It is through these that He ordinarily works, but the creationist also believes that He can suspend
or override these natural laws and use His divine power even as He
did in creation. It is for this reason that the creationist prays; he asks
God to guide the affairs of this universe so that what he wishes may
be accomplished if it is in accordance with His will, but he also asks

God to intervene directly if what he wishes accomplished cannot be accomplished through the operation of natural laws.

Time and the Age of the Earth

What about the matter of time, the age of the earth? This is a problem separate from the problem of creation, though clearly it is one closely associated with it. Here the creationist probably has an advantage. It would be conceivable for the wide variety of living things to exist and to have originated as he postulates in a world that is very old or in a world that is very young. Aside from Scriptural limitations, the creationist is free to postulate either a young or an old earth. He looks then to Scripture for guidance; this is a topic which we will discuss later. The evolutionist, however, must have an old earth. Evolution cannot operate if the earth is judged to be only thousands or tens of thousands or even hundreds of thousands of years old.

Confessional Statements on Creation

Creation in the Lutheran Confessions

It has often been argued that there is no article on creation in the Lutheran Confessions, and therefore Lutherans are free to accept either creation or evolution. Of course, it is true that there is no particular or specific article on creation. The reason for this is very simple: the doctrine was not in controversy at the time the Lutheran Confessions where written. The Confessions grew out of controversy and dealt only with topics that were in controversy. At the same time, we need to recognize that there are many references to creation in the Lutheran Confessions and that these assume the Genesis account to be historical. The Lutheran Confessions, therefore, support the approach of the fiat creationist.

To begin, with there are references to creation in the three ecumenical creeds. The Apostles' Creed speaks of "God, the Father almighty, maker of heaven and earth." The Nicene Creed says, "I believe in one God, the Father almighty, maker of heaven and earth and of all things visible and invisible." The Athanasian Creed says, "The Father is uncreated, the Son is uncreated, the Holy Spirit is uncreated."

There are innumerable references to creation in the specifically Lutheran Confessions. In Article XXIII of the Augsburg Confession, which deals with the marriage of priests, Genesis 1:27 and 1:28 are quoted.[1] The confessors assumed these passages to be historical, for unless they are historical the argument employed here falls.

In Article XXVII on monastic vows, Genesis 2:18 is quoted, once more as an historical statement.[2]

Article XXIII of the Apology of the Augsburg Confession, dealing with sacerdotal marriages, quotes both Genesis 1:28 and Genesis 1:11. Again the confessors regarded these statements as historical, not mythological or allegorical.[3]

The First Article in both the Small Catechism and the Large Catechism deals with creation and the special work of the First Person of the Trinity.[4]

The Formula of Concord, Solid Declaration, in dealing with original sin in Article I, refers to creation and states, "in the article of creation Scripture testifies not only that God created human nature before the Fall, but also that after the Fall human nature is God's creature and handiwork."[5] Here again the confessors simply assume the Genesis account to be historical.

The Apology in Article II on "Original Sin" quotes Genesis 1:27 and describes man as "created in the image of God and after His likeness," once more a clear reference to the historicity of the Genesis account.[6]

In the Formula of Concord, Solid Declaration, Article VII on the "Lord's Supper," Chrysostom is quoted as applying Genesis 1:28 to the question of the efficaciousness of the words of institution. The confessors quote these words favorably and in a way that makes clear that they were regarded by Chrysostom as literal and historical.[7]

In the Epitome of the Formula of Concord, Article VI, paragraph 2, on "the Third Function of the Law" there is a reference to "our first parents" who "even before the Fall did not live without the law, for the law of God was written in their hearts when they were created in the image of God."[8]

References to a Historical Adam

The Lutheran Confessions also refer repeatedly to Adam and assume his historicity. In Article XII of the Apology on "Penitence" there is a reference to the Gospel which the confessors say was "first . . . given to Adam, later to the patriarchs, then illumined by the prophets, and finally proclaimed and revealed by Christ among the Jews, and spread by the apostles throughout the world."[9] The confessors here clearly assume the historicity and individuality of Adam, since they put him on a parallel with other individuals who are clearly persons.

In the next section of the same article[10] there is another reference which assumes the historicity of the father of us all, for we are told, "Adam was rebuked and terrified after his sins; this was contrition." Subsequently, in the same article[11] Adam is mentioned alongside David and other individuals whose historicity is never questioned. In Article VIII of the Smalcald Articles dealing with "Confession" there is a reference to both Adam and Eve, for the confessors say, "All this is the old devil and the old serpent who made enthusiasts of Adam and Eve. He led them from the external word of God to spiritualizing and to their own imagination and he did this through other external words."[12] In that same article there is another reference, for the confessors say, "enthusiasm clings to Adam and to his descendents from the beginning to the end of the world."[13]

The Large Catechism article on "Baptism" has still another reference to Adam, for it asks, "What is the old man? He is what is born in us from Adam, irascible, spiteful, envious, unchaste, greedy, lazy, proud, yes, and unbelieving; he is beset with all vices and by nature has nothing good in him."[14]

Thus, it is clear that the Lutheran confessors accepted the Genesis account as an historical account of actual events in which an individual Adam and an individual Eve played a significant role.

Creation in the Confessions of Other Traditions

The earliest generally accepted Reformed confession, the Second Helvetic Confession of 1566, has one chapter, Chapter 7, on creation, and another chapter, Chapter 8, on the fall. These chapters assume that the Genesis account is historical. The Heidelberg Catechism of 1563 in question 7 answers the question, "Whence, then, comes this depraved nature of man?" with the words, "From the fall and disobedience of our first parents, Adam and Eve, in paradise, whereby our nature became so corrupt that we are all conceived and born in sin." The Belgic Confession of 1561 has an article on "Creation," Article 12. It continues in Article 14 to discuss the creation of man and his fall. These articles, too, simply assume the historicity of the Genesis account.

The Westminster Confession, the basic confession of the Presbyterian church, has one chapter, Chapter 4, dealing with creation, and another chapter, Chapter 6, dealing with the Fall. In the Westminister Confession it is assumed that the Genesis account is historical. It might be noted that in most of the Reformed confessions there is an article on "Providence" between the article on "Creation" and the article on "The Fall." This seems to be a general Reformed approach.

The Thirity-nine Articles, the basic confession of the Anglican church, speaks of the true God as "the Maker and Preserver of all things both visible and invisible" in Article 1. Article 9 deals with original or birth sin. As with the previous confessions, these articles assume the historicity of the Genesis account.

The Dordrecht Confession of 1632, a basic Mennonite confession, begins with an article entitled "Of God and the creation of all things." Article 2 deals with the Fall of man and refers to Genesis 3 as an historical account.

Baptists have been traditionally anti-creedal, and yet a number of documents have been produced which have the appearance and effect of a confession. One of these is the New Hampshire Confession in 1833, which is entitled "Declaration of Faith." While Article 3, "Of the Fall of Man," makes no direct reference to Adam and Eve, it speaks of the fall as an historical event. The "Abstract of Principles" adopted by the Southern Baptist Theological Seminary in 1859 and by the Southeastern Baptist Theological Seminary in 1950 has an article, Article VI, dealing with the fall of man. While again there is no direct reference to Adam and Eve, there is a clear acknowledgement of the historicity of the fall account. In the "Report of Committee on Baptist Faith and Message," adopted by the Southern Baptist Convention in 1925, there is a detailed paragraph entitled, "The Fall of Man" which states: "Man was created by the special act of God, as recorded in Genesis. He was created in a state of holiness under the law of his Maker but through the temptation of Satan he transgressed the command of God and fell from his original holiness and righteousness; whereby his posterity inherited a nature corrupt and in bondage to sin, are under condemnation, and as soon as they are capable of moral action, become actual transgressors." It is interesting that this statement of Baptist faith and message was adopted in 1925 in the middle of the controversy on evolution sparked by the Scopes trial.

The 25 "Articles of Religion," written by John Wesley and adopted by the Methodist Conference in Baltimore in 1784, has an Article 7 entitled "Of Original or Birth Sin." It refers to Adam and assumes his historicity.

A very recent confession of faith is the "Confession of Faith of the Huria-Kristen Batak Protestant," which was produced by the Batak Church of Indonesia in 1951. In Article 3 the church confesses, "We believe and confess God, the Father, created, preserves and governs all things visible and invisible." In Article 5, dealing with "Origin of Sin," this statement is made: "Thus, although the first human beings, Adam and Eve, were good and able to act in conformity with God's will, they nevertheless transgressed the commandment which God had given them because of the seduction by the Devil and turned away from God. Sin is transgression." The confession goes on to say in Article 6, dealing with sin, "We believe and confess: since Adam and Eve fell into sin, sin has been passed on to all their descendents."

Thus other traditions, too, have recognized or assumed the historicity of the creation account and the fall of our first parents.

Notes

1. Citations are from *The Book of Concord*, ed. Theodore G. Tappert (Philadelphia: Fortress, 1959). This citation is from AC XXIII 5.
2. AC XXVII 20.
3. Ap XXIII 7, 8.
4. SC II 1, 2; LC II 9-16.
5. FC SD i 34.
6. Ap II 18.
7. FC SD vii 76.
8. FC Ep VI 2.
9. Ap XII 53.
10. Ap XII 55.
11. Ap XII 155.
12. SA Part 3 VIII 5.
13. SA Part 3 VIII 9.
14. LC IV 66

4

A Systematic Study of Creation

According to Scripture, creation is the work of the Triune God. There are clear references to creation as the work of the Second Person of the Trinity (Prov. 8:26-30; John 1:3, 10; Heb. 2:10) and as the work of the Holy Spirit (Job 26:13; Ps. 33:6). These are in addition to references to the Second and Third Persons of the Trinity in the Genesis account itself.

Systematicians distinguish between *opera divina ad extra* and *opera divina ad intra*. The former are divine works relating to the world; the latter are works within the Godhead, such as the generation of the Son and spiration of the Holy Spirit. Creation is an *opus divinum ad extra*. All such works are the works of all three persons of the Trinity. Sometimes this work is referred to as an *opus proprium*, a work attributed to the Father, though really the work of the Triune God.

Creation contrasts with both pantheism and dualism. Pantheism identifies the creation with God. God is nature. In its crudest form pantheism finds God in all natural objects. A more subtle form of pantheism is the identification of God and nature. God is not a person, but rather a force.

Dualism postulates an eternity of matter/energy. It solves the problem of the origin of this matter/energy by assuming that it has always existed. Yet to suggest that matter/energy had no beginning boggles the mind and requires far more than "the faith of a mustard seed." It is certainly easier to believe that God created matter/energy "in the beginning" than to believe that matter/energy is eternal.

According to Scripture, creation is a part of the natural knowledge of God (Rom. 1:19f.). Reason suggests that matter/ energy had a beginning, and that it was the result of a plan by an all-knowing and all-wise God. Atheism is an exceptional approach to the question of whether God exists or not; rationally, the average person recognizes that God exists because he looks about him in creation.

God's purpose in creation was to glorify Himself. Creation existed for Him, for His honor, and for His glory.

Creation Statements

One of the clearer statements of the doctrine of creation is to be found in the "Brief Statement of the Missouri Synod's Doctrinal Position" (1932). There Article V reads: "We teach that God has created heaven and earth, and that in the manner and in the space of time recorded in the Holy Scriptures, especially Genesis 1 and 2, namely, by His almighty creative Word, and in six days. We reject every doctrine which denies or limits the work of creation as taught in Scripture. In our days it is denied or limited by those who assert, ostensibly in deference to science, that the world came into existence through a process of evolution; that is, that it has over immense periods of time developed more or less out of itself. Since no man was present when it pleased God to create the world, we must look for a reliable account of creation to God's own record, found in God's own book, the Bible. We accept God's own record with full confidence and confess with Luther's Catechism: 'I believe that God has made me and all creatures.' "

This statement is expanded in "A Statement of Scriptural and Confessional Principles," adopted by The Lutheran Church—Missouri Synod in 1973.

Interpreting Genesis 1—3

How are the first chapters of Genesis to be understood? Are they meant to be history? Or are they meant to be allegory? Or myth? Or saga?

It is very clear that there are different literary genres in the Bible. While there is a literal meaning for every statement of Scripture, the literal meaning is not necessarily the literalistic meaning of the words themselves. It is quite clear, for example, that poetry may contain images that are not to be understood literalistically. Prophecy is composed to some extent of pictures. In parables we must be very careful that we understand the point of comparison (*tertium*) and do not seek literal meanings in details which have been added simply to complete the picture.

It must also be recognized that within an account which is basically historical there may well be poetry, with its imagery and its figures of speech. There also may be accounts of prophetic utterances. For example, Genesis 2:23, stating the reaction of Adam to the creation of Eve, is Hebrew poetry. The *protevangelium* in Genesis 3:15 is also poetry.

The literal meaning, then, is not necessarily to be understood in the sense of the literalistic meaning; that is, not every detail of a particular account is necessarily literalistically true. As we pointed out, not every detail in the parables has a meaning. Instead, we must seek the *tertium*, the point of comparison. This same principle applies to prophecy, particularly to the last chapters of Daniel and to the Book of Revelation. It was this mistake of interpreting literalistically that the Jews made in seeking to understand the prophecies of the Messiah's kingdom, and it is this mistake that is made by present-day chiliasts in seeking to understand the prophecies of Daniel and Revelation. Cerinthus, who was active at Ephesus about A.D. 100 and was reputed to be an opponent of St. John, made this mistake in interpreting some of the prophecies of Revelation in a literalistic way.

In the third century the school of Alexandria, especially Origen, supported the allegorical interpretation of Scripture. Origen held that passages of Scripture which relate historical events or speak of earthly things often have a deeper meaning, different from the literal one, and he said we must distinguish between the literal sense, the allegorical or mystical sense, and the moral sense. He was particularly disturbed by the reports of the sins of some of the great saints of the Bible, such as Noah's drunkenness and David's adultery, and he believed that these reports were unworthy of the Scriptures. While he did not deny the literal sense of these reports, he believed that the literal report often had to be disregarded or even discarded. Origen's way of interpreting was opposed particularly at Antioch; yet it came to be the generally accepted way of interpreting the Scriptures. By the time of the Middle Ages it was generally accepted that Scripture passages have a fourfold meaning: the literal; the allegorical or mystical; the moral; and the anagogic; which was essentially an eschatological meaning.

Luther on the Interpretation of Genesis

It was against this fourfold interpretation that Luther and the others reformers had to contend. Luther insisted that each statement of Scripture had only one meaning. It became especially necessary for him to contend against the allegorical interpretation of the Bible. Luther does this repeatedly in the first volume of his works, which deals with the book we are most concerned with, the Book of Genesis. For instance, in discussing the length of the creation days, he says, "Nor does it serve any useful purpose to make Moses at the onset so mystical and allegorical. His purpose is to teach us not about allegorical creatures and an allegorical world, but about real creatures and a visible world apprehended by the senses. Therefore, as the proverb has it, he calls 'a spade a spade,' i.e., he employs the terms 'day' and 'evening' without allegory, just as we customarily do. The evangelist Matthew, in his last chapter, preserves this method of expression when he writes that Christ rose on the evening of the Sabbath which began to dawn into the first day of the week (Matthew 28:1). If, then, we do not understand the nature of the days or have no insight into why God wanted to make use of these intervals of time, let us confess our lack of understanding rather than distort the words, contrary to their context, into a foreign meaning.

"Therefore so far as this opinion of Augustine is concerned, we assert that Moses spoke in the literal sense, not allegorically or figuratively, i.e., that the world with all its creatures was created within six days, as the words read. If we do not comprehend the reason for this, let us remain pupils and leave the job of teacher to the Holy Spirit."[1]

A little later, talking about the primeval light, Luther refers to the suggestion of the medievalists that the phrase "He separated light from darkness" meant that he separated the good angels from the bad. "But this is toying with ill-timed allegories (for Moses is relating history); it is not interpreting Scripture. Moreover, Moses wrote that uneducated men might have clear accounts of the creation. Such preposterous ideas should, therefore, not be propounded here."[2]

In another section Luther says, "The distance between the rivers troubles Origen, for he has in mind a garden area of the size they are among us. Therefore he turns to allegory. Paradise he takes to be heaven; the trees he takes to be angels; the rivers he takes to be wisdom. Such twaddle is unworthy of theologians, though for a mirthful poet they might perhaps be appropriate. Origen does not take into consideration that Moses is writing history and, what is more, one that deals with matters long since past."[3]

Still later he says, "According to our ability, we have treated all these facts in their historical meaning, which is their real and true one. In the interpretation of Holy Scripture, the main task must be to derive from it some sure and plain meaning, especially because there is such a variety of interpreters—Latin, Greek, and Hebrew too. Almost all of these not only do not concern themselves with the story, but bury it and confuse it with their nonsensical allegories."[4]

Finally, at the beginning of Chapter IV Luther says, "The chapters which now follow are less subject to debate and are clearer. Moreover, they support our conviction; for nobody can fail to see that Moses does not intend to present allegories but simply to write the history of the primitive world."[5]

It might be pointed out that while some of the church fathers used an allegorical interpretation, they frequently toyed not with the idea of creation extending over a long period of time but rather with the idea that it was instantaneous. This position was suggested by Origen, Hillary, Augustine, and Jerome.

Two Creation Accounts?

There are many who believe that Genesis 1 and 2 present two creation accounts. The first of these is said to extend from Genesis 1:1 to Genesis 2:4a; the second from Genesis 2:4b to Genesis 2:25. This is one of the alleged evidences for the documentary hypothesis, that Genesis as we know it represents the edited work of a number of authors. Proponents of this idea suggest that the editor did not quite succeed in weaving the accounts together but has presented them more or less side by side in the two chapters. Thus, it is alleged that the second chapter does not mention the creation days, and it is further alleged that the sequence of creation is different in Chapter 2 from the sequence presented in Chapter 1.

Most critics believe that the first two chapters of Genesis were written by separate authors. Genesis 1 is believed to be the priestly account (P), written in the 6th century B.C. Genesis 2:4bff. is believed to be the Yahwist account (J), written in the 10th century B.C. Much is made of the verbs for "create" and "make." The word for create (*bara*) is the theme word of Genesis 1, whereas "make" (*asah*) is found in Genesis 2. Still, it should be pointed out that both *bara* and *asah* occur eight times between Genesis 1:1 and Genesis 2:4a. It is clear that Genesis 1 is no more the chapter of the verb *bara* than it is of the verb *asah*. While it is true that the verb *bara* does not occur following Genesis 2:4a, the verb *asah* occurs only twice thereafter in contrast to the eight times it occurs in Genesis 1. Genesis 1 is a skeleton sketch of the events that occurred during the seven days of the creation week written in outline form using poetic prose. Genesis 2 flows in the manner of a more standard historical narrative, providing a focused view of the events of creation that occurred on one of the seven days referred to in the first account of creation.

Much is also made of the different terms used for God in these two chapters. In the first chapter Elohim is used exclusively; it occurs there almost 30 times. Starting with the fourth verse of chapter 2, Yahweh Elohim is the only name used for God, and it occurs there 11 times. This difference in the name assigned to the deity is frequently used as an evidence against the Mosaic authorship of Genesis 1 and 2. Critics have suggested that in Genesis 2 the name originally present was Yahweh and that Elohim was added later. There is no textual evidence for such a theory, and the fact that Yahweh Elohim is used only in Genesis 2 and 3 and nowhere else in the Pentateuch (with the exception of Ex. 9:30) argues strongly against the later insertion of Elohim into Genesis 2. It has been suggested that in a certain sense Elohim is a more impersonal name for God, and this name is used for God when He set up an impersonal cosmos in Genesis 1. In Genesis 2 we have the creation of man and a more personal relationship, so that God's personal name, Yahweh, is introduced. The generic word for God, which may refer to a heathen god as well as to the true God, is perhaps not specific enough for the account of Genesis 2. The name Yahweh was applied only to the one God, the true God, whom the Israelites worshiped.

Questions Answered in Genesis 1 and 2

There is certainly no need to regard these two chapters as presenting two separate accounts. It appears that in these two chapters God is answering three questions. First of all, He is answering the question, "Where did all the matter/energy in the universe come from?" Then, since we are living on planet earth, He is answering the question, "How did planet earth originate?" As members of the human species we are most interested in the origin of the human race, and He answers that as the third question.

In Genesis 1:1 He answers the question concerning from whence everything came. In Genesis 1:2 to 2:3 He answers the question of the origin of planet earth. From Genesis 2:4 until Genesis 2:25 He satisfies our curiosity regarding the origin of the human race. This last section is to be read and understood against the background of Genesis 1. God assumes that we are familiar with the account of the origin of planet earth and goes back to fill in details regarding the origin of the human species.

Details of Creation

We have commented on some details of the creation account in connection with what Scripture teaches about creation. In the text itself there are several other interesting details. It appears from the text itself that the only *creatio ex nihilo* is in Genesis 1:1. God created the matter/energy out of which the universe was fashioned, and then He took six days to organize it. The six days are days of organizing the matter/energy that He called into being at the beginning.

It is interesting that the first day should be devoted to the creation of light. Today we regard light as primarily a form of energy rather than as a material substance. There was a time when philosophically we were most concerned with matter; today we recognize that matter is merely a container for energy and that energy is the really important gift of God to us.

In the light of this it is noteworthy that the first day's creation involved the creation of light, a form of energy, rather than the creation of a material substance.

There are those who believe that the creation of the "firmament" reported in Genesis 1:6 suggests the Babylonian concept of a three-storied universe. However, the Hebrew concept is not that of a solid iron vault separating the heavens (the abode of the gods) and the earth (the abode of man), but rather that of something that is stretched out. The word "firmament," which occurs in the King James Version, undoubtedly has connotations of something solid, but that is not the meaning of the original Hebrew, which emphasizes the "stretched out" condition of the sky. A better translation would be "the sky."

It is also of significance to note that on the fifth day we have the creation of animals which occupy the seas and the air. We have already referred to the Biblical categories of classification. It should be noted that according to the Biblical account there were birds before there were reptiles. Geologists believe that the reptiles were the ancestors of birds. Thus, interpreting the days of Genesis as long periods of time does not really solve the geological problem. There are still conflicts because the sequence is wrong.

Another difference in the sequence of events is to be seen in the fact that according to the Biblical account seed plants existed before there were any animals. While the geological record suggests that plants came before animals, it also suggests there were simple animals before the seed plants had evolved. Thus, once more the sequence in the geological record does not agree with the sequence in the Biblical account.

It is also worth noting that at the beginning animals and man were herbivores (Gen. 1:29). After the flood God specifically provides meat as a food for man (Gen. 9:3ff.).

Also significant is the fact that in Genesis 2:5-6 we are told, "For the Lord God had not caused it to rain upon the earth, and there was no man to till the ground; but a mist went up from the earth and watered the whole face of the ground." This suggests that originally the earth was provided with moisture by mists and springs, and that there was no rain. It may well be that there was no rain until the time of the flood, which would explain the ridicule leveled by the people of Noah's day for his building a ship on dry land. It would also explain the rainbow, which may well have first appeared after the rain of the flood. We can also imagine how disconcerting it would be for people to see rain for the first time if it were previously unknown.

The rivers of Eden are mentioned in 2:10ff. It is, of course, impossible to identify these exactly. It is quite likely that changes followed the flood and that these rivers no longer exist or exist only in part in the post-diluvian world.

One question that arises is the nature of the tree of the knowledge of good and evil and of the tree of life. Were these unique species? Perhaps it is hardly necessary to assume that they were special creations. It may be that God simply designated one tree as the test tree, the tree of the knowledge of good and evil. Western tradition suggests that this was an apple; that interpretation is not supported by rabbinical commentaries. There are at least two suggestions in rabbinical literature: the apricot and the grape. Indeed, there are some who believe that it was a vine rather than a tree, and that in some way or other a poison similar to alcohol was introduced into man through the eating of the grapes and that this poison accounted for the physical consequences of the fall. While such speculation is intriguing, the Bible gives no answer.

There is an interesting reference to the tree of life at the end of chapter 3. There we are told that God put cherubim and a flaming sword at the east of the garden to guard the way of the tree of life. God's reason for doing this was lest man put forth his hand and take also the tree of life and eat and live forever. Some commentators have suggested that man might indeed have become immortal through eating of the tree of life but that his existence would have been little more than a senile, vegetative one. He would have continued to live, but age would have taken its toll. They believe that God did man a favor by barring access to the tree of life so that death could become a reality and he might be relieved of the senility which comes as time takes it toll. Once more it is intriguing to speculate on a question to which Scripture gives no answer.

Notes

1. Martin Luther, *Lectures on Genesis, Chapters 1—5*, Vol. 1 in the American Edition of *Luther's Works*, gen. ed. Jaroslav Pelikan (St. Louis: Concordia, 1958), p. 5.
2. Ibid., p. 19.
3. Ibid., p. 90.
4. Ibid., p. 231.
5. Ibid., p. 237.

5
Special Problems of Creation

Time of Creation

The King James Version of the Bible has in the center column of Genesis 1 the date 4004 B.C. This date was first placed in the margin of the Authorized or King James Version of the Bible in 1701. It was taken from the chronological scheme of the Irish archbishop of Armagh, James Ussher, an Anglican who published it in his "Annals of the Old and New Testament" from 1650 to 1654. It has been reported that the Ussher date was made even more precise by the famous Hebrew scholar, John Lightfoot (1602—75), master of St. Catherine's College of Cambridge, who is said to have determined that the creation of Adam took place on October 23, 4004 B.C. at nine o'clock in the morning, 45th meridian time.[1] Brewster ridicules this suggestion and says, "Closer than this, as a cautious scholar, the Vice-Chancellor of Cambridge University did not venture to commit himself." Lightfoot's writings, however, do not support this criticism. He did indeed suggest that the creation of Adam took place at 9:00 a.m., but he made this suggestion in connection with his belief that Adam fell into sin on the very day of his creation. He also suggested that creation occurred in September, around the time of the autumnal equinox. All of this was more in the nature of a pious opinion seeking to understand and explain the Genesis account rather than an attempt to fix the age of the earth.[2]

Archbishop Ussher was not the first to seek to establish a chronology. Calvisius made similar calculations, which were in use for a long time in Lutheran circles. Abraham Calov in his *Systema Locorum Theologicorum* places the exodus in the year 2453 after the creation

73

of the world. Ussher had actually placed it in the year 2513, so that the two chronologists were some 60 years apart on the date.

Datings such as these have been based on the assumption that the genealogies of Genesis 5 and 11 represent father-son relationships. A superficial study of these chapters would suggest that this is indeed the case, since the general pattern is to name the individual, indicate how old he was when a named son was born, and then indicate the number of years he lived until his death.

Yet when we compare the genealogical record of Genesis 11 with the genealogical record of Luke 3 we find an individual, Cainan, inserted between Shelah and Arphaxad. Except for this individual the genealogies are parallel. It is clear from Luke's account that Cainan lived, and it is also clear that any chronology based on the genealogies of Genesis 5 and 11 are off by at least the time between the birth of Cainan and the birth of his first son.

Yet this would certainly also suggest that the genealogies are not to be used as chronologies. We know that abridgment of genealogies is quite common in Scripture. In the very first verse of Matthew's gospel Christ is called "the Son of David, the Son of Abraham." In the same chapter in verse 8 three names are omitted between Joram and Ozias. The purpose of these genealogical records does not appear to be to give us an exact chronological account of the times, for if that were the case there would be no omissions. Rather, it seems that God wanted to give us the names of the most important men who lived between Adam and Abraham and wanted to give a brief account of what occurred in that period.

In this case, why should God have given us information on the ages of the patriarchs? Chiefly He did so to show how the human race could have increased in numbers so rapidly. Because men attained great ages they were able to beget large numbers of sons and daughters and so populate the world rather quickly.

An even more striking evidence that these genealogies are not to be used as chronologies is the fact that if they are so employed Shem becomes a contemporary of both Abraham and Isaac. Indeed, unless care is taken and recognition is given to the fact that Abram was not the oldest son of Terah, it will appear that Shem was also a contemporary of Jacob.

The reading of the Bible history scarcely suggests that the great apostasy leading to the call of Abram from Ur of the Chaldees had taken place during the lifetime of Shem. It would appear reasonable to expect Shem, if he were alive, to have warned against leaving the worship of the true God for the worship of idols and to have presented himself as the number one witness to the folly of such action. Yet there is absolutely no suggestion that Shem was alive at the time of this apostasy.

It is clear that we cannot say with certainty how old the earth is. It is also evident that creationists can work with an an old earth or with a young earth; they are not limited. It is also obvious that evolution requires millions and billions of years if it is to be even remotely possible.

Geologists' figures for the age of the earth continue to increase. Two University of Chicago scientists, Schramm and Haineback, have suggested on the basis of radioactive dating with Rhenium-187 that the universe may be as much as 20 billion years old. At the same time other scientists are questioning the age of the earth and have suggested that the earth is no more than 10 billion years old on the basis of a reevaluation of the value for the Hubble constant. The clock used to measure the age of the universe may not be accurate. Data by Aaronson, Mould, and Huchra suggest that the Hubble constant changes with distance,[3] and in that case the dates may be quite unreliable.

While we would agree that theoretically creationists are able to work with an old earth, we must also say that even though Scripture gives us no clear evidence of the precise age of the earth it certainly suggests that we are dealing with a young earth rather than with the old earth of 10 to 20 billion years as suggested by the evolutionists.

If we accept the historicity of the creation and fall accounts and believe that our first parents were created on the sixth day, it is scarcely conceivable that God would have waited millions and billions of years to send the promised Redeemer.

The Gap Theory

There are those who suggest a period of time between the original creation and the organization of planet earth. This idea was suggested and publicized by the Scofield Reference Bible. It is postulated that there was a hiatus of a very long period of time between Genesis 1:1 and Genesis 1:2. Many who follow this suggestion believe that the world was originally created for the angels, and that this explains their not being mentioned in Genesis 1. The creation of this angel world, they believe, is reported in Genesis 1:1. Sometime after the angel world was created, the evil angels led by Satan fell into sin. As a punishment for this sin, the world in which they lived was destroyed and the evil angels cast into hell. It is this condition of the earth which is reported in Genesis 1:2: "The earth was without form and void."

Proponents of this theory believe it accounts for the passage of a considerable amount of time, and they believe that in this way it is possible to reconcile the Bible with the findings of those who believe that the earth is billions of years old. They also believe that this theory accounts for the bizarre fossils we find, the dinosaurs, etc. These, they believe, are the remains of animals created for the angel world but destroyed when that world was destroyed.

The individuals who accept this interpretation want to accept the Bible literally and historically. They are looking for a solution to two problems, the time problem and the fossil problem.

However, this theory does not fit with the Scripture. Genesis 1:2 does not suggest disorganization but rather that the early world was unorganized. It would seem that God first created the matter/energy that makes up the universe and then used six days to organize this matter into the universe that we know. So the "without form and void" condition represents a lack of organization—not a disorganization which may have followed the advent of sin.

At the end of the creation account we are told, "God saw everything that He had made, and behold it was very good." In this verse we have two superlatives: the "everything" and the "very good." This could hardly be said if a part of the world had already been destroyed and if the angels had fallen into sin. The angels as well as the rest of creation were still in a state of perfection at the end of the sixth day.

Preadamites

Were there human beings, individuals who had attained the biological status of *Homo sapiens*, before Adam and Eve? It has been suggested that this is the case. Conservative scholars who have supported this concept have done so in order to explain the rapid spread of the human race. They have also attempted to silence those who have ridiculed the Biblical account by asking whom Cain married. They believe that before Adam and Eve an entire race of human beings existed and that these continued to exist after Adam and Eve were created.

Those who support this idea usually suggest that Adam and Eve were the first human beings who were morally responsible. In other words, these were the first members of the species *Homo sapiens* who possessed an immortal soul. It has even been suggested that God touched on the shoulder a single male from this evolutionary population that had attained the biological status of *Homo sapiens*, gave him a soul, and said, "You're Adam." Similarily, He tapped a female on the shoulder, gave her a soul, and designated her as mother Eve. Adam and Eve were now morally responsible, and it was this pair that fell into sin in the Garden.

Their children inherited their souls from them. When we are told that "when Adam had lived a hundred and thirty years he became the father of a son in his own likeness, after his image, and named him Seth" (Gen. 5:3), we have a description of the conception and birth of Seth, who inherited an immortal soul from Adam and Eve. These direct descendants of our first parents did have immortal souls and in that way were different from the Preadamites. They intermarried with the Preadamites, and their descendants inherited the souls of the sons and daughters of Adam. It is suggested that the "sons of God" mentioned in Genesis 6:2 were the direct descendants of Adam and Eve who had inherited an immortal soul from them. The "daughters of men" were the descendants of the Preadamites.

There is certainly nothing in the Scriptures to suggest a race of Preadamites. There is no reason why Adam and Eve in the course of the centuries they lived should not have had a large number of children, and there is no reason why these should not have intermarried. The long lives of the patriarchs provided an opportunity for a rapid increase in the number of people and the rapid populating of the earth.

At the same time, we should recognize that the cities of the early days were not the metropolises which we know today. They were simply places where an extended family lived. We would probably call them settlements rather than cities.

The Meaning of "Min"

A critical point in any discussion of the theory of evolution is the meaning of "species" and its relationship to the "kinds" of Genesis. There is no doubt that this very topic played a part in the development of Charles Darwin. At Cambridge he learned that the Bible taught the fixity of species, and when as a result of his observations he reached the conclusion that new species arose, he was convinced that the Bible was in error and was untrustworthy.

As we have indicated, this concept of fixity of species came from the taxonomic categories of Linnaeus. The misunderstanding also arose from the equating of the Latin Vulgate's *species* with the "species" of the modern biologist.

We must recognize that the Bible does not use the term "species." The Hebrew word used, *Min*, is probably best translated "kind." The word certainly does not mean "species" in the same sense in which we use the term today. Moses would scarcely have used a term which was unknown to his contempories and which men would have not understood for thousands of years after the Book of Genesis was written. The Bible was written for people of all times, and that certainly included the contemporaries of the writer. It is also unlikely that Moses would have used a term having so many meanings, as has the term "species" today.

We also need to recognize that the language of the Bible is the commonsense, everyday language of our newspapers. This language does not change; technical, scientific language does change. In popular terminology we understand what a "kind" of plant or a "kind" of animal is. We may have new "species" of tomatoes, but they are still the same "kind." There may have been changes within the species, yet tomatoes have not developed into cantaloupes or watermelons. There may also have been changes within the dog "kind," but these have not developed into lions or bears.

In terms of the generally accepted definition of a species—that is, a species understood as a group of individuals who interbreed, whose offspring are fully fertile, who occupy a definite geographical range, and who are separated from other species by morphological and/or physiological differences—it is clear that new species have arisen. We cannot accept the fixity of species concept which Linnaeus developed and which has caused problems ever since. True, most of the demonstrable instances of the development of new species have arisen in very artificial situations and under laboratory conditions. In these cases, it is unlikely that the particular new species could have arisen out in nature. Nevertheless, they are new species in the generally accepted sense of the term. Moreover, there is every reason to believe that new species may arise out in nature, however rarely that occurs.

In all fairness, it should be pointed out that it is unreasonable to expect to be able to demonstrate the origin of new species in the field. The very nature of the problem requires that we be satisfied with laboratory demonstrations of the development of new species. For if we are to say that a form is a new species, we must be able to identify the parents and demonstrate that the new species does not interbreed successfully with the parent species. That is almost impossible under field conditions.

Classification Problems

It must be recognized that there is more agreement on the identification and delimitation of the category "species" than on the identification and delimitation of other categories. Biologists have great difficulty in agreeing on categories either below the species level or above the species level. For that reason, "species" is probably the most concrete term in the entire system of classification.

At the same time, we recognize that there are a great many problems with defining "species." Darwin himself defined species as follows: "In determining whether a form should be ranked as a species or as a variety, the opinion of naturalists having sound judgment and wide experience seems the only guide to follow."[4] It is readily recognized that such a definition is based on an authoritarian approach, even though scientists pride themselves on their objectivity. The fact of the matter is that there is a great deal of subjectivity in determining the bounds of a species.

In another place Darwin wrote, "I look at the term species as one arbitrarily given for the sake of convenience to a set of individuals closely resembling each other, and it does not essentially differ from the term variety which is given to less distinct and more fluctuating forms."[5]

The very nature of the problem makes it difficult to determine objectively whether two organisms belong to the same species or not. For one thing, there is a great deal of arbitrariness in classification, and in some cases this is inevitable. In our modern system of classification there is much emphasis on similarity of structure. This becomes especially true in the classification of fossils, since we cannot apply the breeding test criterion to determine their classification.

Indeed, breeding tests are difficult to carry out even with living species. We recognize that there are organisms which interbreed out in nature but which do not interbreed in captivity. That is the major problem we face in attempting to perpetuate threatened species in zoos. It is for that reason that the birth of an animal in captivity often attracts newspaper attention.

It is also true that forms which are normally separate sometimes interbreed when brought into contact. Some insect species apparently do not interbreed out in nature but will interbreed when brought together in a breeding cage in the laboratory. There are a number of instances of plant forms which are separated geographically or by their environment which will breed if they are brought together. For example, the American buttonwood or sycamore, *Platanus occidentalis*, is found in the eastern part of the United States. *P. orientalis* occurs in the eastern Mediterranean region. They have been considered separate species. The artificial hybrid between them, *P. acerifolia*, is vigorus, highly fertile, and shows perfectly normal cell development.

Another plant example is that of the catalpas. *Catalpa ovata* is found in China, and *C. bignonioides* is found in the eastern United States. The artificial hybrid between the two is fully fertile. In this case the habitats are similar, and the two parents could presumably exist side by side.

There are also wide degrees of difference in external form and appearance within the species of different kinds of animals. In some cases only slight morphological differences are noted between distinct species. In other forms there may be wide morphological differences without any barriers to free interbreeding. Consider the human species and the wide variety of human beings that are found in the different races of man.

Environmental affects often create differences which in the absence of breeding tests appear to be great enough to warrant classifying the organisms as different species. A number of experiments have been carried out in plants suggesting that changes similar to those found between the species can be brought about by environmental factors.[6]

There is a major problem in classifying forms that are normally self-fertilizing or are completely asexual. This is true especially in the plant world. If the form does not normally produce sexually, classification must be based on structural differences.

Other classification problems pop up from time to time. Roger Lewin reports that the house mouse of northern Denmark and Scandinavia is *Mus musculus* as defined by its anatomy and nuclear DNA, but it is *Mus domesticus* in the composition of the DNA of its mitochondria. The Scandinavian *Mus musculus* has suffered an inflow of alien genes to the point where its mitochondria or genome is indistinguishable from that of another species. Yet a species is "a group of individuals whose common gene pool is protected against the inflow of alien genes." Are these separate species? To which species does the house mouse of nothern Denmark and Scandinavia belong?

Other cases have also been reported in the literature. Two of the California fruit flies, *Drosophila pseudoobscura* and *D. persimilis*, reveal a pattern that is similar to, although less clear-cut than that of the European mice. In the case of the mice it is known that along the boundary of the two species there is a hybrid zone where occasional breeding across species lines occurs, but this gives rise typically to sub-fertile offspring.[7]

There is a particular problem of defining species in plants. Not only are plants different from animals, but, according to Levin, the characteristics and diversity of higher plant genetic systems and reproductive modes preclude the application of a universally plant species concept.

In a discussion of the nature of plant species, he reaches the conclusion that plant species lack reality, cohesion, independence, and simple evolutionary or ecological roles. He says, "The concept of species for plant taxomonists and evolutionists can only serve as a tool for characterizing diversity in a mentally satisfying way. . . . The species has had a special status as an evolutionary unit because it is thought to be more natural than higher categories and more amenable to definition and empirical demonstration."

There are three features that have been suggested as making species a unique evolutionary unit. The first of these is their apparent reality in that they are real objective units, the delimitation of which is definite and not open to argument except in borderline cases. It is this concept that Levin believes is lacking in plants. The second is "cohesion," an apparent integration of their populations. He believes that species consist of populations, each of which is an expression of an integrated gene pool, and once more he believes that plant species lack this trait.

A third feature is independence, by which he means that species represent the stage of evolutionary divergence at which the once actually or potentially interbreeding population systems are segregated into systems incapable of interbreeding and thus are capable of pursuing independent avenues of adaptation. Once more he believes that this concept cannot be applied to plants.

Thus, he concludes that in the final analysis species concepts are only tools that are fashioned for characterizing organic diversity. Focusing on the tools draws our attention away from the organisms. He quotes Raven with approval as saying, "the species concept, lacking a universal definition, has very little predictive value, but provides a kind of false assurance that they have a number of key biological properties."

It is apparent that there are major problems in classification on the species level. It is not always possible to determine whether or not two organisms belong to the same species. While the category "species" is probably the best we have, it is far from the objective category we would like to have.

Levin quotes Ehrlich and Holm as stating, "The idea of good species . . . is a generality without foundation—an artifact of the procedures of taxonomy." He further quotes Spurway and Haldane as suggesting that our concept of a species "may result from the structure of our language and the structure of our brain."[8]

Creationists are often challenged to identify the "kinds" of Genesis with the various taxonomic categories, and they are faulted when they say that this cannot be done with any exactness. Yet it is evident that there is an equal difficulty and haziness in defining "species." In many ways this scientific category is as elusive as "kind."

Species and Evolution

In any case, the question of whether or not new species originate does not really solve the problem of evolution. It is clear that Darwin thought that it did. He believed that if he could demonstrate the origin of new species he would have proven the theory of evolution. This was due largely to the fact that he had learned at Cambridge that the Bible taught fixity of species and had learned from his scientific associates that all the evidence in biology supported the concept of fixity of species.

Actually, the problem of evolution involves far more than the origin of species. It must simply be pointed out that the fact of change within species or even the change from one species to another does not prove evolution.

In this connection we must distinguish different ideas of the degree of change, for the question is not whether change takes place but rather the extent of that change. It is clear from Scripture that change must be accepted and expected; it does indeed take place. The psalmist contrasts the changelessness of God with an ever-changing creation (Ps. 102:25-27).

So we must certainly grant the fact of change. We sing "Change and decay in all around I see, O Thou who changest not, abide with me."

The problem that Darwin had was that he extrapolated from the fact of change and from the evidence for the development of new species in the biological sense to the concept that all forms of life had developed from a single or a very few ancestors. Modern evolutionists do the same thing.

Macroevolution and Microevolution

In any discussion of the problem of evolution, it is necessary to distinguish between macroevolution or megaevolution and microevolution. Some have referred to macroevolution as the general theory of evolution and to microevolution as the special theory of evolution. In this way they have drawn a parallel with the general theory of relativity and the special theory of relativity.

There is little controversy regarding microevolution. This is the concept that living things change. Creationists accept this. They recognize, too, that there may even be the development of new species. They insist, however, that demonstrating the development of new species does not prove the general theory of evolution or macroevolution.

Macroevolution is the concept that all living things have developed from a single common ancestor or a very few common ancestors. It is this theory that creationists believe is contrary to available scientific evidence and is also contrary to the Biblical account.

Unfortunately, a great many people believe that the evidence for microevolution proves macroevolution. This is by no means the case. In reality, evolutionists extrapolate from the evidence for microevolution to macroevolution. We have already commented on the hazards of extrapolation.

Often the creationist position is caricatured by stating flatly that creationists deny the fact of change. This is by no means the case. What they are denying is the existence of any evidence for macroevolution, and they reject the procedure of extrapolating from the evidence for microevolution to the theory of macroevolution.

Notes

1. Edwin Tenney Brewster, *Creation: A History of Non-evolutionary Theories* (Indianapolis: Bobbs-Merrill, 1927). pp. 108f.
2. George Bright, ed., *The Works of the Reverend and Learned John Lightfoot D.D.* (London: Scot, Basset, Chrivel, and Wright, 1684), I:692, 1020f.; II:1322.

3. Beverly Karpus Hartline, "Double Hubble, Age in Trouble," *Science* 207 (1980):167—69.
4. Quoted in Ernst Mayr, *Systematics and the Origin of Species* (New York: Columbia University Press, 1942), p. 115.
5. Quoted in Donald A. Levin, "The Nature of Plant Species," *Science* 204 (1979):382.
6. W. B. Turrill, "Experimental and Synthetic Plant Taxonomy," *The New Systematics*, ed. Julian Huxley (Oxford: Oxford University Press, 1940), pp. 55—57.
7. Roger Lewin, "Invasion by Alien Genes," *Science* 220 (1983):811.
8. Levin, pp. 381—84.

6
Evolution

Attempts at Reconciliation

The controversy over creation was relatively late in arising. It was astronomy and the nature of the solar system which first brought about a confrontation between science and some churchmen. The controversy regarding preservation, which had significant philosophical implications, never resulted in a direct confrontation. Until the 18th and 19th centuries the doctrine of creation was sacrosanct. It was generally agreed that God had indeed created heaven and earth; the natural knowledge of God testifies so persuasively to this that there were no challenges to this doctrine. The position of Bruno (1548—1600), who suggested a plurality of worlds and who challenged many of the religious ideas of the day—including God's existence and His creative work—attracted little support. The evolutionary views of the Greeks were known but hardly accepted.

When the theory of evolution was seriously suggested, there were indeed those who sought to reconcile these new scientific ideas with the Biblical account. Probably the most troubling problem was the fossil record and the associated problem of the age of the earth. The paradigm of the time was catastrophism based on supernatural intervention and particularly on the account of the Noachian deluge.

Probably the earliest suggestion in an attempt to effect a reconciliation was the suggestion that the days of Genesis be regarded as long periods of time, comparable to the geological ages. It was pointed out that there was at least some agreement on the sequence in that plants originated before animals and in the fact that man was the climax of creative activity. What was not pointed out was the disagreement in the sequence of other creative acts. For example, according to the Bibical account the birds antedated the reptiles (Gen.

85

1:21-25), and seed plants came into existence prior to any animal life (Gen. 1:12-20).

However, this came to be a very popular approach. It solved the question of the fossil record, for during these long periods of time it was quite plausible that there should be extensive evolutionary development. It also solved the problem of the presumed great age of the earth.

It is apparent that this was the first step in moving away from the view that the Genesis record was historical. Once it was admitted that the days of Genesis might not be ordinary days but could be understood as long periods of time, it was difficult to maintain the historicity and the literal interpretation of other aspects of the creation account. This was the problem that Bryan faced at Dayton, Tennessee, and his concession to Darrow that the days of Genesis might indeed have been long periods of time was the basic cause of his downfall and of the poor defense he made of the position he wished to uphold.

It was not long until there were those who suggested that these first chapters of Genesis were saga. They were indeed based on historical events, but they were not to be understood as history in our usual sense of the term. Rather, they were a "beefed-up" account of what had actually happened. Thus, it was postulated that God indeed did create heaven and earth but not necessarily in six days and in the sequence pictured there. It was conceded that the human race might indeed be descended from a single pair, but these first parents of the human race were not necessarily specially created. It was conceded that Genesis 3 reported a fall into sin but not necessarily as a result of the temptation by the serpent.

From the viewpoint that this account was saga, it was but a few steps to regarding it as myth; that is, it was viewed as totally ahistorical, a series of stories—parables or allegories—intending to convey some great truth. Thus, it was said that the basic thrust of Genesis 1 and 2 was that God was behind the process of creation. The basic thrust of Genesis 3 was that man had sinned. The basic thrust of the flood account was that God punishes wickedness, and the basic thrust of the tower of Babel account was that God punishes arrogance and rebellion. Those who held to this point of view generally postulated the beginning of history with the end of Genesis 11 and the account there of the call of Abram. It was suggested that the first 11 chapters of Genesis were pre-history, even though there is no evidence from the text that a different literary genre begins with the account of the call of Abram in Genesis 11:27.

All this took place within what was nominally the Christian community. Obviously, there were those who totally disregarded Genesis. Such individuals, many of whom denied the very existence of God, understandably were unconcerned with the Genesis account and with any attempts at reconciliation.

Today creationists often find their bitterest opponents within the church. There are those who insist that theology must fit the Procrustean bed of science. The new god is science, and therefore theology must adjust its teaching to the latest scientific findings. Too often the question in church circles in not, "What do the Scriptures say?" but rather, "How must we change our understanding of Scripture because of the latest scientific finds?"

This is not to suggest that the approaches, findings, and research of the various academic disciplines are to be ignored in understanding what the Scriptures say. By no means. They have a role, and it is an important one. But it is a ministerial role, not a magisterial one. They are to help us understand the Scriptures; they are not to judge the Bible and its truthfulness.

One of the questions that needs to be considered is whether science and Scripture are complementary or supplementary. Do they look at the same phenomena from entirely different points of view? Or is their point of view generally identical, with each adding something to our understanding of reality?

Those who hold that science and Scripture are complementary suggest that they are using two different approaches and that they are not talking about the same thing. They suggest a compartmentalization, that we be willing to accept a scientific point of view which is entirely at odds with a Scriptural point of view and regard both as being in keeping with reality. Thus, they suggest that from a Scriptural point of view God created heaven and earth by His almighty power in a period of six ordinary days; from a scientific standpoint, the universe developed by natural processes over a long period of time. They believe that both these statements need to stand without any attempt to reconcile them, since they are both "true." These individuals suggest that we keep our everyday life out in the world separate from our spiritual life.

Those who hold the point of view that science and religion are supplementary believe that they add different aspects to a common basis. In areas in which both are interested there is only one standard of truth, and we must seek to determine that truth. It is not possible, the proponents of this idea believe, to hold that God created heaven and earth in six ordinary days by His almighty power and also to hold that the universe evolved by natural processes over a long period of time. These individuals also hold that both science and theology have a common interest in at least some of the phenomena of daily life. Thus, Scripture speaks of people who are dead; the scientist also judges that an individual is dead. The Bible talks about the rising and setting of the sun; the scientist has an interest in studying this very same phenomenon. The Bible is interested in the relationship of human beings to one another; the scientist is also interested in these relationships. It is this point of view which seems to fit best with the Bible's own claims.

Mary Hesse says, "It is false to say that science and religion are talking about different things, or that they use different methods, or that science deals with 'how' and religion with 'why.' These deny the concern of God for the material world He created. There may be no satisfying synthesis this side of heaven, but Christian thinkers can serve God by striving for such synthesis."[1]

The God of Gaps

Some have referred to "the God of gaps" and have thereby put their finger on an important criticism of those who hold a complementary view of the relationship of science and theology. Such individuals suggest that God be used as a sort of *deus ex machina*. They call on God to explain phenomena for which there is no scientific explanation. It is very evident that the God of gaps shrinks as we increase our understanding of the universe. There are fewer and fewer areas in which we must appeal to this God for explanation.

Descriptions and Explanations

At the same time, it is probably worth pointing out that the scientific optimism, which suggested that because the world was governed by cause and effect relationships the day would come when we would be able fully to explain all phenomena, has all but disappeared. The fact of the matter is that we have given up the quest for an explanation of what the physicist calls "initial properties." At one time it was confidently believed that such phenomena as electricity, magnetism, and gravitation would be explainable on the basis of cause-and-effect relationships. Today we recognize that we shall never be able to explain these phenomena. At best we can describe them.

Unfortunately, many people are willing to accept descriptions or even tautological statements as explanations. Consider the phenomenon of gravity. We ask, "Why do we always fall down? Why don't we sometimes fall up?" And we readily answer, "Because of the law of gravitation." If the individual is not satisfied, we quote the law to him and in most cases he finds the scientific jargon in which the law of gravitation is stated to be so impressive that he raises no further questions. But the fact of the matter is that by saying that two bodies attract one another with a force equal to their masses and inversely proportional to the square of the distance between them, we have not really offered any explanation. We have simply described a phenomenon which we observe.

Because we recognize that we shall never be able to explain many of the phenomena about us, the so-called initial properties, we have given up the quest for explanations in these cases and have agreed that we will have to be satisfied with descriptions. But these are descriptions and not explanations, and they are one of the clear evidences that science is itself limited. Its goal is to explain the world about us; that goal is not always attainable.

We must stand in awe of God and must recognize the limitations of man's wisdom and understanding (Ps. 104:24; Rom. 11:33ff.). Compared to God, man has somewhat less than the I.Q. of a chicken, and for that reason he often "lays an egg." It is not surprising that his efforts to improve on the world God created so often have disastrous results, as is evident from our many environmental problems.

Contradictions

It might be pointed out that sometimes two statements are made which appear to be directly contradictory, but when all the circumstances are known we find they are both true. This is one of the possible explanations of the alleged contradictions in the Bible. For instance, it could be said that Tom Lincoln settled in Hurricane Township of Perry County, Indiana. Another historian might state that Tom Lincoln settled in Carter Township of Spencer County, Indiana. At first glance it would appear that at least one of these individuals is in error, since it would seem unlikely that the two different names could both be right. The explanation is quite simple. The first statement applies to the township name and county name when Tom Lincoln settled there. The second statement applies to the present name of the township and of the county.

Evidences for Evolution

Similarity Proof of Descent

Much of the support for the idea of a common origin of all living things is based on the assumption that similarity is evidence of descent from a common ancestor. This premise is a slight alteration of a statement describing what is clearly observable. It is indeed true that those who are related tend to resemble one another, and it is also true that the closer the relationship, the greater degree of resemblance. However, it is not true that individuals who resemble one another are necessarily related.

We might argue that all robins lay blue eggs. This is an observation which can readily be made. However, it is not true that all blue eggs are laid by robins. Yet basically this is what the evolutionist is arguing when he suggests that the degree of similarity is a function of descent from a common ancestor.

We certainly would agree that similarity may suggest relationships, but we would hardly agree that similarity proves relationship.

David Wake of the University of California, Berkeley, is quoted at a recent conference as saying, "For many years evolutionary biologists have equated morphological similarity with close genetic relationship. This is clearly not necessarily the case."[2] It might also be noted that the evolutionist selects his similarities. Where the similarities or dissimilarities do not support his thesis, he is inclined to judge them to be irrelevant. Often they are cited as examples of convergence, the development of similar traits as adaptation to a similar or identical environment. Those which fit his preconceived notions of evolutionary relationships are cited in support of his thesis; those which do not support this point of view are overlooked or explained away.

The Argument from Classification

The evolutionist argues that the very fact that we can set up a system of classification is an evidence for evolution. He argues that the pigeonholes are actually the result of relationships. Yet the fact of the matter is that the system of classification is set up to reflect the degree of relationship, an argument in a circle, since the system is based on what it is said to prove.

We have discussed the system of classification in connection with our discussion of the species problem. There we pointed out that the categories do indeed have value and that the category of "species" is probably the most valid category we have. At the same time we pointed out that there is no agreement with regard to the nature and extent of the category "species." This is even more true of the other categories of the classification system. Neither is it always possible to place an organism in a given category. Sometimes after the characteristics for a given category have been established, organisms are found that have the characteristics of several categories. The little microscopic organism *Euglena* has both plant and animal characteristics. It has chlorophyll and manufactures its own food. This is clearly a plant characteristic. On the other hand, it is capable of locomotion because it has a long whip-like hair, a flagellum, and by means of this it moves through the water. This is certainly a distinctly animal characteristic.

This same thing is true of bacteria. Many of them have cilia or other means of locomotion. They lack chlorophyll and cannot manufacture their own food, an animal characteristic. Yet in other characteristics they resemble very closely the blue-green algae which are clearly plants.

Many taxonomists solved this problem by setting up a third kingdom in their system of classification, the Protista. Into this pigeonhole they have placed relatively simple, one-celled organisms which do not show sharply differentiated plant and animal characteristics. Thus, they establish another pigeonhole to solve the problem.

Still other taxonomists have suggested two super-kingdoms, the Prokaryota and the Eukaryota. The Eukaryota they divide into the plants, the fungi, and the animals. The Prokaryota are also divided into several kingdoms. There are other differences of approach by various taxonomists. Plant scientists recognize divisions as the highest category within a kingdom; zoologists call these phyla.

To say the least, then, numerous problems have arisen in modern taxonomy as the result of an attempt to redo the classification system.

Phylogenetic Trees

Very often these assumed evolutionary relationships are presented as phylogenetic trees. The forms associated together in species, genera, classes, or phyla are supposed to have descended from a single common ancestor. It is generally recognized that all such phylogenetic trees are highly speculative. Allan describes them as being invented and based on what we read into classification rather then deduced from a true knowledge of descent.[3] In classifying organisms taxonomists have usually examined characteristics of external morphology— the external appearance of the organism. Today it is generally agreed that classification must be based on other factors as well. We have pointed to the general dissatisfaction with the present system of classification that has been expressed by taxonomists themselves.

Today most of the phylogenetic trees look shrub-like or bush-like, that is, they are much-branched instead of being straight-lined. Kraus says that there is a growing number of scholars who are coming to feel that the two-dimensional representatation of phylogenetic relationships is not an adequate way of conveying the story of evolution; it is quite apt to be misleading in that it neglects the very nature of evolution. Yet such two-dimensional representations continue to appear in the literature.[4]

Phylogenetic trees which deal with the past face another problem. It is not possible to examine the genetic makeup of organisms no longer alive. The only evidence that can be used in their classification is their external appearance, and this makes real classification less certain. Indeed, as we have pointed out, it is difficult to do breeding tests even on those organisms which are alive. The very task of making all these detailed observations as to whether organisms are capable of interbreeding is an overwhelming one.

Parallel Mutations

We have pointed to the fact that while siblings resemble one another, it is not true that individuals who resemble one another are always closely related. There is evidence to support the correctness of this principle in the well-known phenomenon of parallel mutations. This is the occurrence by mutation of similar characteristics in different species. For instance, the fruit flies, *Drosophila melanogaster* and *D. simulans*, two separate species, have both experienced mutations of eye color to prune, ruby, and garnet; of body color to yellow; of bristle shape to forked and bobbed; of wings to cross veinless, vesiculated, and rudimentary.

It might be assumed by those who regard similarity as proof of descent from a common ancestor that two flies, both of whom have yellow bodies, have descended from a common ancestor with a yellow body, but this is not necessarily the case. The same type of mutation has occurred in both species, and the two yellow-bodied flies have not inherited that trait from a common ancestor but from separate ancestors. This phenomenon of parallel mutations is not confined to *Drosophila*. It is a widespread phenomenon and has been clearly established in a number of forms.

It is true that evolutionists argue that the existence of parallel mutations is itself evidence of evolution. They argue that parallel mutations are possible only because the organisms are closely related and have the same sort of germ plasm.

However, there are instances in which parallel mutations or parallel variations are known not to involve the same ancestral germ plasm. Dobzhansky says,

> Here is a caveat—phenotypically similiar or mimetic mutants are produced also at different fully complementary and not even linked genes within species . . . . A few of the mimetic genes may conceivably have arisen through reduplication of the same ancestral genes. But for the majority such a supposition is quite gratuitous. Our powers of observation are limited and what to our eyes are phenotypically similar changes may actually be due to different genes.[5]

Rensch says that similar or identical organs may arise from quite different anatomical substrata.[6]

The same result may be accomplished in a variety of ways. Such is the case with albinism, a widespread phenomenon throughout the biological world. It is found not only in most animals but in plants as well. It would be ridiculous to argue that two albino organisms inherited the trait from a common ancestor and that their albinism is evidence of descent from this common ancestor. Indeed, we know that albinism may be brought about in a great many ways. There is no single way in which an absence of pigment is brought about. Mayr recognizes the problem, pointing out that so-called similarity is a complex phenomenon that is not necessarily closely correlated with common descent, since similarity is often due to convergence.[7]

The reasoning of those who insist that if plants and animals had been separately created it would not be possible to classify them is highly questionable. Our God is a God of order. It is but natural that organisms which are supposed to occupy the same place in the scheme of life should have similar characteristics. There is no reason at all why God should have to follow a separate pattern in the creation of such organisms.

The Evidence for Evolution from Homology

The second type of evidence for evolution is drawn from homology, a detailed comparision of structure after structure in different organisms. When this is done we find not only that the skeletons are similar but also that in many instances there is a bone-for-bone correspondence. Organisms as diverse as man, the giraffe, and the whale have seven cervical vertebrae.

Furthermore, biologists distinguish between homologous and analogous structures. Homologous structures are those which correspond to one another. For instance, the wing of a bird and the wing of a bat perform the same function; they are analogous. However, structurally they are quite different, and for that reason they are not regarded as being homologous. On the other hand, the wing of a bat is similar in structure to the forefoot of a dog and to the arm and hand of man. They are therefore homologous, but since they do not serve the same function they are not analogous. The fact that the wing of a bat resembles the arm of a man more than it resembles a wing of a bird is pointed to as evidence for the fact that the bat is more closely related to man than to the bird. It is homology that is believed to imply common ancestry.

Once more this argument from homology is based on the premise that similarity is evidence of descent from a common ancestor. And once more we should like to point to the phenomenon of parallel mutations. This clearly shows us that similar structures need not indicate descent from a common ancestor.

Moreover, again in this area the evolutionist selects his similarities. There are times when organisms which are very similar are not classified as being closely related. The platypus, one of the strange mammals of Australia, is not regarded as a link between birds and mammals. It has a bill, but the bill is believed to resemble the bill of a duck only superficially. It has webbed feet and tarsal spurs, but these too are believed to be only superficial resemblances. Because it has hair and produces milk it is classified as a mammal.

Today the argument from homology is not stressed as much as it once was. Many evolutionists themselves are of the opinion that the evidence from homology is of little importance in establishing the "fact" of evolution.

The Argument from Vestigial Organs

The third evidence for evolution depending on the argument that similarity is evidence of descent from a common ancestor is the occurrence of what are known as vestigial organs. These are organs for which no function has been demonstrated. It is postulated that these organs were once functional but that in the course of their evolutionary history they lost their usefulness and gradually deteriorated. In the human body, for instance, the appendix and caecum in the digestive tract, the coccyx at the end of the vertebral column, the tonsils, ear muscles, and a few other structures are cited as instances of vestigial organs. It is believed that these once had a function and that they deteriorated through disuse.

The argument that these have deteriorated through disuse is a Lamarckian argument. Evolutionists do mental gymnastics in order to meet this criticism. They have developed the concept of "loss mutation." It is believed that an organism can lose certain structures without being at a disadvantage in the process of natural selection. In other words, the loss is not a handicap and would not be selected against. But if such loss mutations existed, we should have also expected that the individual who retained the trait would not be at a disadvantage either. And we would expect to find human beings with a fully developed appendix and caecum, a tail, functional ear muscles, and the like.

Moreover, the fact that a function has not been demonstrated for an organ is no evidence that it has no function. It is quite possible that these structures have a function that has not been discovered. For many years the endocrine glands—glands of internal secretion, such as the thyroid, the pituitary, and the adrenals, which pour their products into the blood stream—were regarded as vestigial organs. They could be seen and described anatomically, but no function was known for them. Today, of course, we know that these structures are very important for life.

A good example of recent discoveries in this area are the discoveries regarding the thymus. At one time it was not possible to assign any function to it. Now we know that it plays a key role in the establishment of a functioning immunologic apparatus. If the thymus is removed in early life before the immune system is fully developed, or if it does not develop in embryonic life, there is a disturbance of the immune functions. Yet once immunologic mechanisms are well established, the effects of a thymectomy are negligible. Moreover, if in an adult we destroy the cellular basis for immunologic reactions, a thymectomy is again associated with serious defect in immune functions. Thus, the thymus is necessary not only for establishing normal immunological potential during development but also in restoring such potential after it has been destroyed or damaged and possibly for maintaining it as it becomes depleted with time.

It is also possible that an organ such as the appendix, which can be removed without any discernible effects, may have a function which is taken over by other structures after it has been removed. The margin of safety phenomenon, which consists in man's having more tissue of a specialized type than he really needs, is an example of this. Man can live with only one kidney or one lung, but God has provided him with two as a sort of margin of safety. Organs may also take over functions which they do not ordinarily have. The spleen, for example, produces red corpuscles before birth, but in the adult it ordinarily does not. In cases of severe hemorrhage, however, it may resume this function until the emergency is over.

Once more, this argument is based on the assumption that similarity is evidence of a relationship, and again the evidence from parallel mutations is relevant. It should also be pointed out that today the argument from vestigial organs does not receive a great deal of emphasis from evolutionists.

The Argument from Comparative Physiology and Biochemistry

Another argument based on the premise that similarity is evidence of descent from a common ancestor is the argument from comparative physiology and biochemistry. The various physiological processes and the chemical makeup of various cells and tissues in different organisms are compared.

It is often pointed out that protoplasm itself seems to be basically one substance. Throughout the living world chromosomes seem to consist of DNA, basic proteins and nucleic acid. Very similar or even identical enzymes and hormones are found in large groups of animals.

Much of the work in this area has been done with blood. It is readily available tissue, and one which lends itself in a peculiar way to very careful analysis.

Obviously, the chief premise of this argument is once more that similarities are evidence of descent from a common ancestor. It is assumed that the reason for similarities in physiological processes and in the chemical structure of tissues is that these organisms have descended from a common ancestor, and it is further assumed that the degree of similarity is a measure of the closeness of the relationship.

Dobzhansky cautions against this sort of reasoning. He says that to an evolutionist the fact that certain enzymes are widely distributed in most of earth's organisms is very impressive. But to conclude that these chemical constituents are produced everywhere by the same genes is going far beyond what is justified by the evidence. He points out that what we really know is merely that some enzymes extracted from different organisms facilitate the same chemical reaction. Second, the functional similarity of enzymes is not necessarily conferred upon them by identical genes in different organisms.[8]

Mabry, Alston, and Turner point to an inconsistency in the explanation of similarities by some evolutionists. They point out that the ability of two different organisms to synthesize the same secondary compounds may reflect the common ancestor, or, alternately, it may be a case of parallel evolution. The evolutionist again chooses his similarities.[9]

This second explanation of parallel evolution is used when organisms that are not believed to be closely related produce identical or very similar compounds. For example, the makeup of the insulin in sperm whales is identical with that in pigs and is quite different from that in the sei whales. Fitch and Margoliash have pointed to several striking exceptions in cytochrome c sequences. They found on the basis of these sequences that the penguin seems closely related to the chicken, whereas they would expect "birds of flight" to be more closely related to each other than to the penguin. The kangaroo was found to be closely associated with non-primate mammals, whereas most zoologists maintain that the placental mammals, excluding the primates, are more closely related to each other than to the marsupials. Third, they discovered that the turtle appears more closely associated in their studies with birds than with its fellow reptile, the rattlesnake.[10]

In blood relationships the evolutionist once more selects his similarities. In comparing the blood of man with that of the primates it has been found that man is only distantly related to the lemurs and tarsiers. He is more closely related to the Old World monkeys than he is to the New World monkeys, and he is most closely related to the great apes. This would tend to confirm the opinion that most evolutionists have held.

However, there are other blood relationships which do not match this particular type of evidence. The chimpanzee, which is supposed to be closest to man, has blood group A and O but no blood group B or AB. The orangutan, gibbon, and baboon have A and B but no O. The gorilla has a B-like group but neither A nor O. The macaques, however, seem to have all of the blood groups, and this is true of other

Old World monkeys and the New World monkeys (though these blood groups may not be identical with the corresponding human factors).[11]

It is certainly striking that the macaques, the other Old World monkeys, and New World monkeys seem to have all of the blood groups, whereas the great apes, who are supposed to be most closely related to man, lack at least one of these blood groups. Could it not be argued that man is more closely related to these than to the great apes? It is also striking that in some cases the "O" blood group should be the one missing, since it is believed that the "O" blood group was the original blood group in humans, that A was acquired later, and that B was acquired still later in the course of evolutionary history. Hooton admits that these investigations create a problem and says that the interpretation of these findings concerning blood groups is not altogether clear. He suggests that they may have originated as more or less parallel mutations in different stocks. Once more the evolutionist in such an explanation is choosing his similarities. Moreover, this explanation presents some difficulties, since it does not explain the absence of blood group O, apparently the original blood group, in some of the higher apes.

While there are indeed many similarities in the physiology of organisms and in their biochemistry, there are also many dissimilarities and many similarities that are ignored because they prove the wrong things. Some diseases are limited to an odd assortment of organisms. The trypanosome of sleeping sickness attacks man, antelopes, and other African mammals and domestic cattle. Is this evidence that man is closely related to these animals? Rabies attacks man, the dog, and a few other animals. Is this evidence of a relationship? Malta fever affects only man and goats, while the plague occurs chiefly in man and rats. Are these evidences of similarities?

There are other similarities that prove the wrong thing. The hemoglobin of New World monkeys appears to resemble human hemoglobin rather closely; yet the New World monkeys are not believed to be closely related to man. The hemoglobin of tarsiers is similar to, if not identical with, elephant hemoglobin. The paramecium, a one-celled protozoan, has the vertebrate form of hemoglobin. The cyclostomes, simple vertebrates, have the invertebrate form of hemoglobin. Hemoglobin is also found in the root nodules of leguminous plants.[12]

It had been thought that hemoglobin occurred only in the nitrogen-fixing root nodules of the legumes. Because this legume hemoglobin is very similar to that of animal globin genes, it was suggested that the gene of leghemoglobin was transferred to legumes from an-

other eukaryote outside the plant kingdom relatively recently in evolutionary history. However, it has now been found that hemoglobin
occurs also in the nitrogen-fixing root nodules of *Parasponia*, a member of the Ulmaceae.[13]

Doolittle, in a computer-based study of amino acid sequences,
reaches the conclusion that such a systematic study "may allow a
complete reconstruction of the evolutionary events leading to contemporary proteins. But sometimes the surviving similarities are so vague
that even computer-based sequence comparison procedures are unable to validate relationships. In other cases similar sequences may
appear in totally alien proteins as a result of mere chance or, occasionally, by the convergent evolution of sequences with special properties." In his computer study Doolittle was able to develop what he
regarded as an optimal alignment, a normalized alignment score, and
a measure of the statistical significance of the match. He believes that
NAS greater than 200 almost always indicates a genuine relationship
and that the significance of scores between 140 and 200 depends on
the lengths of the two sequences being compared; if they are longer
than 200 residues, the evidence for common ancestry is very strong.
While he has a number of instances which he believes suggest a common ancestor, there are others which are believed to be "an extraor-
dinary statistical coincidence" because they are not believed to be
related by descent. Again the evolutionist chooses his similarities.[14]

Actually, the complexity of physiological and biochemical processes is quite incredible. It requires a great deal of faith to believe
that these complexities could have developed by chance. Consider
what we have learned about DNA. Is it plausible that this developed
by chance? Is it not easier to believe that this developed as a result
of the planning of an all-wise God?

It is evident that many of the chemical reactions in the body
occur step-wise. It is easy to determine the beginning product and
the end product, but it has not always been easy to determine the
intermediate steps. In many cases these intermediate steps are toxic
or harmful if they accumulate. Many of the inherited metabolic diseases of man involve an inability of the individual to complete one of
the intermediate steps in the breakdown of these complex substances.
The result is an accumulation of an intermediate product which may
do a great deal of harm to the individual. Again, could these complex
reactions have developed by chance?

The Evidence from Embryology

Another field supposedly furnishing evidence for the theory of
evolution and also based on the argument that similarity is due to

descent from a common ancestor is the field of comparative embryology. Here we have Haeckel's famous recapitulation theory or biogenetic law, "Ontogeny Recapitulates Phylogeny." Haeckel suggested that in the course of embryonic development (ontogeny) the organism repeats the evolutionary history of the phylum (phylogeny). In the process of man's development he begins as a single fertilized cell, the protozoan stage. Then he develops through a sort of jellyfish stage and a worm stage. Finally he becomes a chordate. This process, we are told, is merely a repetition of his evolutionary history, an abridgment of the stages he passed through in the course of his evolutionary development.

Embryology is also said to give a clue to relationships. These may be masked in the adult, but it is said that there are often similarities during embryonic development, which give a clue to actual relationships.

Development through various evolutionary stages can also be traced in the various systems. Man's kidneys first pass through a worm stage, then through a frog stage, and finally become human. His heart develops first as a pulsating tube—the worm stage. Then it becomes a two-chambered structure—the fish stage. It continues and becomes three chambered—the frog stage. It then develops into a four-chambered stage, but there is a connection between the right and left sides of the heart—the reptile stage. Only at birth does the heart finally become fully human.

The development which is probably referred to most frequently by evolutionists is the development of the so-called "gill slits" or "branchial grooves" and "gill arches." These are found in the throat and resemble superficially the gill slits and gill arches of fish. They are supposed to be evidences that at one time man passed through a fish stage.

The argument from embryology also emphasizes the fact that in the early embryonic stages mammals are all very much alike. Indeed, until about the eighth week of development it is difficult to tell a human embryo from the embryo of any other mammal. This is regarded by evolutionists as evidence that they are descended from a common ancestor.

The argument from embryology has often been regarded as a very telling one in support of evolution. It would almost seem as if these organisms are repeating their ancestral history. Yet much of the development referred to is just what we would expect. It is to be expected that organs and systems should develop from simple to complex. The human being starts out as a single fertilized cell not because he was once protozoan, but because that is the simplest form possible. In the case of the heart it is but natural that there should be development from simple to complex. In the early stages only a pulsating tube is needed. Why should a complex four-chambered heart spring into being at once? As the need develops for a more complicated transportation system, the heart itself becomes more complicated. The connection between the right and left sides of the heart is there so that before birth most of the blood can be shunted around the lungs. Oxygen is supplied before birth not by the lungs, but by the placenta, and there is no reason to send all of the blood to the lungs. The development of the heart meets the needs of the developing organism.

It is also striking that structures do not always function in the way in which the organs they resemble function. The real test is not structure but function. If the function is not present, the structural resemblance may indeed be superficial. The worm kidney (pronephros) and the frog kidney (mesonephros) are probably not functional in excretion. It is generally agreed that the pronephros does not carry out this function. Some have suggested that the mesonephros may function as a temporary excretory organ; others do not believe it ever has this function. In man and in some other animals it is relatively small; in the rabbit and in the pig it is large. Its small size in man makes it doubtful that it functions as an excretory organ in early human development. In later embryonic development the pronephros and mesonephros are incorporated into the reproductive systems. Only the last kidney (the metanephros, which is distinctly human) is used in excretion. It functions already before birth.[15]

This is true also of the so-called gill slits. If they really represent a fish stage they should be functional in respiration, but they are not. As a matter of fact, except for the more cephalic, which occasionally break through, they are never completely open in man but are closed by a membrane. They develop as an inpocketing from the neck and an outpocketing from the pharynx. In later embryonic life they are incorporated into various other organs. The first becomes the Eustachian tube, which connects the throat and the middle ear, and the tympanic cavity of the middle ear. The second is greatly reduced and is incorporated into the palatine tonsils. The third, fourth, and fifth become incorporated into the thymus, the parathyroids, and the postbranchial bodies. In no way are any of these associated with the respiratory system or with respiratory processes.

The gill arches, too, are incorporated into other organs. The anterior branches persist on both sides to form the internal and external carotids, the arteries going to the head. The third gill arches form portions of the internal carotids. The right side of the fourth gill arch forms a part of the right subclavian artery, which feeds the arm. The left side of the fourth gill arch forms the aortic arch. The sixth arch forms the ductus arteriosus, which is cut off at birth.[16]

We need to be very careful in naming and assigning functions to structures which resemble superficially other structures whose function is known. In the *Euglena* there are structures the names of which would suggest that they are parts of the digestive system. There is what has been called a mouth, a gullet, and a food reservoir. All these names would imply that these structures are associated with the ingestion and digestion of food. And, superficially, they look as if they would serve that purpose. The mouth appears to be an opening which might well serve for taking in food. The gullet appears to connect the mouth and the food reservoir, and food reservoir resembles a structure which might well be used for storing food.

Yet these structures as far as we know are not associated with the food-getting and digestive processes in the *Euglena*. The animal manufactures its own food, and there is no evidence that under any circumstances it takes in food through the mouth. In short, we have structures which superficially seem to have a given function. However, when we examine them carefully we find that they do not have the functions which their names imply and that their resemblance to these structures is obviously only superficial.

Today the recapitulation theory is not as important in knowledgeable circles as the popularization of evolution in many textbooks would indicate. Already by 1920 it had been rejected by most knowledgeable scientists. Ehrlich and Holm refer to it as a "crude interpretation of embryological sequences," and they say it will not stand on close examination. Its shortcomings have been pointed out repeatedly, but the idea still has a prominent place in "biological mythology." Ehrlich and Holm believe that the resemblances of early vertebrate embryos are readily explained "without resorting to mysterious forces compelling each individual to climb its phylogenetic tree."[17]

Haeckel and other recapitulationists were forced to assume a principle of terminal addition (i.e., that evolutionary change occurs by adding new stages to the end of an unaltered ancestral pattern of embryonic development) and a principle of condensation (i.e., that early development must be continually speeded up during evolution to make room for new terminal additions).

Recapitulationism collapsed, it is believed, when it became unfashionable as embryologists grew more interested in efficient causes of embryogenesis than in reconstructing phylogeny, and it finally proved inconsistent with a new higher level theory when Mendelian genetics ruled out any universal principle of terminal addition.[18]

When evolutionary change speeds up reproductive maturation relative to somatic growth, it is believed that pedomorphosis results, that is, an adult descendant looks like a juvenile ancestor. Pedomorphosis is the result of two processes: progenesis, an absolute acceleration of maturation without comparable acceleration of somatic growth; and neoteny, retardation of growth without comparable retarded reproductive maturation. Gould is quoted as believing that progenesis and neoteny yield "rapid and profound evolutionary change in a Darwinian fashion without the specter of macromutation" by producing novel combinations of adult and juvenile morphology through relatively minor alterations in genetic mechanisms regulating growth.[19]

Today it is coming more and more to be recognized that embryonic development can be explained on the basis of increasing complexity and developing needs just as reasonably as on the basis of recapitulation. De Beer says that failure to recognize the principle of parallelism of increasing degrees of complexity was a grave error in the theory of recapitulation. Many invertebrates, for example, excrete nitrogen in the form of ammonia. Fish and amphibia excrete it as urea, and adult birds excrete nitrogenous waste as uric acid. The bird embryo first excretes ammonia, then urea, and finally as an adult it excretes uric acid. This certainly seems to be an instance of recapitulation.[20] Yet Needham points out that this probably represents the order and sequence in which biochemical reactions of increasing degrees of complexity can be performed. He points out, too, that the production of urea by the chick embryo by means of the arginine-arginase system is not identical with that which occurs in fish and amphibia.[21]

Wald has referred to a situation in tadpoles and their supposed resemblances to fishes and frogs as "the most striking instances of recapitulation we know." Wald says that tadpoles resemble fishes in a number of biochemical characteristics, whereas adult frogs have a biochemistry similar to that of the land vertebrates. Simpson points out that tadpoles are adapted to live in water and adult frogs are adapted to live on land. Wastes are secreted as ammonia in water, urea out of it. He points out that when amphibians go from land to water, as some do, the changes tend to go in the opposite direction from recapitulation.[22]

Stebbins believes that seedling similarity in plants, which at first seems to exemplify recapitulation, is the result of an entirely different phenomenon. He believes that the genetic factors which alter the growing tip of the plant so that it produces appendages of a more specialized type often begin their action relatively late in development. Thus, a number of plants follow the same general plan for a relatively long time, and it is only relatively later in their development that specialization appears. Genetic factors, he believes, not recapitulation, account for seedling similarities.[23]

De Beer has studied extensively the evidence of embryology. He believes that embryology cannot with any degree of certainty reconstruct ancestral types, though he believes that embryology may give some indication of affinity. The descendant, he says, may be derived from a larval form of the ancestor, and in such a case the resemblances between the young form of the descendant and the young form of the ancestor may convey little or no information concerning the adult form of the ancestor. He suggests that in many cases the embryonic or undeveloped ancestor resembles the adult descendant. For instance, the adult modern man is believed to resemble the young Neanderthal man or the newborn ape, a suggestion developed by Bolk.[24]

Thus it is suggested that man is a neotenic ape. Somatic growth in man is "absolutely and relatively retarded compared to that of the apes, and man retains into adulthood the short face, bulging brain case, hairless skin, and slender erect neck of the fetal ape." Gould believes that the fetal rates of brain growth, facial elongation, and so on continue far longer after birth in man than in other anthropoids. As man grows older his face becomes wrinkled, a characteristic already of the very young ape. Cartmill, however, asks how, after all, could the adult brain be enlarged or the face shortened except by prolongation of the rapid fetal growth of the brain or the slow juvenile rate of facial elongation?[25]

Vertebrates, De Beer believes, have developed from larval echinoderms. Recapitulation, he says, is now discredited and generally abandoned.[26] His ideas, which have gained rather wide acceptance, are almost the opposite of recapitulation. Instead of completing embryonic development to its final stages, for some reason or other the embryonic development of higher organisms stop at a certain point, and this stoppage results in the development of a higher form. Many of man's traits are regarded as fetalizations. This is the case of the unique relations between the head and the spine, the position of the face and orbit relative to the brain case, the inability to rotate the great toe, certain peculiarities of hair distribution, and the late appearance of skin color.

Most of the objections which apply to recapitulation also apply to the newer theories of De Beer and his colleagues. The development we find is only that which we would expect in the course of development from simple to complex. Moreover, with the suggestion of the number of types of possible embryonic and evolutionary resemblances, it is only natural that we should occasionally find some superficial resemblance to one of the types suggested. If it does not fit with one, it may fit with one of the others that have been suggested, for in this area again the evolutionist is prone to choose his resemblances.

Evidences Representing the End Product of a Long Period of Evolution

There are a series of other evidences which are not based on similarity but which presumably represent the end product of a long period of evolution. These are the evidences from color patterns, particularly in insects. It is believed that the patterns observable at present have evolved in the course of time from relatively simple patterns and from neutral colors. Playing a part in this whole discussion is the question of survival of the fittest. These patterns which have evolved are believed to have had substantial survival value and to have enabled their possessors to have survived when other members of the species were eliminated.

Protective Resemblance

The first of these color patterns is what has been called protective resemblance. In this category are instances of organisms supposedly protected against predators by blending into their background. Two types of protective resemblance have been distinguished: resemblance to the general background, a sort of camouflage; and the resemblance to a particular object in the background. There are a great many examples of these phenomena. Fish, for instance, are dark-colored above, so that they blend in with the dark bottom when observed from above. However, they are light-colored on their underparts, so that they blend in with the sky when observed from below. Bright green parrots are relatively inconspicuous in the tropical vegetation of South America. Some animals, such as the chameleon, even have the power to change their color depending on the background.

There are also examples of the second type of protective resemblance. The grayish caterpillars of certain geometrid moths, when disturbed, hold themselves rigid at an angle to the twig on which they rest, thus looking like branches of the twig. The wings of some katydids, longhorned grasshoppers, and mantids are green and have net-veined structures like leaves. The famous Kallima butterfly of India has wings which when folded are colored and marked like a dead leaf.

Many evolutionists believe that originally these animals lacked protective resemblance and that in the course of their evolutionary history they acquired it as a means of survival. Those members of the species which did not develop these traits were quickly exterminated by predators, and only those who had such protection survived.

There is no doubt that there is some degree of resemblance to the background in animals. However, its extent seems to have been exaggerated by the evolutionists, and, as Robson and Richards point out, there is no evidence that this has developed as a result of selection and evolution.[27] McAtee goes so far as to conclude from his experiments that the whole idea of protection is largely a myth. He studied the stomach contents of a large number of North American birds and found that protection did not exist for some of the prey species thought to be protected. These supposedly protected species were eaten just as often as those that were not supposed to be protected.[28] After reviewing the various ways in which animals changed color, the Milnes came to much the same conclusion. They believed that protective coloration in land animals is generally overrated. Changes in the chameleon, for instance, appear to have no relationship to the background of the animal.[29]

A real difficulty in discussing protection is the problem of determining the visual powers of the predator. We know that some insects are able to see parts of the spectrum that we humans cannot see. Ants, for instance, can apparently see ultraviolet light, which we do not see, and they cannot see some of the red zones which we can see.[30] Levy and McCrea report that flower colors are perceived differently by insect pollinators than by human observers. Phlox are pink; a mutant is white. Their studies, however, demonstrated that the pink forms appear violet-blue to honey bees and the white forms as "highly reflective blue-green." There are many animals who apparently do not see red light. Some newer zoo exhibits take advantage of this in providing exhibits of nocturnal animals that are illuminated with red light. We are able to observe the animals who are active because they do not see the red light and sense that they are in the dark.

It can be demonstrated that the color pattern of these protected organisms is different under ultraviolet light from the pattern that appears under visible light. It may be that many of the animals which appear to have a sort of protective resemblance do not have that protected resemblance when viewed by their predators.

Other factors which play a part are the size of the object relative to the observer's field of vision and the relative length of time that the organisms spend against the protected background. In general, animals that are at rest tend to blend into the background, but as soon as an animal moves he is observed. Still another factor to be considered is what Robson and Richards call the "capricious incidence" of protective resemblance. It is well developed in some organisms and yet entirely absent in others.[31]

Protective resemblance should be characteristic of prey species. However, in some cases predators have what appears to be protective coloration. To meet this objection two other theories have been proposed: the theory of aggressive resemblance and the theory of alluring resemblance. According to the first, a predator resembles his environment in order that he may sneak up on his prey and catch him unawares. Animals such as the polar bear blend into the background to such a degree that they become invisible to the animal that is to serve as food. However, it should be noted that in order to catch their prey they must move, and movements do attract attention. It is hardly likely that a predator would remain invisible to his prey when he is advancing to capture it.

Alluring resemblance is found in organisms that are passive in the pursuit of their prey. Instead of creeping up on the prey, they entice the prey to come to them. There is a spider in Java which supposedly entices butterflies as its prey by its resemblance to the excretion of birds. There is a lizard in Algeria with red spots on its tongue; these resemble a desert flower to such an extent that insects are attracted to it.

Warning Coloration

Some organisms do not blend in with the environment but actually stand out from it. These are brilliantly colored animals who presumably use their bright colors as a warning that they are in some way undesirable or dangerous. They advertise the fact to protect themselves against being eaten inadvertently.

A good example of an animal supposedly warningly-colored is the skunk. Instead of having the dull brownish-gray agouti pattern of most wild animals, the fur is solid black with a conspicuous white stripe. Other example of organisms supposedly warningly-colored are the yellow-jacket, the Gila monster, and the blister beetle.

There are difficulties with this theory, too. It is really impossible to say that an animal which is distasteful or unpalatable to man is also distasteful or unpalatable to the predator. The studies of McAtee on the stomach contents of birds emphasize this. The chinch bug is said to be warningly-colored and is supposed to have an objectionable taste, but McAtee found that this bug was eaten by 29 species of birds, three of which ate more than 100 bugs in a single meal. Either the bug is not distasteful to the birds or the birds do not learn.[32] Reighard worked with a number of brilliantly colored reef fish in the Gulf of Mexico. These were believed to be warningly-colored and distasteful to potential predators. Reighard conducted a series of experiments and found that some of the highly colored reef fish were eagerly eaten by their predator, the gray snapper, when they were away from the reef. He concluded that the reef fish were protected in their normal habitat, not by the fact that they are warningly-colored but by the fact that the gray snapper usually takes its prey with a swift rush. In the neighborhood of a sharp reef, it does not dare risking injury to itself.[33]

Once more it would seem that there is some significance to warning coloration. Predators do seem to recognize bright colors as an indication of some undesirable trait. Yet it is doubtful that predators can discriminate minor variations of color and taste. It is this ability, though, which birds would have to have had if conspicuous patterns were developed by evolution. It is difficult to believe that brilliant color developed in one step. Generally it is assumed that this was a gradual process in which one insect or a few insects were slightly more brightly colored than other members of the species. But there is no evidence that birds or predators can discriminate between such minor variations. Robson and Richards summarize their discussion on warning coloration by saying that the great extent to which certain groups usually supposed to be distasteful are preyed upon can only make one hesitate to regard them as specially protected. They conclude by saying that even though a selective attack constituting a very small part of the total predation might lead to important evolutionary changes, the degree of selective attack recorded, unless deceptively low, is minimal compared with the enormous changes that such attacks are supposed to have brought about.[34]

Mimicry

Another explanation for bright color patterns in animals is the theory of mimicry. According to this theory, an edible species imitates or mimics an inedible one. Actually, because some inedible species have developed patterns which appear to represent mimicry, two forms of mimicry have been suggested: Batesian mimicry, according to which an edible species mimics or imitates an inedible one; and Muellerian mimicry, according to which two or more inedible species have evolved the same pattern. Muellerian mimicry assumes that some members of the inedible species will be eaten until the predator learns to avoid animals with that particular pattern. When two or more inedible species evolve the same pattern, they economize on the number that are eaten for this type of experimentation and thus spread this particular loss among them.

Most examples of mimicry are from insects and spiders. Usually tropical species are involved, but probably the most commonly cited example of mimicry is that of the viceroy butterfly (Basilarchia archippus), which is said to mimic the monarch butterfly (Anosia plexippus). The viceroy is the mimic and the monarch the model. The monarch is distasteful to humans—it feeds on the milkweed which has an acrid juice—and presumably also to predators, and it is protected by this trait. Another type of mimicry is that supposedly found in harmless or mildly venomous snakes, which mimic the highly poisonous and warningly-colored coral snakes.

There are a number of factors which need to be evaluated in discussing the theory of mimicry. In the first place, there is seldom any real proof that the model is distasteful. The experiments that have been carried out are by no means conclusive. While there is some evidence that some insects are distasteful to birds, and while it is a fact that insects feeding on plants with acrid or poisonous juices are among these, it has by no means been established that the majority of those insects and spiders regarded as models are distasteful.

Another difficulty concerns itself with the supposed enemies of insects, particularly butterflies and moths. It has generally been assumed that since these are aerial insects, their chief enemies are birds. McAtee, in examining the stomach contents of 80,000 birds, found only 87 adult butterflies, and 69 of these were found in a single species of bird, the pigeon hawk. His findings certainly throw doubt on the contention that birds are important predators of moths and butterflies.[35]

Even if birds really are the chief predators of butterflies and moths, there is no evidence that they see the same parts of the spectrum that we see. There is evidence that some birds— chickens, doves, and kestrels—do not see colors as we do. If birds do not see the same visual areas that we do, presumably the pattern they see is different too.

Most suggestions regarding mimicry are made on the basis of museum specimens. They are discovered not out in nature but by an entomologist working with his collection in a museum. Sometimes, however, museum specimens, because of the way in which they are dried and mounted, are more alike than living specimens.

Robson and Richards summarize their discussion of mimicry by concluding that the data we have are not sufficiently quantitative to be conclusive. They point out that there are few, if any, pairs of model and mimic in which all the desirable evidence is available for that particular pair. They believe that it is dangerous to use the mimicry theory as one of the main lines of support for natural selection and evolution.[36]

Sexual Selection

Another explanation for brilliant colors among animals, one which was stressed especially by Darwin, is sexual selection. Evolutionists have assumed that characters such as the bright color of the male bird are due to the fact that in the course of time females have always chosen the most brightly colored males as their mates. It is generally assumed that both sexes were originally dull-colored. Gradually, however, individual males developed some color, and this aided those particular individuals in gaining a mate. These brightly colored males became the fathers of the next generation and passed on the bright colors to their descendants. This process continued for many generations, and in the course of time many of the males acquired the bright color that characterizes them in some of the species. In addition to the brilliant color of the male, other characteristics that are believed to have developed as the result of sexual selection are the mane of the lion, the crests of certain male birds, the feathery tails of some crustaceans, and the weapons used in fighting such as spurs, antlers, horns, and teeth.

In evaluating this suggestion we need to recognize that in very few cases does the female actually exercise choice with regard to the male with whom she mates. Among most animals it is the male who makes the choice, if any choice is made. Yet there are few instances in which the female is brightly colored. The only instances in which female choice may occur are in such birds as the ruff, the blackcock, and probably the various species of the bird of paradise.

This theory presupposes that the female has an aesthetic sense. There is no evidence at all that any animal has the sense of beauty that man possesses. If they cannot be appreciated by the female, there is really no reason for the development of these brilliant colors.

Many evolutionists have suggested that these characters regarded as having developed by sexual selection are intended as display characters, to call attention to the male, and are not intended to appeal to the aesthetic sense of the female. It should be pointed out, however, that at least in some cases sexual display cannot be favorable to the male who has developed this particular behavior pattern. In the case of some of the newts, courtship takes place after the little package of sperm, the spermatophore, has been deposited on the bottom of the pond. This courtship behavior cannot favor one newt over another newt, for how can the female know which newt has produced which spermatophore? The same situation occurs in some of the migratory birds. In warblers the courtship display occurs after the birds have already paired off for the season.

Huxley believes that this sort of behavior favors the species as a whole, that it stimulates the female so that more eggs are produced and fertilized.[37] But this cannot account for the development of display characteristics. If this were the case, the male who developed the behavior pattern characterizing this courtship display would not have been favored. He would not have become the father of more progeny than the male who did not develop the pattern. The latter, too, would have left progeny, and within the species there would have been some males showing this pattern and others not. Yet so far as it is known all males in a given species show the pattern and not just certain groups of males.

It should also be pointed out that some characteristics that are supposed to have developed by sexual selection are actually harmful to the organism. That is the case with the train of enormously overgrown tail-covert feathers found in the peacock, which are so long and cumbersome that they are actually a handicap in flight. The beautifully adorned wings of the male argus pheasant are of little value in flight, for the male bird is able to fly for only short distances.

Robson and Richards conclude that most secondary sexual characteristics should be classified as apparently of no value so far as the survival of the form is concerned. They also point to the sporadic distribution among species of such structures. In some groups they are very common; in others they are quite rare.[38] Huxley says that it has now become clear that the hypothesis of female choice and selection between rival males, irrespective of general biological advantages, is inapplicable to the great majority of display characters. While he believes they have developed by selection, he believes that other factors are also involved. He points out the intrasexual selection between males of the same species would be of advantage only in polygamous species. Still, he believes that Darwin's theory, though wrong in many details, was essentially right, since no other explanation for the bulk of charactistics concerned with the display in the male is possible.[39]

Notes

1. Mary B. Hesse, *Science and the Human Imagination* (New York: Philosophical, 1955), p. 155.
2. Roger Lewin, "Seeds of Change in Embryonic Development," *Science* 214 (1981):43.
3. H. H. Allan, "Natural Hybridization in Relation to Taxonomy," *The New Systematics*, ed., Julian Huxley (Oxford: Oxford University Press, 1940), p. 516.
4. Bertram S. Kraus, *The Basis of Human Evolution* (New York: Harper & Row, 1964), p. 30.
5. Theodosius Dobzhansky, "Evolution of Genes and Genes in Evolution," *Cold Spring Harbor Symposia on Quantitative Biology*, XXIV (1959), 22.
6. Bernhard Rensch, *Evolution Above the Species Level* (London: Methuen, 1959), p. 279.
7. Ernst Mayr, "Biological Classification: Toward a Synthesis of Opposing Methodologies," *Science* 214 (1981):511.
8. Dobzhansky, p. 23.
9. Tom J. Mabry, R. E. Alston, and B. L. Turner, "The Biochemical Basis of Taxonomy," *The Science Teacher* XXXII, 9 (December 1965), 20.
10. Walter M. Fitch, and Emanuel Margoliash, "Construction of Phylogenetic Trees," *Science* 155 (1967):283.
11. Alexander S. Wiener, and J. Moor-Jankowski, "Blood Groups in Anthropoid Apes and Baboons," *Science* 142 (1963):68; and Earnest Albert Hooton, *Up From the Ape* (New York: Macmillan, 1946), p. 46.
12. Harold F. Blum, *Time's Arrow and Evolution* (Princeton: Princeton University Press, 1951), pp. 182—88.

13. Cyril A. Appleby, John D. Tjepkema, and Michael J. Trinick, "Hemoglobin in a Non-leguminous Plant, *Parasponia*: Possible Genetic Origin and Function in Nitrogen Fixation," *Science* 220 (1983):951—53.
14. Russell F. Doolittle, "Similar Amino Acid Sequences: Chance or Common Ancestry?" *Science* 214 (1981):149—59.
15. Bradley M. Patten, *Human Embryology* (Philadelphia: Blakiston, 1946), pp. 549—60.
16. Ibid., pp. 460f.; Hooton, pp. 218f.
17. Paul R. Ehrlich and Richard W. Holm, *The Process of Evolution* (New York: McGraw-Hill), 1963, p. 66.
18. Matt Cartmill, "Recapitulationism: Issues Evolutionary and Philosophical," *Science* 199 (1978):1194f.
19. Ibid.
20. G. R. De Beer, "Embryology and Evolution," *Evolution*, ed. G. R. De Beer (Oxford: Clarenden Press, 1938), p. 60.
21. Joseph Needham, "The Biochemical Aspects of the Recapitulation Theory," *Biological Reviews* V (1930):150f.; and J. Needham, *Advances in Modern Biology* (Moscow, 1935), IV, 239. Quoted in De Beer, p. 60.
22. George Gaylord Simpson, "Organisms and Molecules in Evolution," *Science* 146 (1964):1537.
23. G. Ledyard Stebbins, Jr., *Variation and Evolution in Plants* (New York: Columbia University Press, 1950), p. 492.
24. De Beer, pp. 58—61.
25. Cartmill, *loc. cit.*
26. De Beer, pp. 375f.
27. G. C. Robson and O. W. Richards, *The Variations of Animals in Nature* (New York: Longmans, Green, 1936), p. 313.
28. W. L. McAtee, "Effectiveness in Nature of the So-Called Protective Adaptation in the Animal Kingdom, Chiefly as Illustrated By the Food Habits of Nearctic Birds," *Smithsonian Miscellaneous Collections* LXXXV, 7 (1932):144.
29. Lorus J. Milne and Margery J. Milne "How Animals Change Color," *Scientific American* CLXXXVI, 3 (1952):64.
30. Kenneth D. McCrea and Morris Levy, "Photographic Visualization of Floral Colors as Perceived by Honey Bee Pollinators," *American Journal of Botany* 70 (3). Quoted in *Bio-Science* 33 (1983):713f.
31. Robson and Richards, p. 234.
32. McAtee, p. 44.
33. Jacob Reighard, "An Experimental Field Study of Warning Coloration in Coral-Reef Fishes," *Department of Marine Biology of Carnegie Institute of Washington,* Papers from the Tortugas Laboratory, II, 9 (1908):261—321.

34. Robson and Richards, p. 251.
35. McAtee, p. 60.
36. Robson and Richards, pp. 264f.
37. Julian Huxley, *Man in the Modern World* (London: Chatto and Windus, 1950), pp. 89, 92.
38. Robson and Richards, p. 296.
39. J. S. Huxley, "The Present Standing of the Theory of Sexual Selection," *Evolution*, ed. G. R. DeBeer (Oxford: Clarendon Press, 1938), pp. 20, 21, 24. Huxley, *Man in the Modern World*, pp. 86f.

7
Problems for the Creationist

There are two areas which present problems for those who wish to reconcile the account of creation in Genesis with the facts and evidences that we find. These are the fossils and the geographical distribution of plants and animals. The fact that there are a great many forms found as fossils which do not exist today would seem to indicate that a great deal of change has taken place. The fossil record would present no problem were most of the fossils similar to those forms which we know today. But the fact of the matter is that most of them are different, and in many cases quite different, from the plants and animals that we know on our time level.

Then, too, the fact that we find certain species of plants and animals limited to small areas of the earth's surface is difficult to explain on the basis of the Biblical account. According to Scripture, land animals must have radiated out from the point at which the ark was grounded, and it is difficult to understand why certain groups of animals are absent from large areas of the world's surface.

The Fossils

Fossils are the hard parts of plants and animals which have been preserved by petrification. Sometimes bones and teeth are preserved by having their pores filled in with mineral matter, and in this case the hard material, the bone or tooth, remains intact and unaltered. In other cases the original substance of the hard part is dissolved away and replaced, often particle by particle, by mineral matter, such as silica or carbonate of lime. Wood is commonly preserved in this way, and the process may be so delicate that the cells and other microscopic structures of the wood are preserved even after the organic matter has disappeared. In addition to fossils themselves, we find evidences of plants and animals no longer alive in the form of casts, footprints, insects preserved in amber, whole animals preserved in ice, and the like.

We must recognize that fossils are quite common; furthermore, that most of them are quite different from the plants and animals we know today. Indeed, one of the problems is the quantity of material that has not yet been examined. Museum storehouses are literally jammed with fossils that have not yet been carefully examined.

It is also true that we find the fossils grouped together so that certain kinds of fossils are characteristic of certain rock layers.

The evolutionist believes that the fact that many fossils are quite different from the forms we know today is evidence that evolution has taken place. He believes, too, that in many cases it is possible to arrange the fossils in a sequence so as to show how evolution has taken place.

Evaluating the Fossil Evidence

The fossil record has some problems peculiar to itself. There is a real problem, for instance, in classifying organisms which we know only as fossils. The paleontologist has only the remnants of the skeleton to work with, and often there are only fragments. Davis points out that the paleontologist must infer the major part of each functional system, the functioning of these systems, and the conditions under which they function. Certainly, as he says, these limitations are extremely difficult, often even insurmountable. The problem is great enough in working with those forms which have similar forms alive on our time level, but it is even greater in the case of those forms which have no existing counterparts or lines that have died out completely.[1]

Boyd calls attention to five "grave defects" in using bones as a basis for classification of human and pre-human remains. Some of his criticisms apply also to the fossils of animals and plants. He points out that skeletal characteristics alter rapidly in response to the environment. The form of the skull, for instance, depends partly on the muscles that are attached to it. Differences in skeletal structure may not indicate a difference of specific magnitude at all. Two forms with different skeletons may well belong to the same species; these differences may be due to an environmental effect not passed on to descendants. Then, too, the characters of the skeleton are dependent upon the action of a number of genes, any or all of which can bring about extensive changes within the species. It is a fact that the skeletal system is the system most likely to be affected by environmental changes which have no genetic effect and which therefore have no effect on future generations. Boyd refers to the changes which muscles make on the skeleton. In addition, nutrition plays a part; witness the results of calcium deficiency in producing rickets. Disease may take its toll; prior to the practice of examining dairy herds for bovine tuberculosis, the disease frequently spread through contaminated milk to humans and resulted in a great many hunchbacks. Endocrine disorders may affect the skeletal system; acromegaly may distort the skeleton and give the individual human an almost prehistoric look.[2]

The Fossil Record: An Incomplete and Non-Random Sample

The chance of a given organism being fossilized is very slight. It is estimated that it would be no greater than one in one million. Indeed, Simpson estimates that the available fossils represent only a fraction of one percent of the species which have existed during the evolution of life. Immediate burial is a first prerequisite for fossilization, and this should be such as to exclude the air in order to prevent oxidation of the organism. Usually this burial is effected by water-borne sediment. Thus, the record is not only very incomplete, but, as Stebbins points out, a strongly biased sample. In most places where organisms die their remains are quickly destroyed by other organisms such as the bacteria and fungi of decay. Since fossils are preserved chiefly under water, in water, or in water-soaked ground, nearly all the deposits of terrestrial animals and plants are in or near ancient river or lake beds. Organisms which live in such habitats are more likely to be preserved than those which lived in uplands or on mountainsides. This means that periods of the earth's history when shallow seas, lakes, and large rivers were widespread are more strongly represented in the fossil record than are those periods when mountain ranges were high and there was a much larger proportion of dry land.[3]

Another problem is that almost no organism is preserved in its entirety. Soft parts are very rarely preserved as fossils; the larger or harder an animal structure is, the greater its chance for being preserved. Insects, which are both small and fragile, are preserved in only a few deposits. Plants are most often represented by leaves, wood, and particularly pollen, parts which botanists find difficult to use in classification, since classification is based largely on flower parts. Still another problem is that many past periods are represented by fossil beds which are found only in a small number of places on earth.

It is particularly significant, then, that the fossil record not only represents a minute sample, but that it is also a non-random sample. We have a reasonably good picture of life in the shallow seas and in swampy and boggy areas, but we have a very poor picture of the life of the past in mountains, plains, and deserts.

Reading the fossil record is really very similar to attempting to reconstruct a book in which only random pages are extant. We may indeed have parts of the account, but there is a great deal of conjecture involved in reproducing the missing sections.

Stebbins says that the bias inherent in the fossil record is exactly the wrong kind for evolutionists who wish to learn how the major groups of organisms originated. In modern floras and faunas, the greatest diversity of races and species exist in mountainous habitats, where climate, soil, and other factors vary greatly in a small area. In such regions, he says, new habitats are opened up much more often than in the flat lowlands, and as a result what he regards as stages in the origin of modern species can be found most easily in upland regions or on islands which are hilly or mountainous. But he points out that these are the places in which the chances that fossils would be preserved are the lowest. He does, however, believe that in spite of these imperfections the paleontologists have been able to supply us with a great deal of information regarding the course of evolution.[4]

Ehrlich and Holm also believe that fossils must be viewed as a very biased sample of the remains of past life. In addition to some of the problems pointed out by Stebbins, they call attention to the fact that factors favorable to the preservation of plant remains often are not suitable for animal preservation. Acid conditions, which might preserve leaves, will dissolve shells and bones. They agree with Stebbins that the fossil record is nevertheless sufficiently ample and diverse that paleontologists have been able to recognize many patterns and have been able to describe the processes thought to be responsible for their development.[5]

Davis says that the paleontologist has threads of a cross-section disconnected and fragmented because of the deficiencies in the record and that, further, his study is limited by being restricted to a single system, the skeletal system. All these deficiencies inherent in the record present a real problem, he believes, to the evolutionist.[6]

Lewin, in a recent article on problems of extinction at the time of the end of the Cretaceous period, says, "The notorious paucity of the fossil record combines with a greatly varying sedimentation rate to make time resolution of faunal changes little short of a nightmare."[7]

Difficulties of Fossil Reconstruction

Another related problem concerns the reconstruction of forms from their fossil remains. Cuvier thought that, given an ungulate-like tooth, he could infallibly predict that it would be associated with a particular sort of hoofed foot, even though the feet had not yet been found. It was not long until people came to believe that Cuvier could restore a whole animal from one fragment of the bone.

It is true, of course, that a great deal can be learned from a single bone of, let us say, a human being. Often it is possible to predict the age, sex, height, and other physical characteristics quite accurately. However, it is not possible to predict the exact physical appearance. It should be remembered, too, that this sort of thing is done with living human beings on the basis of thousands and thousands of measurements. Accurate restoration of extinct forms from one or a few fossil bones is simply not possible. Simpson classified this supposed ability as "folklore." He goes on to say that this marvelous ability is ascribed to paleontologists to their great distress. He criticizes many of the restorations that have been made and says that a prudent paleontologist is sometimes appalled at the extent of restoration indulged in by anthropologists. Some of them, he says, seem quite willing to reconstruct the face from a partial cranium, a whole skull from a piece of a lower jaw and so on.[8]

There have been instances in which the restoration did not match the animal when it was finally found. Such was the case with many restorations of the mammoth, which were found in various museums before the whole animal was found encased in ice in Siberia. There have been other suggestions, too, which have been shown wrong. W. D. Matthew suggested that the Sauropods, one of the extinct lizard-like reptiles, could not walk on land. He believed that they were so heavy that they would have collapsed without water to support their weight. It was his opinion and that of a number of other paleontologists that these animals lived in the water at the edge of the ocean, in marshes, or in lakes, where part of their weight was supported by the buoyancy of water.[9] However, a set of fossil footprints was excavated by Barnum Brown indicating quite clearly that the Sauropods did walk on land.[10]

One of the current controversies is over the possibility that the dinosaurs were warm-blooded. The traditional view has been that the

dinosaurs, which have always been classified as reptiles on the basis
of their skeletal anatomy, were, like other reptiles, cold-blooded creatures whose body temperature fluctuated with that of the environment. Today there are a number of individuals who argue that
dinosaurs were warm-blooded creatures and that this explains how
they were able to dominate the land for some 140 million years.

One important issue is the level of activity displayed by the dinosaurs. Reptiles generally have the reputation of being slow, sluggish creatures, not capable of much sustained activity. This inactivity
is often attributed to their being cold-blooded. Only by taking advantage of environmental heat sources (such as basking in the sun) can
reptiles warm their bodies and raise their metabolic rates to a level
that permits a high degree of activity. Some investigators have
reached the conclusion that dinosaurs do not fit the picture of slow,
sluggish reptiles. They believe that the long limbs and erect posture
of dinosaurs require a great deal more agility and speed than would
be possible in a cold-blooded animal. Marx believes that the whole
controversy may never be resolved to everyone's satisfaction. "Since
dinosaurs cannot be rounded up and studied directly, both sides have
to rely on their interpretations of the fossil record, which is incomplete, and on analogies with the physiology and anatomy of modern
animals. All of the arguments—both pro and con—contain many opportunities for disagreement."[11]

Known Variations Within Living Species: Their Significance for Fossil Classification

Even assuming that forms are quite different, it is not possible
to state with certainty that all fossils which are different actually
belong to different species. It is quite possible, and indeed probable,
that many of them are varieties of the same species. This would reduce
the number of species known as fossils which are not extant today.

There is a real pressure on paleontologists to split species. It may
be a subtle unconscious pressure, but it is there nevertheless. For if
the individual is the first one to discover a new species of an extinct
form, his name is incorporated in the literature together with an
account of his discovery. However, if it is a subsequent specimen of
a known form, he receives at best a footnote in some journal. Consequently, paleontologists are under pressure to minimize similarities
and to emphasize differences.

There are tremendous variations within living species. Some species, it is true, are quite uniform, others are quite diverse. Certainly *Homo sapiens* is a diverse species, as is apparent to anyone who examines illustrations of the races of man. There is a similar variety in the domesticated dog. If we today were to find the fossilized bones of all the varieties of dogs from, let us say, the tiny Chihauhua to the bulldog to the Great Dane, it is likely that we would conclude that we had at least several different species represented. But we are living in the age when these animals exist, and we are able to recognize that they are all members of the same species.

This is true also of the various forms which go through several stages in their life-cycles. The larvae of butterflies are quite different from the adult. Many of the Coelenterates (jellyfishes of various sorts) show a polyp and medusa stage. In the polyp stage they frequently resemble plants; in the medusa stage they frequently look like the common jellyfish.

Similarly, there are various species in which polymorphic forms occur. In ants, for instance, there are not only two kinds of females, as in bees—the workers and the fertile queen—but also several kinds of workers. There is a sexual dimorphism—bright colored males and dull colored females—in birds. In some forms there are seasonal variations. In the varying hare, the ermine, and the ptarmigan, the animals are white in winter and more or less brownish in summer. Many birds are brightly colored during the breeding season and more or less dull colored at other times of the year. There are also seasonal generations in insects and short-lived invertebrates. Individuals hatching in the cool spring are quite different from those hatching in the summer. Dry-season individuals are different from wet-season individuals. Mayr points out that seasonal generations have caused confusion and much complication of nomenclature in butterflies.[12]

If all of this is true in the case of forms which are alive today and can be carefully examined, imagine what the results are in studying fossil remains. It is quite possible—indeed, even probable—that substantial numbers of the forms classified as separate species are actually varieties rather than species.

Hybrids and Fossil Histories

Evolutionists not only show the general development of living organisms from the fossil record, but they have also developed series showing the evolutionary development of individual forms. Perhaps the best known of these is the fossil history of the horse. It is traced from an animal about the size of a fox terrier, known as *Hyracoth-erium* or *Eohippus*, through several forms said to represent steps in its evolutionary development, down to our present horse. In general, the trend in horse evolution is supposed to have been toward a reduction in size, a lengthing of the limbs, a reduction and loss of toes, and a change in dentition, so that the modern horse lives as a grazer. *Eohippus* had an arched back and had four toes on its front feet, with three toes and the remnants of two others on its hind feet. Its teeth had low crowns and rough surfaces. The modern horse has one toe on each foot and is a grazer rather than a browser.

It is quite possible that all organisms arranged in such a series actually belong there. It may well be, however, that some of the fossils are remnants of interspecific and intergenetic hybrids. These are sterile and make no contribution to the course of evolution. For instance, it is possible to mate a female horse and a male ass. The offspring is a mule, which is ordinarily sterile and cannot reproduce. If we did not know these three forms today—the horse, the mule, and the ass—and found them as fossils, it is conceivable that they might be arranged in a series to show how the ass evolved into the mule and the mule evolved into the horse. There is no way of doing genetic testing on fossils and no way of identifying sterile organisms. While it is true that there is great likelihood of the individual belonging to a fertile group of organisms, the possibility of a sterile hybrid cannot be ruled out. It is very apparent, too, that such hybrids might well appear as links between the forms from which they are derived.

Supposedly Extinct Forms That Are Still Alive

It is possible that some forms regarded as extinct are still alive in some parts of the globe. We commonly believe that most of the globe has been explored. However, there are still several land areas where this is not the case, and there is one very large area of the globe which has not been explored at all, the sea depths. We know that very bizarre and unusual forms are found there. Some have indeed been seen, but many have never been seen by man. Canadian and U.S. scientists recently announced the discovery of at least eight new species living near hot vents in a volcano a mile beneath the surface of the Pacific Ocean. Possibly some of the forms regarded as being extinct are still very much alive in these unexplored areas.

For instance, for many years it was believed that the Dawn Redwood, *Metasequoia glyptostroboides*, had been extinct for almost 20 million years. However, in 1944 its existence in the wild was reported by a Chinese forester, who found it towering above a small temple in the midst of rice paddies northeast of Chungking in the province of Szechwan in central China. Later small groves of these trees were found growing in sheltered mountain ravines in the Shuihsa valley. Far from being extinct, the tree is still very much alive. It has been brought to the United States and seems to thrive in our climate.

Another living fossil is the ginkgo or maiden-hair tree. It has been planted extensively here in the United States. It is unknown in the wild and is believed to have been preserved by the Chinese, who planted it in their cemeteries. It is found only in such places where it has been planted and preserved by man.

Another fossil that has been found alive is a fish, the coelacanth, *Latimeria chalumnae*. The first living specimen was taken off the coast of Africa in 1937. Until that time it was believed to have been extinct for from 50 to 120 million years. Since that time a number of specimens have been captured, most of them between Madagascar and Mozambique.

One of the echinoderms was known from fossils in lower Paleozoic rocks and was thought to have become extinct in early Ordovician times about 400 million years ago. A living Somasteroid echinoderm is now known to have survived in tropical eastern Pacific waters bordering on Southern Mexico.[13]

McKenzie reports the discovery of a new ostracod "living fossil" in samples of recent marine sediment collected from several Pacific islands. Members of this genus are very similar to a superfamily characteristic of the Devonian and Pennsylvanian periods.[14] Still another recently discovered living fossil is *Neopolina galatheae*, which was discovered off the west coast of Mexico during explorations conducted in connection with the International Geophysical Year. It was thought to be extinct since Paleozoic times, possibly as much as 500 million years ago.

Heinz Lowenstam of the California Institute of Technology recently recovered some mollusks which appear to be a new species related to fossils 350 to 600 million years old and thought to be extinct. These living Monoplacopherans were found in the Pacific Ocean bottom sample 400 meters deep, about 80 kilometers southwest of Los Angeles. Local fishermen had previously turned up many dead specimens.[15] Lowenstam was able to bring up several living specimens.

Yentsch, Lewis, and Yentsch report that some hystrichospheres, resting dinoflagellate cysts from Precambrian times, are indistinguishable from organisms found in modern marine sediments.[16]

The discovery of these living fossils does not suggest that we shall find alive most of the forms which we today regard as extinct. It is quite unlikely that we shall sometime find dinosaurs living in a "lost world." But it does suggest that some forms believed to be very ancient may have survived down to the present day.

Perhaps most significantly, this point demonstrates how hazardous it is to argue the non-existence of an organism from its failure to appear in the fossil record. These forms were all believed to have become extinct because they left no fossils. This was the reason for stating, let us say, that the coelacanth became extinct 50 to 120 million years ago, or that *Neopilina* became extinct 500 million years ago. These were all believed to have become extinct because they left no fossils, and it may well be that other organisms have existed much earlier or later than they appeared in the fossil record. It is hazardous, for example, to argue that man appeared late in the earth's history because we do not find human fossils in what are regarded as the earliest rock layers.

Absence of Transitional Forms

Another problem of the fossil record is the absence of what are generally known as missing links—transitional forms—to show the development of different phyla, classes, or orders. In mammals the earliest and most primitive known members of every order already have the basic ordinal characters. This is true of almost all orders of all classes of animals, both vertebrate and invertebrate. It is also true of the classes and of the phyla of the animal kingdom and presumably it is also true of plants. Darwin was much bothered by this problem. He titled one of the chapters of his book, "On the Imperfection of the Geological Record." Simpson points out that the absence of these transitional fossils is a serious problem, which cannot easily be dismissed. He says that in the larger groups—classes, orders, and phyla—transitional groups are not only rare but practically absent.[17]

Merrell says that the gaps in the fossil record usually seem to occur at crucial stages, where, if evolution is a gradual process, transitional forms connecting major groups ought to be found. He says that failure to find any transitional fossils has led many authorities to postulate a different evolutionary mechanism for the origin of the higher taxonomic groups. But he believes that no special mechanism is demanded by the evidence.[18]

The Cambrian and Cretaceous Outbursts

There are two geological periods which are particularly interesting. The first of these is the Cambrian period, when there is literally a sudden outburst of living things of great variety. Very few of the groups which we know today were not in existence at the time of the Cambrian period. And this is one of the earliest periods in the earth's history, believed to have begun about 540 million years ago; it is the first period in the Paleozoic era. All of the animal phyla are clearly represented already in the Cambrian period except two minor soft-bodied phyla, which may have been present without leaving fossil evidence, and the chordates. Even the chordates are believed to have been present, since an object which looks like a fish scale has been discovered in Cambrian rock and phosphatic dermal fragments of one of the heterostracan fish dating from the late Cambrian period have been discovered in northeastern Wyoming.[19] It is quite striking that this large number of phyla should have originated already in the Cambrian period, and it is also striking that no new phyla have developed since.

There has been a similar development in plants with most of the woody angiosperms, the flowering plants, appearing in great abundance in the early Cretaceous period. Since the Eocene epoch there have been few, if any, new genera. Just as there was a sudden outburst of animals in the Cambrian period, so there was a sudden development of plants in the Cretaceous period.

Extinction Problems

The geological record is thought to indicate that many species of plants and animals became extinct near the end of the Cretaceous period. Certain groups of organisms, such as planktonic foraminifera and calcareous nannoplanktons, were almost completely eliminated during a very brief span of geological time. Significant physicial and chemical changes of the oceans at the end of the Cretaceous have been revealed by analyses of the lithology and of the stable isotope compositions of fossil calcareous plankton in deep-sea drilling cores. However, it has not always been clear if the changes were the causes or the effects of mass mortality.

Recently a number of suggestions have been made regarding these extinctions, and they have been attributed to extraterrestrial causes primarily on the basis of anomalously-rich traces of iridium being found in sediments directly above the Cretaceous-Tertiary boundary. The assumption of a fallen asteroid or a disintegrated comet seems to offer the best explanation for the iridium anomaly, but the various scenarios have not produced convincing arguments that meteor impact should cause a selective extinction at the end of the Cretaceous period as registered by the paleontological record.

It has also been suggested recently that the catastrophic environmental changes were the consequences, not the causes, of mass mortality in the oceans. The finding of anomalous iridium contents at the Cretaceous-Tertiary boundary in various regions, including areas of continental sedimentation, is believed to be good evidence that mass mortality was related to the impact of a large extraterrestrial body from the solar system. Various possibilities of mass mortality in connection with the impact of a large meteorite have been suggested. The dust from the impact may have prevented photosynthesis of plants leading to starvation of animals all the way up the food chain. The meteorite may have been a comet containing cyanide, which poisoned the marine plankton. Finally, a flash-heating of the atmosphere during the entry of a meteorite may have caused catastrophic extinctions. It has been argued that there is no evidence of the craters we would expect from such a theory. However, it has also been suggested that two impact craters from this period have been found in southern Russia.

Thus, it has been postulated that there was a catastrophic near extinction of marine plankton, which was the consequence of mass mortality in the surface waters of the oceans, and that dinosaurs became extinct because of thermal stress after such a terminal Cretaceous catastrophe. The extinction took place within a few ten thousands of years after this event; it was not instantaneous.[20]

Other mass extinctions of marine forms are believed to have occurred at the end of the Ordovician, Devonian, Permian and Triassic periods.[21]

It is believed that at the time of the Cretaceous-Tertiary extinction the marine reptiles, the flying reptiles, and both orders of dinosaurs became extinct. It is also believed that there were dramatic extinctions among the microscopic floating animals and plants; both calcareous planktonic foraminifera and the calcareous nannoplankton were nearly exterminated with only a few species surviving. On the other hand, there were some groups that were little affected, such as land plants, crocodiles, snakes, mammals, and many kinds of invertebrates. One worker concludes that about half of the genera living at that time perished during the extinction event.

Deep sea limestone exposed in Italy, Denmark, and New Zealand show iridium increases of about 30, 160, and 20 times respectively above the background level at precisely the time of the Cretaceous-Tertiary extinction. It has been suggested that the impact of a large earth-crossing asteriod would inject about 60 times the object's mass into the atmosphere as pulverized rock. A fraction of this dust would stay in the stratosphere for several years and be distributed world-wide. The resulting darkness would supress photosynthesis and result in the extinctions that are supposed to have occurred. It is suggested that an asteriod struck the earth, formed an impact crater, and some of the dust-sized material ejected from the crater reached the strat-osphere and was spread around the globe. This dust effectively pre-vented sunlight from reaching the surface for a period of several years until the dust settled to earth. Loss of sunlight suppressed photosyn-thesis, and as a result most food chains collapsed and extinctions resulted. Day was turned into night for a period of several years, after which time the atmosphere returned relatively quickly to its normal transparent state.

A temporary absence of sunlight, such as is suggested, would effectively shut off photosynthesis and thus attack food chains at their origins. The food chain in the open ocean is based on microscopic floating plants, which it is believed show a nearly complete extinction. The animals at successively higher levels in this food chain were also very strongly affected with a nearly total extinction of the foraminifera and complete disappearance of several other forms, including the am-monites and marine reptiles.

A second food chain is based on land plants. Among these plants, existing individuals would die or at least stop producing new growth during the interval of darkness, but when light returned they would regenerate from seeds, spores, and existing root systems. However, the large herbivorous and carnivorous animals that were directly or indirectly dependent on this vegetation would become extinct. Many smaller terrestrial vertebrates did survive, including the ancestral mammals, and these may have been able to do so by feeding on insects and decaying vegetation.

Among the bottom-dwelling invertebrates of the shallow marine areas, some groups became extinct and others survived. It is sug-gested that there may have been a temporary food chain in this en-vironment based on nutrients originating from decaying land plants and animals and brought by rivers to the shallow marine waters.

One problem is that the extinction of the dinosaurs and the foram-nannoplankton did not occur at the same time. Another prob-lem is the lack of discovery of an impact crater. However, it has been argued that there was about a two-thirds probability that the object fell into the oceans.[22]

Studies at California Institute of Technology have assumed that a comet or asteroid with a diameter of seven miles hit the earth. The impact of such an object would have released the equivalent of one billion megatons of TNT and left a crater 100 miles in diameter. Since no such crater has been discovered, it is assumed that the comet or asteroid landed in the sea. The result would have been a tidal wave about three miles high, which would have enveloped the entire earth in 27 hours. Even in the deep oceans this tidal wave would have been 500 feet high half way around the earth. The layer of dust thrown in the air would have included the iridium that researchers have reported finding. The water ejected from such an impact would have destroyed much of the ozone layer, which protects the earth from ultraviolet rays. The impact would have had the effect of raising the average global temperatures by five to 10 degrees centigrade shortly after impact. This heat would have been followed by a rapid cooling as the dust cloud obscured the sun.

Recent analyses of osmium isotopes believed to have been deposited on the earth's surface some 65 million years ago are thought to support the idea of an asteriod impact causing or contributing to mass extinctions at the end of the Cretaceous. Studies in Denmark and Colorado of osmium-isotope ratios suggest a meteorite-origin explanation for the deviation from expectation.[23]

Another suggested explanation for the extinction of organisms at the end of the Cretaceous is the spillover of water from the Arctic into the other oceans of the world. It is suggested that the Arctic Ocean became isolated from other oceans in the late Cretaceous times. Later salt water from the North Atlantic intruded into the Arctic, while at the same time the lighter Arctic Ocean waters spilled over into the North Atlantic and beyond into the South Atlantic.

The entire ocean surface was covered with the layer of water of low salinity. The low salinity layer caused the extinction of a great many stenohaline planktonic organisms that lived on the surface, whereas beneath the surface layer depletion of dissolved oxygen had a severe impact on organisms with a high oxygen requirement. This resulted in serious climatic disturbances, particularly in a severe, prolonged drought of perhaps a decade or more accompanied by a general cooling. There were other climatic disturbances as well. It is believed that a great many of the dinosaurs died as a result of this drought. In some places water ran out in their territory.[24]

Another period of mass extinction is believed to have occurred at the end of the last Ice Age. The giant mammals were its chief victims. Most paleontologists have assumed that this extinction was brought about by the rapid termination of the glaciation, so that climatic and enviromental changes delivered a fatal blow to many terrestrial vertebrates. Vegetational communities on which they depended were not simply displaced geographically by the post-glacial climate shift but were fragmented. Recently it has been suggested that the real death blow suffered by many species was actually delivered by human hands. Demise of the late Pleistocene mammals was brought about by the advance of big game hunters. Commenting on these reports, Lewin says, "Colleagues working with a superior fossil record and better time resolution cannot readily establish the cause of the late Pleistocene extinction only tens of thousands of years ago. What chance then is there of solving mysteries that are measured in tens of millions of years in the past?"[25] Certainly the record is not as clear as we might wish it. It is a book with many pages missing and many others obscure.

The Persistence of Unchanged Forms

Another problem of the fossil record is that a number of forms have persisted unchanged for long periods of time. The horseshoe crab, *Limulus*, dates back as a genus to Triassic times and is believed to have been unchanged for about 200 million years. Brine shrimp, simple crustacea, are believed to have existed almost unchanged since Lower Cambrian times about 500 million years ago. Among insects, the ants are believed to have reached their limits of specialization some 30 million years ago and are thought to have survived with very little evolutionary change since that time.

Among the vertebrates, the lampreys and hagfishes still have the fundamental structure of the Agnatha, the earliest vertebrate group. A shark, *Scapanorhynchus owsteni*, is already represented by teeth in what is believed to be upper Cretaceous rock; yet it has been found living off the coast of Japan.[26]

Stanley says,

All fossil beetles known from deposits representing the recent Ice Age belong to still-living species; this situation implies that beetle species normally persist, almost unchanged, longer than a million years—perhaps much longer. Well-preserved teeth and bones tell us that an average species of mammal has survived for perhaps two million years. The seeds of higher plants serve as diagnostic features for species recognition, and fossil seeds reveal that half of all seed-bearing species alive three million years ago also populate the modern world. On a smaller scale, nearly all species of mosses and liverworts in existence four or five million years ago are still clinging to the damp dirt. Comparisons of fossils and living seashells reveal that half of all the species of mollusks that populated seafloors seven million years ago are still with us. Among the foraminifera—tiny amoeba-like sea creatures with shells that have left a superb fossil record—the average duration for species has exceeded 30 million years![27]

He goes on to say that when over long stretches of geological time, there is no change in the key aspects of body form that enable us to recognize the species, we can be almost certain that the species underwent no evolution, save for a bit of fine tuning.

Catastrophism and Uniformitarianism

The major geological controversy of the 19th century was the controversy between the catastrophists and the uniformitarians. This controversy dealt with the question of the geological record. Prior to this time most of the observations that were made by the geologists were explained on the basis of the Noachian deluge of Genesis. One of the first individuals to question catastrophism was Lyell, who had such a marked influence on Darwin. Uniformitarianism postulated that the present is the key to the past. It suggested that forces seen shaping the earth's surface today acted in the same way and with the same results in the past. Uniformitarianism deals primarily with the rates of change.

This principle is not to be confused with the principle of uniformity, which suggests that processes go on in the same way throughout the universe and that they have gone on in the same way throughout time. Uniformity is clearly Biblical, since the God of the Bible is the God of order. He is not the capricious god of the heathen, who enjoys changing the rules and playing cat-and-mouse games with human beings. Uniformity deals with the validity and applicability of natural laws; uniformitarianism deals with the rate at which these processes go on.

For many years uniformitarianism dominated the science of geology.

In 1669 Nicholas Steno developed the principles that still remain the keystones of modern stratigraphy today. They describe the initial conditions of sedimentary deposition and include such principles as superposition (that in any stratigraphic succession the youngest strata are on top), original horizontality (that strata are deposited horizontally or nearly so), and lateral continuity (that strata originally continue in all directions until they either terminate against the boundaries of the dispositional basin or thin to zero).

In the early 19th century William Smith ("Strata Smith") and George Cuvier added the principle of faunal succession, thereby providing the means for correlating discontinuous geologic formations. Originally the rocks were divided into three successive groups by Giovanni Arduino, a mining inspector in Italy in 1759. The scale today has become very complex, so that more than a 150 eons, eras, periods, epochs, and ages are recognized by geologists. This is the basis for the geological time scale suggesting that the earth is billions of years old, and it is a time scale based on uniformitarianism.

Today, however, there has come to be an acceptance, though a grudging one, of the possibility of at least some catastrophism. Recently it was stated, "It is a great philosophical breakthrough for geologists to accept catastrophe as a normal part of Earth history." This new approach was characterized as "a currently important, perhaps revolutionary, shift in collective professional perspectives among paleontologists as well as geologists." A particular area of recent interest has been the end of the so-called Cretaceous period. As we noted, this is believed to have been marked by major changes in plants and animals including the dinosaurs, who at the time of their extinction appeared to be well equipped to resist any threat to their survival. In recent years the idea of asteroids striking the earth, a catastrophe of major importance, has attracted considerable attention. Uniformitarianism has given way to at least some catastrophism.[28]

The Fossil Record in Summary

Careful study suggests that the evidence from the fossil record is not so overwhelmingly in favor of evolution as it first appears. To be sure, the fossils do present a difficulty for creationists to which in the present state of knowledge there is no complete answer. There is no doubt that there were a great many climatic changes both before the flood and after it, and these made it impossible for many animals to survive in the post-diluvian world. But there are many puzzles also for the evolutionist, some of which we have outlined. He has real difficulty in explaining the extinction of large numbers of animals. For instance, there has been no reasonable explanation of the extinction of the dinosaurs at the end of the Mesozoic period. The dinosaurs existing at that time seem to have been equipped to meet any environmental problem. They seemed well adapted to their environment and adequately equipped with defense mechanisms.

Another puzzle is the sudden freezing of the mammoths. Many of these are preserved in the ice in Siberia. The food in their digestive tracts has not yet been digested, which would indicate that the digestive processes were stopped by the cold within a very short time. Even with temperatures of near absolute zero, it is difficult to understand how the cold could have penetrated to the digestive tract in time to stop the digestive processes there.

Many evolutionists recognize that they have problems and acknowledge the precariousness of the fossil evidence. Huxley says that the material on which the paleontologist is forced to rely is unrepresentative. He believes that much theory depends on fossils of organisms which probably are relatively unimportant in evolution. He refers to the presidential address of Professor Hawkins to the Geology Section of the British Association at Blackpool in 1936. Hawkins drew far-reaching conclusions as to the method and course of evolution on the basis of the echinoderms, mollusks, and brachiopods. No trends in vertebrates and no trends in land animals were discussed by him.[29]

Nilsson, a botanist, says, "My attempts to demonstrate evolution by an experiment carried on for more than 40 years have completely failed. At least I should hardly be accused of having started from any pre-conceived antievolutionary standpoint." Later he says, "It may be firmly maintained that it is not even possible to make a caricature of an evolution out of paleobiological facts. The fossil material is now so complete that it has been possible to construct new classes, and the lack of transitional series cannot be explained as being due to scarcity of material. The deficiencies are real, they will never be filled."[30]

Arkell and Moy-Thomas tell us that we simply do not know the true explanation of many paleontological relationships. They tell us that we are in the position of an observer who for the first time becomes aware of black men and white men and mulattoes in the United States. From the mulattoes he might infer that the negro and white population are more closely related to each other than to their negro and white forebears in Africa and Europe, or that there is a trend from black *to* white or vice versa. They believe that at best paleontologists' results are hypothetical and more or less subjective.[31]

Davis goes so far as to say that the facts of paleontology conform equally well with other interpretations which he believes have been discredited by neo-biological work. Among the other interpretations he mentions divine creation, innate developmental processes, Lamarckianism, and the like. He believes that paleontology by itself can neither prove nor refute such ideas.[32]

Punctuated Equilibrium

The new theory of punctuated equilibrium, which has been espoused by Gould, Niles Eldredge, and their associates since they announced the theory in 1972, is an indication that the fossil record does not support the current theories of gradual development. Gould's ideas are similar to those developed by Richard Goldschmidt. He spoke of what he called "hopeful monsters," suggesting that the first bird hatched from a reptilian egg.[33] Goldschmidt spoke of a sort of sudden-jump evolution, and it is this idea which Gould and his associates have espoused. They believe that transitional forms were hardly to be expected because evolution did not come about through gradual development but by a sudden jump followed by a plateau of hundreds of thousands or millions of years.

The problem to which the proponents of punctuated equilibrium address themselves is the question of the large changes observed in evolutionary history and the rapidity with which they appear in the geological record. Another issue that they deal with is stasis—the apparent persistence of species with little or no morphological change for hundreds of thousands or millions of years. What appears to them to be an inadequacy of the current synthetic theory is that this yields small but continuous changes, whereas evolution as seen by the punctuationists occurs by large and rapid bursts of change followed by long periods without change. Goldschmidt called attention to this problem when he said, "The decisive step in evolution, the first step towards macroevolution, the step from one species to another, requires another evolutionary method than that of sheer accumulation of micromutations."[34]

Stebbins and Ayala believe there are two major problems for the synthetic theory: the large morphological changes observed in evolutionary history, together with the rapidity with which they appear in the geological record; and stasis, the apparent persistence of species with little or no morphological change for hundreds of thousands or millions of years. The apparent dilemma, they believe, is that the mechanism suggested by the modern synthetic theory yields small but continous changes, whereas the fossil records suggest large and rapid bursts of change followed by long periods without change. They too refer to the work of Goldschmidt, who insisted that the first decisive step in evolution, the step from one species to another, requires another evolutionary method than that of sheer accumulation of microromutations.[35]

In discussing punctuated equilibrium, which he accepts, Stanley points to the problem of a mechanism for this new theory when he raises the question, "What is the genetic basis for major restructuring of life in quantum speciation events . . . ?" He answers, "At present we have no certain answer." He suggests that in a small population, especially one living in an unusual environment, some of the disadvantages of biological restructuring can be tolerated while the advantages are exploited.

He also suggests that punctuated equilibrium solves the problem of adaptive radiation which troubled Darwin. He believes it explains the rapid formation of a wide variety of new forms of life from a single ancestral group. Stanley believes that paleontology suffered a major decline after failing to support Darwin's popular view of gradualistic evolution. "Darwin's dismal appraisal of fossil records pushed the science of paleontology into the background in the study of evolution for more than a century."[36]

Gould believes that many features of organic architecture and developmental pathways have never been adaptations to anything, but arose as by-products or incidental consequences of changes with the basis in selection. Functionless, non-adaptive structures have played a significant role in evolution; one of these is the human brain, which Gould and his colleague Vrba believe is unrelated to its original adaptation.[37]

Gould believes that there are counterforces involved, that sometimes the negative interaction of a species level disadvantage is counterbalanced by an individual level advantage. He believes that this explains overspecialization, which he says is "a central evolutionary phenomenon that has failed to gain the attention it deserves because we have lacked a vocabulary to express what is really happening." Gould believes that many of the problems of Darwinism are the result of emphasis on the role of selection on individuals. He believes in what he calls "a concept of hierarchy" in which selection acts on higher level "individuals" such as demes (members of a species who live in a particular area and who are therefore capable of free interbreeding) and species. He believes, then, that selection may act on larger groups. Darwin thought primarily of selection acting on individuals.[38]

Gould believes that punctuated equilibrium will provide "more than a comfortable extension" of the modern synthetic theory of evolution, "but much less than a revolution." He believes that neither of Darwinism's two central themes will survive: first, gradual evolution as the result of small genetic changes (mutations) and recombination; second, the ordering of this genetic variation by natural selection. Gould holds that the essence of the Darwinian argument is embodied in punctuated equilibrium in a more abstract and hierarchically extended form. The modern synthesis he believes is "incomplete, not incorrect."[39]

In support of the principle of stasis, Gould quotes MacGillavry, who writes, "During my work as an oil paleontologist I had the opportunity to study sections meeting these rigid requirements [of long, well-represented sequences]. As an ardent student of evolution, moreover, I was continually on the watch for evidence of evolutionary change. . . . The great majority of species do not show any appreciable evolutionary change at all. These species appear in the section [first occurrence] without obvious ancestors in underlying beds [and] are stable once established."[40]

Perhaps the fossil record is not as supportive of substantial change as it is represented as being.

Geographical Distribution

Except for the earthworm and the ant, there are no plants or animals which are approximately universal in their distribution over the globe. Most are confined to somewhat limited areas, and in some cases the range is very narrow indeed. This is believed by evolutionists to demonstrate that particular species, genera, and orders have evolved in a particular area. It is suggested that the limited range is due to the fact that this is the area in which they evolved. The present geographical distribution is regarded as the end product of a long period of evolution.

Plant and animal geographers distinguish six areas of geographical distribution. They are: (1) Nearctic, which includes Greenland and North America as far south as Mexico; (2) Palearctic, which includes Europe and the northern part of Asia; (3) Neotropical, which includes Central and South America; (4) Ethiopian, which includes Africa, Madagascar and the southern part of Arabia; (5) Oriental, which includes the southern part of Asia, Malay States, Sumatra, Borneo, Java, the Celebes, and the Philippines; and (6) Australian, which includes Australia, New Zealand, Tasmania, New Guinea and the Pacific Islands. Each of these geographical realms has characteristic plants and animals differing from those found in other realms.

Biologists also distinguish different ecological zones—forests, grasslands, deserts, etc.—in each of these broader areas. Zones are also distinguished in the ocean. Organisms are frequently limited not only to a particular geographical realm but also to a specific ecological zone.

It is interesting that the Biblical system of classification is based on such broad ecological zones rather than on structure, as is our own system of classification.

What is particularly striking about these geographical realms is the peculiarities of the plants and animals found there. North and South America, for example, differ very markedly in their large mammals. South America has a number of what are considered rather simple mammals, such as the anteater, the sloth, and the armadillo. Members of the camel family are found only in South America, though fossil camels are found in North America, and Asia has camels today. Evolutionists believe that originally North America and South America were separate. The Isthmus of Panama was submerged, they believe, and during this period different plants and animals evolved in North and in South America. They suggest that camels originally crossed into North America from Asia by means of land connections across the Bering Sea. Later the Isthmus of Panama emerged, making possible an exchange of plants and particularly of animals between North and South America, and during this period the camel traveled down into South America. The number of families of land mammals in South America increased from 32 to 39 and then fell back to 35. They believe that at this time, too, the Canadian porcupine and the opossum traveled up from South America into North America. Subsequently, camels became extinct in North America; this was believed to have occurred during the great mammalian destruction of the late Pleistocene epoch, but they did not become extinct in South America where they are still found today.

Primitiveness of South Fauna

When one examines the animals of the northern and southern hemispheres, one is struck by the primitiveness of the fauna of the southern hemisphere, particularly of Australia. The Australian zone is noted for the prevalence of egg-laying mammals, the monotremes, and the marsupials, pouched mammals. One of the three genera of lungfish, considered to be primitive fish, is found only in Australia. Except for the wild dog, which may have been introduced by early man, the rabbit, which was introduced in historical times, and some rodents, there are no placental mammals in Australia.

Peculiarities of Island Fauna

Islands, too, tend to be characterized by a very limited fauna. Some, such as the British Isles, are known as continental islands; these have plants and animals quite similar to those of the nearby continents and are not so limited in their variety. Oceanic islands, however, which are separated from the continental masses by deep water and which are typically composed of igneous (volcanic) rock ordinarily have only a very limited number of plants and animals, and these usually are somewhat unique. Generally they have no mammals except for bats. Most of the animals there are those which can be carried on floating material or can be borne by the wind, such as snails, lizards, insects, and land birds. Plants, too, tend to be quite different. Of the Hawaiian plants, for example, 83 percent of the species are found only on these islands. It should be noted that the studies which impressed Darwin most were made on the Galapagos Islands off the coast of Ecuador. Forty percent of the plant species and 96 percent of the reptiles of the Galapagos Islands live only there.

Animal geographers report that a whole family of birds of 60 species is known only from the Hawaiian Islands. Of the 260 species of birds on Madagascar, half are found nowhere else. Forty-three species of birds are known only from Jamaica; 74 species of birds are known only from the Bismarck Islands; 15 species of Greenland plants are found only there; and about 75 percent of the New Zealand plants are unique to those islands.

Forms Absent from Certain Areas

Furthermore, there are large areas from which certain groups of animals are excluded. There are no bears in Africa. New Zealand and Hawaii lack snakes; indeed, the Hawaiian Islands have only seven species of reptiles, and these are skinks and geckos. Australia and New Zealand lack placental mammals except those which appear to have been introduced. Though the Ethiopian region has the richest mammalian fauna, it lacks entirely the monotremes and the marsupials.

Geographical Distribution and Evolution

As we have indicated, evolutionists believe the present observations made on the distribution of plants and animals represent the end product of a long period of evolution. They believe that species, genera, families, and orders have evolved in almost all areas of the earth. They suggest that relatively simple forms, the ancestral forms of the present organisms, got to these areas in some way or another, and in the course of evolution the present species developed. They believe that isolation played an important role in this process of evolution.

Thus, they suggest that Australia has been isolated at least since Permian times with a short-lived continental link at the end of the Cretaceous period. This explains not only the presence of the marsupials but also the absence of placental mammals. Much is made of the rise and fall of land bridges, which ultimately connect land areas and isolate them.

Continental Drift

Today continental drift plays an important role in explaining the distribution of plants and animals. This theory was quite popular after it was first suggested by Wegener. Subsequently, it fell into disrepute and only relatively recently has it been revived. Today it is widely accepted. One author described it as having in the space of the last 25 years "made the transition from lunatic fringe to accepted dogma, the paradigm of the geological sciences."

According to this theory, there was at one time a single continent, Pangaea, representing two major land masses sutured together: Gondwanaland, centering around the South Pole; and Laurentia, in the vicinity of the equator. These masses gradually drifted northward, Laurentia splitting into North America and Eurasia, and Gondwanaland splitting up to form Africa, South America, Antarctica, and the Arabian and Indian peninsulas. The drifting was very slow and depended on the movement of plates under the continents. This drifting continues and is supposed to be responsible for some of the pressures which are finally released in earthquakes. Recent studies on rock paleomagnetism have suggested that the poles have wandered considerably during the history of the earth, and this would seem to support the continental drift theory. Today, it is believed that the big picture of sea floor spreading, moving plates, and subduction has been largely filled in, but the smaller scale details are still proving more difficult to fit with the theory.[41]

Continental drift is believed to explain some of the observations made in connection with geographical distribution, since at one time organisms are supposed to have been able to move freely over the original continents. After these were separated, the organisms became isolated.

Geographical Distributions and Special Creation

There is little doubt that the facts of geographical distribution are easier to reconcile with the theory of evolution than they are with special creation. We might indeed postulate that God created the plants and animals and placed them in areas where we now know them were it not for the Noachian deluge. Presumably, all air-breathing animals that were not on the ark died as a result of that cataclysm (Gen. 7:21-23). Most plants, too, presumably perished, though it is possible that a number of them survived as seeds, on rafts of vegetation, or in other ways.

If only those air-breathing animals that were on the ark survived, how did they achieve the present distribution? It is possible, of course, that they traveled by means of land bridges from Mount Ararat to the places where they are now found. The development of land bridges, however, is not as easy as it sounds. It requires tremendous changes in the earth's crust. Heavier rock, it is believed, must be replaced by lighter rocks if submerged areas are to rise. Moreover, the rise and fall of land bridges would presumably require a substantial amount of time.

At the same time, the evolutionists have this identical problem. They too want land bridges to explain the migration of animals from one area to another. And if land bridges radiating from Mount Ararat to various parts of the world are difficult to erect, so are the land bridges of the evolutionist. The one factor that favors him is the amount of time at his disposal.

Some evolutionists have asked, "if all animals radiated out from Mount Ararat, why is it that there are no marsupials in Asia and along the Malay peninsula, where they must have traveled?" It is possible that they became extinct in these areas. Possibly they were able to live in some of the areas for only a very short time and radiated out almost immediately to the places included in the present range. It is not difficult to picture the extinction of certain forms, particularly if they were not adapted for a particular climate.

Exceptions to Expected Plant and Animal Distributions

It should be pointed out, too, that not all of the earth's areas have the distribution we would expect according to the evolutionary scheme. Not all of them fit neatly into the patterns which evolutionists have developed. Islands, for example, frequently have a peculiar flora and fauna, but not always. The island of Java, for instance, has only a few peculiar species of birds among the 500 that have been identified there, and not a single bird genus is limited to Java. The animals of Madagascar just off the coast of Africa are most similar not to those of Africa but to those of Asia. The animals of New Guinea are very similar to those of Australia but quite different from those of other islands to the north and west which are almost as near as Australia. The animals of Sumatra are more like those of Borneo than like those of Java, though Java is closer to Sumatra than is Borneo.

Still other exceptions to expectations could be listed. While many of the patterns of distribution fit with the expectations of the evolutionists, there are enough exceptions to create problems for their theories, too.

Non-Adaptive Nature of Differences

It is also true that many of the differences between species that are close to one another geographically are not adaptive. They ought to be that if they have developed through competition and natural selection. Yet the differences between two such species are not always such as to equip the two for their particular habitats. The differences, for example, between the species of Hawaiian land snails are not adaptive. This is also true of the color polymorphism of the various races of the deer mice and of the marking of *Buarremon inornatus*, one of the tanagers.[42]

Summary

We will have to recognize that the observations we are able to make on the geographical distribution of plants and animals do indeed pose problems for those who support special creation. The evidences from this area fit better with the theory of evolution than they do with the idea of special creation. Yet not all of the observations fit neatly with the theories of the evolutionist, either. These exceptions warrant our reserving judgment at least for the time being.

Notes

1. D. Dwight Davis, "Comparative Anatomy and the Evolution of the Vertebrates," *Genetics, Paleontology, and Evolution*, ed. Glenn L. Jepsen, Ernst Mayr, and George Gaylord Simpson (Princeton: Princeton University Press, 1949), p. 73.

2. William C. Boyd, *Genetics and the Races of Man* (Boston: Little, Brown, 1950), pp. 21f.

3. G. Ledyard Stebbins, *Processes of Organic Evolution* (Englewood Cliffs: Prentice-Hall, 1966), p. 134.

4. Ibid.

5. Paul R. Ehrlich and Richard W. Holm, *The Process of Evolution* (New York: McGraw-Hill, 1963), p. 259.

6. Davis, p. 73.

7. Roger Lewin, "Extinctions and the History of Life," *Science* 221 (1983):935.

8. George Gaylord Simpson, "Some Principles of Historical Geology Bearing on Human Origins," *Cold Spring Harbor Symposia on Quantitative Biology* XV (1950), p. 57f.

9. W. D. Matthew, "The Pose of Sauropodous Dinosaurs," *American Naturalist* XLIV (1910):559f.

10. William King Gregory, *Evolution Emerging* (New York: Macmillan, 1951) I:305f.

11. Jean L. Marx, "Warm Blooded Dinosaurs: Evidence Pro and Con," *Science* 199 (1978):1424—26.

12. Ernst Mayr, *Systematics and the Origin of Species* (New York: Columbia University Press, 1942), p. 26.

13. H. Barraclough Fell, "A Surviving Somasteroid From the Eastern Pacific Ocean," *Science* 136 (1962):633.

14. Kenneth G. McKenzie, "Ostracod 'Living Fossils': New Finds in the Pacific," *Science* 155 (1967):1005.

15. "Biology Briefs," *Bioscience* 27 (1977):574.

16. Clarice M. Yentsch, Carrie M. Lewis, and Charles S. Yentsch, "Biological Resting in the Dinoflagellate *Gonyaulax excavata*," *Bioscience* 30 (1980):251.

17. George Gaylord Simpson, *Tempo and Mode in Evolution* (New York: Columbia University Press, 1944), pp. 105—07.

18. David Merrell, *Evolution and Genetics* (New York: Holt, Rinehart & Winston, 1962), p. 43.

19. John E. Repetski, "A Fish from the Upper Cambrian of North America," *Science* 200 (1978):529—31.

20. Kenneth J. Hsu, Q. He, Judith A. McKenzie, et. al., "Mass Mortality and Its Environmental and Evolutionary Consequences," *Science* 216 (1982): 249—56.

21. David M. Raup and J. John Sepkoski, Jr., "Mass Extinctions in the Marine Fossil Record," *Science* 215 (1982):1501—02.

22. Luis W. Alvarez, Walter Alvarez. Frank Asaro, and Helen V. Michel, "Extraterrestrial Cause for the Cretaceous-Tertiary Extinction," *Science* 208 (1980):1095—1108.

23. J. M. Luck and K. K. Turekian, "Osmium-187/Osmium-186 in Manganese Nodules and the Cretaceous-Tertiary Boundary," *Science* 222 (1983):613—15.
24. Stefan Gartner and James P. McGuirk, "Terminal Cretaceous Extinction: Scenario for a Catastrophe," *Science* 206 (1979):1272—76.
25. Roger Lewin, "What Killed the Giant Mammals?" *Science* 221 (1983):1036—37.
26. G. S. Carter, *Animal Evolution* (London: Sidwick and Jackson, 1951), p. 329. J. R. Norman, *A History of Fishes* (New York: Wyn, 1949), p. 124.
27. Steven Stanley, "The New Evolution," *Johns Hopkins Magazine* 33, #3 (1982):7.
28. Roger Lewin, "Extinctions and the History of Life," *Science* 221 (1983):935—37.
29. Julian Huxley, *Evolution, the Modern Synthesis* (New York: Harpers, 1943), pp. 31f.
30. Heribert Nilsson, *Synthetische Artbuildung* (Lund: Verlag C. W. K. Gleerup, 1953), pp. 1185, 1212.
31. W. J. Arkell and J. A. Moy-Thomas, "Paleontology and the Taxonomic Problems," *The New Systematics*, ed. Julian Huxley (Oxford: Oxford University Press, 1940), pp. 401f.
32. Davis, p. 77.
33. Richard Goldschmidt, *The Material Basis of Evolution* (New Haven: Yale University Press, 1940), p. 390.
34. Ibid., p. 183.
35. G. Ledyard Stebbins and Francisco J. Ayala, "Is a New Evolutionary Synthesis Necessary?" *Science* 213 (1981):967—71.
36. Stanley, pp. 6—11.
37. Roger Lewin, "Adaptation Can Be a Problem for Evolutionists," *Science* 216 (1982):1212f.
38. Stephen J. Gould, "Darwinism and the Expansion of Evolutionary Theory," *Science* 216 (1982):380—87.
39. Ibid., p. 382.
40. Stephen J. Gould, "Punctuated Equilibrium and the Fossil Record," *Science* 219 (1983):439.
41. Richard A. Kerr, "Skepticism Persists as Plate Tectonic Answers Come Harder," *Science* 199 (1978):283.
42. Huxley, p. 242.

8
Problems for the Evolutionist

While it is true that there are observations which fit better with the theory of evolution than they do with the theory of special creation, there are also areas which cannot readily be explained on the basis of the theory of evolution and which fit better with the concept of special creation. One of these is the study of the evolution of man himself. While the fossil record in general is usually regarded as supporting the theory of evolution, the record of human evolution suggests that man branched off very early from other animals and that he has existed as man for a very long time. Creationists suggest that he has existed as a separate species ever since the beginning, for the Bible clearly states that man was created from the dust of the earth (Gen. 2:7). As more and more information accumulates, the gap between man and his supposed anthropoid ancestors widens, as will be evident.

Another area that creates problems for evolution is the suggested mechanism for evolution. The development of Gould's theory of punctuated equilibrium, suggesting sudden evolutionary jumps followed by long periods without any evolutionary change, is an indication of how unsatisfactory presently-suggested mechanisms are.

Still another area that creates difficulties is the whole question of the complexity of living things. It strains credibility to suggest that all of the complexities that we have come to know have developed by chance.

Human Evolution

It is only natural that man should be particularly interested in the story of his own evolutionary development. Far more attention has been given to this subject than to any other paleontological area. In popular accounts evolutionists are represented as saying that man is descended from the monkey. This is not quite what the evolutionist says. He believes that man and the monkey had a common ancestor. Man is supposedly not the great-great-great-great-grandchild of the monkey, but rather the monkey's 32nd cousin.

At the same time, if we were to ask the question as to how this common ancestor would have been classified, there is little doubt that he would be classified as a monkey or an ape. Simpson says that on the subject of the classification of the common ancestor there has been "too much pussyfooting." He says that apologists emphasize that man cannot be the descendant of any living ape—"A statement that is obvious to the verge of imbecility"—and go on to state or imply that man is not really descended from an ape or monkey at all but from an earlier common ancestor. Simpson goes on to say, "In fact that earlier ancestor would certainly be called an ape or monkey in popular speech by anyone who saw it. Since the terms *ape* and *monkey* are defined by popular usage, man's ancestors were apes or monkeys (or successively both). It is pusillanimous if not dishonest for an informed investigator to say otherwise."[1]

One of the problems in connection with human evolution is the paucity of human and pre-human fossils. While it is true that there are a great many fossils of other organisms, the fossil record of man is relatively meager.

A number of explanations have been advanced for this situation. Some have suggested that man was originally a tropical organism and that under tropical conditions of high heat and humidity decay sets in so rapidly that fossilization rarely, if ever, occurs. This would also account for the fact that there are very few primate fossils, since all of the primates other than man are essentially tropical animals.

However, it must be pointed out that man has occupied other habitats as well. The fact that we do find human fossils in regions that are not tropical is evidence of this.

Another explanation for the absence of fossils is that man developed the custom of burying his dead very early in his evolutionary history. Burying the dead is a distinctly human practice. There is little doubt that the practice of earth burial reduces the chance of an organism being fossilized. Fossils, as we have pointed out, are formed only under conditions where oxygen is excluded, and this is not the case with earth burial.

The fact that man practiced earth burial very early in his history—indeed, from the very beginning of his history—is a testimony of his belief in the resurrection of the body. He recognized that the dead were not separated from him forever, but he realized that he would one day see them again. For that reason he had a respect for the dead body and carefully laid it away in the ground to await the resurrection.

Determining the Degree of Evolutionary Development

Many of the comparisons made between man and other primates and between supposedly pre-human fossils and man as we know him today are made on the basis of brain capacity and dentition (tooth structure and arrangement). It is believed that an increase in the brain size indicates a higher development on the scale of evolution, and that the evolution of man has come primarily through the enlargement of his brain, a trend which Gould believes was not directly adaptive.[2]

It is true, of course, that we do find a gradual increase in brain size as we go up the assumed evolutionary ladder. The mean brain capacity of the gorilla, for instance, is 549 cc; for the various *Pithecanthropus* fossils it is 900 cc; for modern man the variation ranges from 800 to 2000 cc. It is interesting to note that the average brain capacity of the Cro-Magnon man was in excess of the average brain capacity of man today, and that the Neanderthalers had a brain size which averaged somewhat larger than that of modern man.[3]

If brain size and cranial capacity are in themselves only relative, the data are meaningless unless it is possible to compare them with the actual weight of the whole organism. For instance, if we compare only the absolute weights it is possible to prove that men are brainier than women, with the implication that men are more intelligent than women, since the average man's brain weighs more than does the average woman's brain. However, when we compare the weight of the brain with the weight of the whole body, we find that a woman's brain constitutes the same percentage of her body weight as does man's brain.

Another factor to be considered is the age of the individual. A child's brain is smaller than that of an adult, but this is no indication that he is relatively unintelligent.

Even when we compare brain size with body weight we do not always get the answers we want. The brain weight of the South American squirrel monkey, *Saimiri* or *Chrysothrix sciureus*, is 1/17th of his total body weight. Man's brain weighs approximately 1/35th of his body weight. Surely no one would argue that the squirrel monkey's brain is more highly developed than that of man.

Actually, the important consideration is the number of folds and convolutions in the brain. It is difficult if not impossible to study these in a fossil form. Soft tissues such as the brain disappear in the process of fossilization.

It is for this reason that Mayr says the size of the brain can hardly be regarded as a criterion of intelligence. He believes that we should be very hesitant to use brain size as any sort of criterion in the genus *Homo*. It is misleading, he says, to believe that the *Homo* stage is reached when the brain capacity reached 700-750 cc.[4] Bennett, Diamond, Krech, and Rosenzweig sum up the problem by saying that we no longer subscribe to the judgment of anthropologists of the last century that size and weight of brains in men indicate their degree of intellectual capacity.[5] While the first results of brain weight and brain size measurements were encouraging when it was found that more capable individuals had larger brains than inferior individuals, it was soon realized that men in different stations of life often differ in health and nutrition as well as in intellect, and it was recognized that these factors might also affect brain weight. It was also discovered that there were striking exceptions to the general relations established; idiots were found with large brains and geniuses with small brains. For that reason, at present it is believed that the important thing is the number of neural interconnections and the chemical processes in the brain. These can hardly be measured in fossil form.

Dobzhansky believes that cranial capacity and brain size are not reliable criteria of intelligence or intellectual ability. He not only points to the cranial capacity of the Neanderthals, but also to the paintings found in the Altamira and Lascau caves. These artists were, he believes, as talented as any of the artists of recent times.[6]

Tooth Structure

The second criterion frequently used for classifying fossil primates is tooth structure. Here we first of all study the general shape of the jaw, the human jaw being arched and the jaw of the anthropoid ape being somewhat square. We also study the size of teeth. Teeth are studied because they resist decay and are often available for such studies.

One question that has received attention is the size of the teeth. There are many supposedly primitive primates and fossil humans which have teeth larger than those which we find in men today. Do larger teeth indicate gigantism? Or are these large teeth to be found in ordinary-sized jaws? Hooton is very critical of conclusions that have been reached from teeth and tooth structure. He says that recent paleontological discoveries of both human and ape remains, in which teeth are accompanied by skull bones and other skeletal parts, indicated that classifying an organism and making inferences as to the degree of evolution achieved on the basis of teeth and bone is precarious. He believes that early human types may have had some teeth that are indistinguishable from those of apes and vice versa. Dentitians which at one time would confidently have been assigned to early humans, he says, have now been found in the crania of apes.[7]

Man's Place in the Scheme of Classification

Man is considered to be a primate. This name was chosen to indicate the primitiveness of this order. Primates are considered relatively simple and undifferentiated animals. They are mammals with a true placenta, covered more or less with a hairy or wooly coat. They have five fingers and five toes. In most cases the digits have flat nails instead of claws. The brain case is large and the brain highly developed. The eyes are generally directed forward and are located in a socket surrounded by a ring of bone.

The order Primates is usually divided into two suborders: the Prosimii and the Simii. The Prosimians do not look particularly monkey-like. They have a rhinarium, the moist outer portion of the upper lip, which runs from the lip to the nose and which may be observed in a dog or a cat. Prosimians also have a frenulum, a membrane which anchors the upper lip to the upper jaw and prevents the upper lip from curling.

The Prosimians are usually divided into three groups: the lemurs, the lorises, and the tarsiers. The lemurs are about the size of a cat and have a snout instead of a face, giving them a somewhat fox-like appearance. Their fur is quite wooly, and they have a long bushy tail. They run on all four feet.

The lorises are usually smaller-bodied than the lemurs. They have large eyes and ears and shorter tails. They move much more slowly and much more deliberately than do the lemurs.

The tarsiers are found mainly in the Malay peninsula and the Philippine Islands. They are called tarsiers because of the exceptional length of the tarsal part of their feet. Tarsiers are about the size of rats. They are rather flat-faced with round heads, enormous eyes, and large ears. They can swivel their heads through a 180 degree turn.

The Prosimians do not resemble man to any great degree.

The suborder Simii is sometimes referred to as the Anthropoidea. It consists of the monkeys, the apes, and man. These have a bowl in back of the eyes and a bony ring around the eye. The tear duct lies within the orbit of the eye. The mammary glands are pectoral, and the cerebrum or fore-brain overhangs the cerebellum or hind-brain. This suborder is divided into three superfamilies: the Ceboidea, or new-world monkeys; the Cercopithecoidea, or old-world monkeys; and Hominoidea, the apes and man. The Ceboidea are divided into two groups: the marmosets, which are an exception to the general primate rule, since they have nails only on their thumbs and claws on other digits; and the true monkeys, which have nails on all digits. The new-world monkeys are found in Central and South America. They differ from the old-world monkeys in that they have a prehensile tail which can be used for grasping branches to aid in locomotion. The familiar monkey of the organ grinder was usually a new-world monkey. New-world monkeys also have a wide space between their nostrils and lack cheek pouches as well as the ischial callosities of the old-world monkeys.

The old-world monkeys, the Cercopithecoidea, have nostrils set close together. Those that have tails never use these as a sort of fifth leg. Many also have cheek pouches. They include the baboons, mandrills, rhesus monkeys, macaques, langurs, and the like.

The Hominoidea lack tails and cheek pouches. One of the families is the gibbon family, which lives in the forests in Southeast Asia. They usually are less than three feet tall and weigh from 11 to 15 pounds. Their bodies are slender with long arms that reach to their toes. They swing from tree to tree.

The anthropoid apes (Pongidae) include the orangutan, gorilla, and chimpanzee. The orangutan lives mainly in trees and walks on his knuckles as well as on his feet. He may reach a height somewhat in excess of four feet and may weigh as much as 165 pounds. The orangutans have the longest arms in proportion to other limbs. The male has a sagittal crest, that is, a ridge of bone running length-wise across the top of the skull as well as a transverse crest at the rear.

The gorillas, which are confined to Central West Africa, live in trees and are omnivorous in their diet. They use the back of the hand to speed their locomotion. They may reach a height of five to six feet with a weight of 400 pounds. Zoo specimens may reach a greater weight because of their easy living and the lack of exercise in a cage. Male gorillas have a sagittal crest.

The chimpanzees are natives of West Africa. They are somewhat shorter and considerably lighter versions of the gorilla. They may reach a height of from five to five-and-a-half feet with a weight of about 110 pounds. They lack a sagittal crest. The lips are long, very mobile, and protrusable. The face is rather nude. They have a well-developed brain; their cranial capacity is about 400 cc. They walk using the back of their fingers. Chimpanzees have large projecting ears; this distinguishes them from the gorillas.

Which of the anthropoid apes is man's closest relative? A variety of comparisons has been made. There are a few characteristics in which man is more like the monkeys than he is like the apes. He and the orangutan, for instance, have 12 ribs as do the old-world monkeys, whereas the African apes have 13. The average number of vertebrae in the tail region is considerably greater in man than in the Asiatic apes.

In many characteristics there are striking resemblances between man and the chimpanzee. The chimpanzee, for instance, presents some of the varieties of skin color found in man. The chimpanzee can also be divided into tasters and non-tasters. Like man, some of them apparently experience a bitter taste from phenylthiocarbamide; to other chimpanzees the compound is tasteless.

King and Wilson report studies that indicate human polypeptid is more than 99 percent identical with its chimpanzee counterparts. They believe that "the genetic distance" between humans and chimpanzees based on comparison of their proteins is very small, "corresponding to the genetic distance between sibling species of fruit flies or mammals."[8]

Yunis, Sawyer, and Dunham report that chromosomal differences between man and the chimpanzee are largely confined to the existence of nine pericentric inversions, addition of telomeric heterochromatin in 18 chimpanzee chromosomes, and differences in the amount of pericentromeric, paracentromeric, intercalated and Y-type heterochromatin. They believe the fine structure and genetic organization of the chromosomes of the two species are so similar that it is difficult to account for their large phenotypic differences.[9]

On the other hand, the adult human foot resembles most closely the foot of the gorilla, and there are other characteristics in which man seems most closely related to the gorilla. Schultz has analyzed 57 characteristics found in man and the anthropoid apes. In 23 of these man resembles most closely the gorilla; in 15, the gibbon; in 12, the chimpanzee; and in 7 the orangutan.[10] Simpson believes that it is clear that man is most closely related to the chimpanzee and the gorilla, which he believes are in turn closely related. He believes that man's relationships to the chimpanzee and gorilla are about equal, although gorillas may have become somewhat more specialized with respect to the common ancestry. Other anthropologists believe that man is most closely related to the chimpanzee.[11]

Miller's studies suggest that man is more closely related to the gorilla than to the chimpanzee. These involved a comparison of human and higher primate chromosomes. She concluded that the general banding patterns of the chromosomes of the gorilla, chimpanzee, and orangutan—but not the gibbon—are similar to those of the human. She believes that the evolutionary distance between the gibbon and the orangutan is relatively great compared to the distance between the orangutan and the other great apes, and also that man is more closely related to the gorilla than to the chimpanzee.[12]

Differences Between Man and the Primates

While there are notable resemblances between man and the primates, and while this is not totally unexpected since God may well have used a similar plan in creating them, there are also a great many differences. Some of these are insignificant; others are substantial. Evolutionists make much of the similarities but tend to downplay the differences. One of the most striking and significant differences is permanent bipedal locomotion—the ability to walk on two feet rather than on all fours—which is a distinctive characteristic of man. From time to time there have been observations on anthropoids in the wild in which these animals, normally quadrupedal, were observed walking or running bipedally while carrying food. However, the distance they traverse in this way is quite limited, and there is general agreement that their normal method of locomotion is quadrupedal.

It was suggested at one time that some of man's problems, such as flat feet, pain in the back, and dropping of the viscera are due to the fact that originally he walked on all fours and that his body mechanically is not equipped for bipedal locomotion. However, the feeling today is that lying prone may create equal, if not more serious, problems. Surgical patients are gotten out of bed as soon as possible to avoid the problems of recumbency and inactivity, and it may also be that some of the problems of weightlessness in space are due to the fact that astronauts tend to be recumbent rather than upright.

The human nose has a prominent bridge and a well-developed, elongated tip which is lacking in the apes. Man has a median furrow in his upper lip; this is lacking in the apes. The lips of man are outrolled so that the mucous membrane is visible as a continuous red line. Thick lips are characteristic of man; the apes have lips that are extremely thin. Man has a chin; apes do not. The dental arch, as we have pointed out, is U-shaped in apes, with the canines projecting sharply at the base of the "U." In man the jaw is smaller, and the dental arch is parabolic. Man lacks the diastema, or gap, found in the upper and lower dental arches in apes. The apes lack the forward convexity of the spine known as the lumbar curve. Only man has it.

Apes' feet are similar to their hands. This is due to the fact that they have an opposable great toe similar to the thumb. The great toe in man is not opposable; only apes have thumbs on their feet as well as on their hands. Here is a characteristic where evolution, if the story is true, made a mistake. The fact that the apes all have thumbs on their feet would suggest that the ancestral condition involved an opposable great toe. Somewhere along the line in the course of man's evolution he lost this trait, which would certainly be an advantage. If man had an opposable great toe he could slip off his shoes and pick up things quite easily with his toes, or even begin to write with his toes if his fingers became tired. Of course, it may also be that God knew we would be wearing shoes and would have no use for an opposable great toe.

Man's foot is arched both transversely and in an anterior-posterior plane. His toes are short, the first toe being frequently the longest and not divergent. Man's body is relatively hairless. What hair is present tends to be more prominent on the ventral surface. Apes have a great deal of body hair, and it is most prominent on the dorsal surface. Man's body is completely devoid of "feelers" or tactile hairs.

Man's brain is two-and-a-half to three times as big as the brain of the largest ape, the gorilla, and his brain is also relatively the largest. The canine teeth in man project only slightly, if at all, beyond the level of the other teeth. All of the apes have projecting canines. The head of man is balanced on top of the spinal column. That of the apes is hinged in front rather than on top.

Man shows a very long period of post-natal growth. He has the greatest weight at birth in relation to body weight in adult life, but he shows the least degree of maturation at birth, being far more helpless and far more dependent on his parents than are any of the apes. He has little instinctive behavior; most of his behavior is learned. There is an advantage to this, since it is impossible to overcome instincts which may themselves prove harmful; witness the attraction that a candle has for moths.

Only man has wavy and curly hair. Some animals show this trait, but the great apes do not. Perhaps this accounts for the desire of some humans, both male and female, to curl or wave their hair, for if they have curly or wavy hair it is clear that they are human and not anthropoids.

Ischial callosities are absent in man. The *os centrale* disappears earliest in man as an independent bone. Rarely do the nasal bones fuse in man, and when they do this fusion occurs very late. In man the facial sutures between the maxillary and pre-maxillary bones disappear earlier than in any of the anthropoids. The great fontanella closes latest in man. Man has an *ossicula mentalia*. He also has a true inguinal ligament and a transverse metatarsal ligament between toes I and II. These are all lacking in anthropoids. There is no baculum in man; the apes have a baculum. Man does not have a simian shelf; the simian shelf is present in the anthropoids. Man has a large, vaulted cranium; the cranium in apes is flattened. The human femur has a *linea aspera*, a ridge for the attachment of muscles. The *linea aspera* is absent in the femur in apes. Man has short neural spines on the cervical vertebrae; the apes have long neural spines on their cervical vertebrae. Man has the highest total number of vertebrae and the highest average number of thoracolumbar and coccygeal vertebrae. He has the longest cervical and lumbar regions in the spine. In man there is less approximation between the thorax and the pelvis than in the anthropoids.

Compared to the anthropoids, man shows the greatest average relative length of the lower limbs and the shortest average relative length in the upper limbs. His arms are short; the ape has arms that are so long that by assuming a slightly stooped position, he can reach the ground with his arms. Cartoonists take advantage of this characteristic and assign long arms to someone who is not in their favor.

The structure of man's kidney is unique.

He has by far the lowest intermembral index and by far the longest thumb in proportion to the length of the hand. Relatively, he also has the longest free portion of the thumb, and his hand is characterized by the straightness of the fingers when the palm is extended.

The position of the pelvis in relation to the longitudinal axis of the trunk is unique. The direction of the *fossa iliaca* is unique. The size of the canine teeth is the same in males and females. Man has the shortest relative length of the phalangeal portions of fingers II to V. He is characterized by a complete permanent adduction of the hallux. He has the shortest height of the face in relation to trunk height and in relation to the size of the brain area of the head. He has the shortest height of the pelvis in relation to trunk height and breadth of the ilium. He has the greatest enlargement of the sacral surface of the ilium.

Man is the only creature who weeps and sheds tears when he is emotionally disturbed. The biological clock, by which the organism alternates periods of activity and inactivity and other forms of behavior, is particularly well developed in primates, but in man this clock no longer shows itself by sharply alternating 12-hour periods of activity and inactivity. In primates their survival seems to depend on the ability to adjust to these alternating 12-hour periods; in man survival depends on his ability to free himself from this 24-hour routine in order to function at more even levels for longer time periods through the entire 24 hours. In monkeys and apes adult males never provide food; in man this is a major responsibility of the male. Monkeys and apes have a rather small territory, and man has a large territory. Monkeys provide no shelter at all, and apes only a temporary nest. Man provides houses, shelters, and fire.

One of the most significant differences is that only man is teachable in the true sense of the word. He can learn from experience and can modify his behavior accordingly. Other animals can be trained, but they cannot be educated. This contributes to another unique and important characteristic of man —his possession of culture, cumulative tradition, the capacity for transmitting experience and the fruits of experience from one generation to another. This is tied in with the fact that he has very few instincts and must learn most of his behavior.

A part of culture and a significant difference between man and the anthropids is man's ability to use language. He can communicate in abstract terms and can convey concepts. While it is true that many animals can communicate, in that they can sound a warning, can call attention to food, and can use sounds to teach their young, today it is believed that only man has the ability to use language.

Animal Speech

Early efforts to teach animals to communicate in the fullest sense of the word were unsuccessful. Still, from time to time it has been suggested that some animals have been able to think, to reason, and to communicate. By 1937 there were more than 70 so-called "thinking" animals—dogs, cats, and horses. In the 1950s a number of such claims were made for dolphins. Of late, however, most of the claims have been made for chimpanzees and gorillas. Original efforts to teach these primates to communicate were unsuccessful. These early efforts failed, it was suggested, because the animals are physiologically incapable of producing the sounds needed for vocal speech. Then came the idea of teaching communication by other means than sound. In the 1960s there was a wave of attempts to teach American sign language and other types of language not requiring vocalization to what were believed to be man's closest relatives. One chimpanzee eventually learned to make and recognize 125 signs. Psychologists from the University of Nevada taught a chimp named Washoe to use 132 signs. A female gorilla named Koko is reported to have learned more than 400 signs.

Today many psychologists and anthropologists believe that these animals did not learn to use language, but rather what had been interpreted as instances of language usage were actually responses to conditioned reflexes. One investigator goes so far as to suggest that all of these are really instances in which *Homo sapiens* was made the servant of the apes. The animals learned that the use of certain signs or symbols was a way of securing reward, and it is this reward that they sought rather than the communication of thought or concepts. Through these signs or symbols "the crafty ape" obliged man to supply what he wanted.

Much has been made of the development by anthropoids of sentences or word combinations. One is said to have designated a watermelon as a "drink fruit," a swan as a "water bird," and a zebra as a "white tiger." It is possible, though, that these are not instances of sentence or word combination at all. The ape may have seen a swan swimming in the water and been moved first to sign the symbol for the water and then the symbol for bird.

One complication has been the subjectivity of researchers in selecting their evidence, a problem not unusual among evolutionists.

For instance, one anthropoid was asked to give the sign for drink, and he made the proper gesture except that he touched his ear instead of his mouth. One researcher explained this deviation by assuming not that the animal was making a mistake but that he was joking. If an animal smiles when asked to frown it may be said to be displaying a "grasp of opposites." Obviously, if mistakes can be explained in this way, a wide variety of what appear to be mistakes at first glance can actually be used to support the individual's thesis and to demonstrate that apes do show insight and can use symbols. It is the old story of selecting your facts.

Perhaps the most significant studies of this question are those which have been carried on with the young chimpanzee named Nim. His full name was Nim Chimpsky, a play on the name of Professor Noam Chomsky of Massachusetts Institute of Technology, a staunch proponent of the idea that language ability is biologically unique to humans. The researcher, Herbert Terrace, expected to be able to prove Chomsky wrong and to show that creatures other than man could indeed conquer syntax and link words together in sentences.

Nim was put through 34 months of intensive sign language drills and was treated as a child would be treated. While the initial results seemed favorable, Terrace reports that Nim never mastered even the rudiments of grammar or sentence construction and that his speech did not grow in complexity. Phrases spoken by children increase both in length and complexity as they grow older; the average length of Nim's utterances remained stuck at around 1.5 signs during the last two of the four years he underwent training. Moreover, during 88 percent of the time he talked only in response to specific questions from his teacher.

As a result of these findings, Terrace began to review the reports and videotapes of other experimenters and reached the conclusion that there were rarely any spontaneous utterances. What seemed at first glance to be original sentences emerged largely as imitations of signs made by the teacher or responses that the anthropoid had learned to associate with reward. Indeed, in Nim's case, in as many as 40 percent of the cases, he merely repeated the signs made by the trainer without adding new ones of his own. Even when he expanded on the signs used by his trainer he tended to use signs that did not add any new information.[13]

Terrace's work has been criticized for a number of reasons, but he has stood his ground and insists that there is little real evidence of anthropoids' ability to use language. Many of these developments with anthropoids are now believed to be instances of the "clever Hans" effect. Around the turn of the century a retired school teacher by the name of Wilhelm von Osten exhibited a German horse which could apparently count by tapping out numbers with his hoof. There is little doubt that von Osten sincerely believed he had taught Hans to solve arithmetic problems and to add and subtract. What his master did not know was that he was involuntarily providing the horse with cues as to when he should stop his hoof taps. Apparently in most cases von Osten gave an unconscious cue by moving his head ever so slightly, and Hans was able to detect head movements as slight as a fifth of a millimeter. In other cases there were changes in facial expression, breathing patterns, or even eye pupil size so that Hans learned when he needed to stop stomping.[14]

This is also true of other studies of animal intelligence. The first serious investigations of animal intelligence were made by George Romanes, a follower of Darwin who published his work in 1882. Today it is believed that though his basic ideas were sound, his work was compromised by his evolutionary zeal to portray the animal mind as a precursor of the human mind. He reported seeing mice in Norway piling mushrooms and berries onto pieces of cow dung and pushing them across the river, using their tails as rudders, apparently imitating their human counterparts on the docks.

Karl von Frisch made much of the so-called dance language of honey bees. The dance meets the definition of language according to James Gould, a Princeton biologist. Still, he believes that the dance and its interpretation are "hard-wired" into the bee nervous system, for bees can perform the dance without ever witnessing it.

Bennet Galef, Jr., of McMaster University of Ontario, is another investigator who is not so ready to agree that animals think, and he debunks many of the myths about how traditions are transmitted through animal communities to offspring. Generally it is believed that tradition spread through complex social learning, such as learning by imitation. He carried on studies of rat dietary preferences. After their preferred diet was poisoned once, Galef's rats shunned the diet, as did their offspring. Yet learning through imitation was not involved, for young rats that had never seen their parents feed showed the same aversion to the diet. Galef determined that the rat's diet imparts a distinct flavor to the lactating mother's milk, and that pups developed their preference through nursing.

Galef is skeptical of other reported instances of learning, such as the behavior of British titmice, who, it is believed, have learned to open the aluminum caps of milk bottles to feed on the cream. He does not believe that this represents learning through imitation but rather trial-and-error learning. He also doubts whether the tradition of food washing among the Macaques at the Japanese Monkey Center can be explained by imitation. Here Galef suspects that the Macaques had human encouragement. He suggests that "the mental map is really in the mind of the experimenter, not the animal."[15]

Sheri Lynn Gish, a research associate at the National Zoological Park, dismisses the notion that dolphins possess a complex symbolical "humanoid" language, claiming that most studies have been descriptive, not quantitative, and have made tremendous assumptions. She believes there are no data to suggest that acoustic communication is the most important form of communication for dolphins. In their natural setting they interact constantly in acoustic, visual, and tactile modes. She said that the acoustic behavior she observed occurred when the dolphins were in turbid water with reduced visibility, or when they were physically separated. Dolphins, she believes, may be able to communicate some simple information, but we do not know how or if they really do.[16]

The gap between man and the anthropids still remains, and the ability to use language is still uniquely human. It is interesting that one suggested cause for the demise of the Neanderthals was their inability to articulate certain sounds necessary for rapidly spoken, complex language.[17]

Pre-human Fossils

Several forms have been found which are regarded as pre-human, evolutionary links between the common ancestor of the apes and man himself. As is the case with human fossils, the number of these has been very small. Several of these were discovered already in the 19th century. One of these was *Oreopithecus bambolii*, which was found in lignite beds believed to date from the Upper Miocene and Lower Pliocene periods. A complete skeleton was found embedded in a roof slab in a coal mine near Mount Bamboli in Italy. It has generally been regarded as an anthropoid ape. It is the only complete skeleton that has been found.

In the south of France in 1856 a jawbone of *Dryopithecus* was discovered in Miocene beds. Eduard Lartet and Albert Gaudry first publicized it as being closer to man than any monkey, but when a more complete, better preserved jawbone turned up in 1890, Gaudry admitted that this fossil monkey resembled man less than the living anthropoids. In 1935 G. E. Lewis located fragments of jaw and teeth in the Upper Miocene strata of the Siwalik hills in India. This find was hailed by Lewis as resembling man more than any other known monkey. *Dryopithecus* had well-developed, projecting canines that were more ape-like than hominoid.

A large ape, *Proconsul*, was discovered by L. S. B. Leakey in Africa. The lower jaw of this form lacks a simian shelf. However, today *Proconsul* is considered closer to the dog-faced monkey (Cynomorpha) than to man. There is some doubt as to whether this form had stereoscopic vision, since the eye sockets faced slightly to each side.

Today pre-human forms have been reduced to three genera: *Dryopithecus, Gigantopithecus*, and *Ramapithecus*. Some 500 fossil fragments of pre-human forms are known. Most of these consist of tooth or jaw fragments.

Philbeam suggests there were three species of ancestors of man, *Sivapithecus, Ramapithecus*, and *Gigantopithecus*, who lived in Pakistan during the Middle Miocene period from 17 to 7 million years ago. He refers to these as the sivapithecids. Sivapithecids are believed to have appeared when some heavily forested areas gave way to mixed environments consisting of dense forests, savannah woodlands, and more open areas. Dryopithecids lived both before and during the Miocene period in heavily forested areas of Africa and Europe. It is believed that they never left these areas for more open environments. The sivapithecids, on the other hand, seem to have lived on the boundary between forest and open areas and to have exploited both.

None of the three species of Miocene hominoids found in Pakistan resemble apes or humans living today.[18]

Homo Erectus

The first important pre-human fossils thought to be directly ancestral to man were discovered on the island of Java. Originally these were known as *Pithecanthropus erectus* fossils; now these forms are classified as *Homo erectus*. They are supposed to date from the Pleistocene epoch about 500,000 years ago. The first of these was discovered by Dr. Eugene Dubois, a Dutch army surgeon who went to Java in 1890 with no indication that he might find human fossils there but who was determined to do so nonetheless. Within a few years after beginning his exploration he had found a skull cap, a lower jaw, two separate molar teeth, a pre-molar, and a femur. The femur was found 50 feet away from the head parts, and a number of investigators have expressed doubt as to whether it belonged with the head parts. The brain cavity is estimated at 914 cc.—intermediate between the anthropoid ape and man. The jaw and the teeth are partly ape-like.[19]

In 1894 Dr. Dubois returned to Holland with 215 packing cases of fossils, and in 1895 he appeared before the Third International Congress of Zoologists at Leyden showing his fossils and describing their discovery.

Along with the *Pithecanthropus* finds, Dubois discovered what came to be known as the Wadjak skulls. These he did not report until 1920, and in 1924 he produced a lower jaw he had found in Java as well as some thigh bones.

The Wadjak skulls were kept under the floorboards of Dubois' room and were not made available to the public. Later Dubois kept the *Pithecanthropus* fragments to himself and made them available to only a select few, and then only through the glass of a bell jar. Toward the end of his life, Dubois became convinced that *Pithecanthropus* finds were not human at all but rather the remains of a giant gibbon-like ape.[20]

The Wadjak skulls have an exceptionally large cranial capacity, one being as massive as those of a Heidelberg man. Carleton Coon considers them to be *Homo sapiens* but notes resemblances between them and *Homo erectus*.[21]

G. H. R. von Koenigswald went to Java himself in search of more fossils. He found a jaw bone, a skull cap, and a right parietal bone, with parts of the left parietal and occipital bones. These findings have been complicated by his discovery in 1936 in Java of the skull of a young child, which has been called the Modjokerto Child. The form is believed to be older than *Pithecanthropus* because of the rock layer in which it was found. The face is missing, but the form has a number of modern characteristics, such as a rounded occipital bone, a parietal area that is larger than the frontal area, and a deep mastoid fossa.

Another find of von Koenigswald was *Meganthropus*, characterized by the giant size of the teeth. There are two of these. The jawbone fragments were larger than any modern or fossil human jaws as well as larger than those of most anthropoid apes. The teeth were distinctly human.[22]

A number of giant teeth have been found in drug stores in China. In 1935 G. H. R. von Koenigswald reported that he had purchased a huge lower third molar in a drug store in Hong Kong. This exceeded in size the largest gorilla third molar, and he believed it represented a new species called *Gigantopithecus*. Later he obtained a worn upper second molar and still later another third molar. These had gotten into the apothecary trade of China where they were used, ground up, for medicinal purposes. Fossils in general are known in the Far East as "dragon bones" and are common ingredients in a number of medicines.

In the case of these large teeth, the question arises as to whether they indicate a race of giants or whether they represent large teeth in a normal-sized individual.

Peking Man

A number of other fossils have been found in China. The first of these was discovered near Peking around 1922. One of the leaders of the expedition making this discovery was Pere Teilhard de Chardin. It consisted of a number of teeth. Later a lower jaw and finally a number of skulls were found. The site of these discoveries was a partially collapsed cave used as a dwelling. These fossils are frequently known as the Peking Man or *Sinanthropus*. The collection consists of some 38 fragments— mostly teeth, jaw fragments, and odd bits of skull. The cranial capacity varies from 850 to 1300 cc., with an average of 1075 cc. The skulls appear to have been bashed in. Some think that the presence of skulls only indicates that these were the trophies of headhunters. This would account also for the fact that there are very few human remains but many animal remains.

When the Japanese forces swept into China in 1941, the Peking Man fossils were crated and sent to a U.S. Marine base near Chingwangtao for shipment to safekeeping in the United States. Before the Marines were able to leave, the Japanese arrived, and in the confusion the bones were lost or stolen. It has been suggested that they were placed on a ship which was sunk before it arrived in the United States.

All this occurred at the time of the outbreak of hostilities between the United States and Japan. The fossils were under the care of Peking Union Medical College and the Cenozoic Research Laboratory. At the beginning of November 1941, the fossils were packed in footlockers similar to those used by the military, and the footlockers were sent to the U.S. embassy, from whence they were to be transferred to the U.S. Marine Corps stationed in the Peking area. The Marines were to be responsible for their safe conduct to the United States. Eventually they were to be shipped on the *S.S. President Harrison*, but the *S.S. President Harrison* never reached China; it ran aground outside the mouth of the Yangtze River. It has been reported that the two footlockers were stored in a warehouse waiting shipment by the *S.S. President Harrison*, and that the warehouse was ransacked and plundered twice by Japanese soldiers. Another report is that they were being taken by train to Tientsin by the last group of Marines to be evacuated before the Japanese took over, and that the train was halted and baggage seized by Japanese troops.[23]

Subsequent attempts to recover the bones have been unsucessful. The story is one of a great deal of intrigue, machinations, and probably outright fraud on the part of people seeking to enrich themselves at the expense of scientists who were very anxious to recover the fossils. Shapiro has a detailed account of this sorry development in his book *Peking Man.*

The forehead in *Sinanthropus* is receding, but there is a distinct bump on the frontal bone; this is missing in *Pithecanthropus.* There is a prominent ridge running down the middle of the skull, a characteristic found today among Eskimos and Australians. The nasal index is unusually broad and compares with that of modern Negroes.

All of these forms—*Pithecanthropus, Sinanthropus, Meganthropus, Giganthopithecus*—today are generally classified as *Homo erectus.* It is interesting to note that they have lost their exotic names. Originally all of them were given different genus as well as species names, no doubt due to the understandable tendency to exaggerate differences and to minimize similarities. However, very careful work has indicated to most anthropologists and paleontologists that these are all representatives of a single species.

Homo Transvaalensis

A number of forms have been found in Africa. Indeed, there are many people who believe that Africa is the cradle of the human race. The various remains seem to represent two populations. A number of these discoveries were made by Professor Raymond A. Dart of the University of Witwatersrand in Johannesburg, Dr. Robert Broom of the Transvaal Museum of Pretoria, and their co-workers. Subsequently, a number of discoveries were made by the Leakeys.

Dart's first discovery was of an infant skull in 1924, the Taungs skull. It was classified as *Australopithecus africanus.* The brain capacity of this form, believed to have been about six years old, was 494 cc., which was believed to represent an adult brain capacity of about 550 cc. Other skulls, which at first were referred to the genus *Plesianthropus*, were believed to have had a cranial capacity of between 435 and 480 cc. Another series of skulls was classified as *Paranthropus*; these had brain capacities of between 435 and 700 cc. Coon believes these forms to have been humans in form but ape-like in size.

One paleontologist has suggested that these australopithecines might represent a race of *Homo* suffering from microcephaly.

The two races, which today are regarded as *Homo transvaalensis*, have been classified as *Australopithecus africanus* and *Australopithecus robustus*. Both were upright and bipedal. *Australopithecus robustus* shows a sagittal crest which is absent in *Australopithecus africanus*. When both forms are found together tools are usually found, and tools are usually thought to be associated with *Australopithecus africanus*, because where *Australopithecus robustus* is found alone no tools were found.

Other anthropologists do not believe that the australopithecines are human. One of these is Oxnard. His studies, he says, "imply that various australopithecines are really not at all that much like humans . . . they may well have been bipeds, tool makers and hunters; but if so it was not in the human manner."[24]

A number of recent finds have been made by the Leakeys— both parents and sons. The first of these finds was made in the Olduvai Gorge in Tanzania. In 1959 a form known as *Zinjanthropus* was found together with the fragments of a child's skeleton. Leakey senior estimated that *Zinjanthropus* lived about 600,000 years ago, but subsequently other scientists using potassium-argon dating techniques reported the age to be about 1.75 million years. The *Zinjanthropus* finds included a very complete cranium with all 16 upper teeth and the wisdom or third molar still in the process of erupting. The cranial capacity was about 530 cc. In spite of the large teeth, Leakey thought the form was hominid. The child found in the same bed was thought to be more like man than *Zinjanthropus* himself.

Homo habilis was discovered later in the same bed and at the same time level as *Zinjanthropus*. His dental features are much more like those of modern man; the molars are much narrower than those in *Australopithecus*. The remains are rather sparse. Primitive stone tools have been found associated with *Homo habilis*, and the measurements are proportionate to those of modern man.

Homo habilis is believed to suggest that man diverged from other anthropoids much earlier than was once thought. It is quite interesting that recent studies have focused on the antiquity of man. Man has been man for at least 3.5 million years, if the dating of Mary Leakey's 1975 find is accepted. In any case, it is agreed that *Homo* appeared two million years ago. *Homo* and *Australopithecus* coexisted until perhaps one million years ago, after which *Homo* survives alone. Without accepting these datings of man's antiquity, it is evident that man has been separate from the anthropoids for a long time—perhaps since the beginning.

The most recent work in studying man's supposed evolution has been carried on in Africa. Some of the most successful workers in this area have been Louis and Mary Leakey, who worked in the Olduvai Gorge in East Africa; their son, Richard; Maurice Taieb, of France's National Center for Scientific Research; and Donald Karl Johanason of Case Western Reserve University and the Cleveland Museum of Natural History. It was the Leakey's other son, Jonathan, who discovered *Homo habilis* in 1961. *Homo habilis* is believed to have lived at the same time as his less-advanced relatives, who have been classified as *Homo erectus* and *Homo transvaalensis*. It is hardly likely that a form that lived contemporaneously was descended from the less advanced form.

One of the important recent discoveries was made at Hadar in the Afar region of Ethiopia in 1974. Here a 20-year-old female was found by Morris Taieb and Donald Karl Johanason.The find, known as Lucy, was a small creature not more than 40 inches tall with the brain capacity one-third that of modern man. The skeleton was about 40 percent complete, making it the most complete early hominid. Lucy's skeleton showed that she was surprisingly short-legged. However, the shape of her pelvis shows that she was bipedal and walked erect. Lucy is believed to have lived between 3.6 and 3.1 million years ago.

A set of footprints found by Mary Leakey at Laetoli in Tanzania must also be considered in this connection. They represent footprints left by two creatures supposedly more than 3.6 million years ago in a layer of volcanic ash. They cover about 73 feet in two parallel paths and like Lucy indicate bipedal, upright locomotion. One is thought to have been four feet tall; the other 4'8" tall. Both these forms are now classified as *Australopithecus afarensis*. Apparently they had forelimbs of comparable length to those of modern humans, but their hind limbs were relatively short. Thus they would have had a very short stride.

One of the questions that must be considered concerns the degree of arboreal behavior. Apparently the opposable great toe had disappeared in Lucy. One worker, Latimer, argues against extensive arboreal behavior. Another points out that the post-cranial morphology of *Australopithecus afarensis* at Hadar was very similar to that of *Australopithecus africanus*, a presumed descendant. Tuttle believes that *Australopithecus afarensis* had essentially a modern bipedal gait and yet retained significant anatomical adaptations to arboreality.

Still another worker reports that the Laetoli prints are much more human-like than can be inferred from the Hadar foot bones.[25] One group of workers believes that Lucy and the individuals leaving the Laetoli prints showed an essentially modern gait. Another group of workers insists that there was a simian behavior in early hominoids and like to describe Lucy as a "missing link."

Another question is whether Lucy had short legs relative to her arms, or whether her arms were long in relationship to her legs. Jungers believed that while Lucy walked upright on two legs, the process was less efficient energetically than in *Homo sapiens*. Her arms are within human range, yet they are relatively long for the rest of her body.

In any case, there is general agreement that the ancestor of man walked on two legs rather than on all four 3.5 million years ago.

Another find was that of Richard Leakey and his colleagues in the area of Lake Turkana in Northeastern Kenya. A form, known as "1470" after its National Museum of Kenya's catalog number, was discovered in 1972. The form, classified as *Homo habilis*, was believed to be more than two million years old. This find and a similar find labeled "1590" show that *Homo habilis* existed alongside *Australopithecus*, so that *Australopithecus* could hardly be man's direct ancestor. In 1975 the same site yielded a *Homo erectus* skull resembling that of the Peking Man with a brain size of 900 cc. This fossil was believed to be about 1.5 million years old. All of this creates problems of ancestry and descent, since it is hardly likely that the form that lived contemporaneously was descended from the less advanced form.[26] Richard Leakey believes that late-surviving small *Australopithecus* individuals were contemporaneous with *Homo habilis*, then with *Homo erectus*. Leakey does not believe the Hadar forms were ancestral to man; Johanason believes they were ancestral to both man and *Australopithecus*. Leakey suggests they were merely a primitive form of *Australopithecus*.

These recent discoveries make it quite clear that man separated from his presumed anthropid ancestors quite early, and that man has been man for a long time. The common ancestor moves farther and farther back in time as more materials become available. Man has been a separate species for a long time. It is perhaps not as farfetched as it seems to postulate that he has been man since Creation.

At one time it was thought that man's evolution was a straight line type of evolution. This is no longer the case. Today anthropologists believe that the story of man's development can best be represented by thinking of multiple strands forming a network of evolving populations diverging and converging, with some strands disappearing and others giving rise to further evolutionary development. It is believed that man's family tree goes back to a primate called *Dryopithecus*, a true ape that appeared some 20 million years age. By 14 million years ago this line had split into three branches. One of these developed into the ancestors of today's great apes. Another produces *Gigantopithecus*, a large ground ape that roamed in Asia and eventually became extinct. A third gave rise to *Ramapithecus*, which became one of the distant ancestors of man.

Sometime between eight and five million years ago it is believed that this ancestral line split into two species, *Australopithecus robustus* and *Australopithecus africanus*. There was also a third species which some believe branched off at the same time and others believe evolved later from *A. africanus*. It was this third species which first deserved the title *Homo*. *Australopithecus* is believed to have been herbivorous, with *Homo habilis* a scavenging part-time carnivore and *Homo erectus* an active predator.[27] Even today it is recognized by anthropologists that there are many questions about the story as it has been developed, for these most cherished scientific theories "are conceded to be based on embarrassingly few fossil fragments," and it is recognized that huge gaps exist in the fossil record.

Other Fossil Finds

A well-known European find is the Heidelberg Man, discovered in 1907 in the sand pit six miles southeast of Heidelberg near the village of Mauer. The find consists of a well-preserved lower jaw with all the teeth in place. The jaw is very large, thick, deep, and chinless. Indeed, the chin falls away as it does in the ape. Yet the teeth are ordinary in size. It may be that the jaw-mouth formation is the result of an endocrine disorder.[28]

An important English fossil discovery is the Swanscombe skull, found on the south side of the Thames River between Dartford and Gravesend. In 1935 Dr. A. T. Marston found a fossilized human occipital 24 feet from the surface. Nine months later he found a left parietal at the same depth but eight yards further back. It is believed that the two bones belonged to the same individual. The bones differ from modern remains of *Homo sapiens* only in the breadth of the occipital and in the great thickness of both bones. The Swanscombe skull is therefore believed to be older than any other European skull except the Heidelberg Man. It appears to be the skull of a female who died in her early twenties. She had the cranial capacity of 1325 cc.[29]

The most striking thing is that these bones, in spite of their apparent age, appear quite similar to those of modern man. Hooton believes there is no denying the conclusion that Swanscombe is either a mid-Pleistocene *Homo sapiens* or something so close that the differences are zoologically inconsiderable.[30]

Galley Hill Man

Another British fossil is that of the Galley Hill Man, which was uncovered by workmen at Galley Hill some miles below London.[31] It was found eight feet down in the gravel and about two feet above the chalk. It seems to represent a male of about 50 years who was 5'3" tall. The Galley Hill Man is thought to have had a brain capacity of about 1350 cc. Some believe this represents a burial, since the various bones were found close together. It is believed that the Galley Hill Man was a contemporary of the Swanscombe Man. The bones of the Galley Hill Man were excavated before they could be examined by competent geologists, and there are some who question whether it dates from the period assigned to it. However, the discovery of the Swanscombe skull tends to authenticate the Galley Hill find.

Rhodesian Man

Another well-known fossil is the Rhodesian Man, found in a cave at Broken Hill in Rhodesia. This discovery was made about 60 feet below ground level. It includes the skull, a left tibia, parts of the left femur, a sacrum, portions of the two pelvises and a part of the upper jaw. The pelvis, the sacrum, and the leg bones belong to a man about 5'10" tall. The other bones may be the bones of a woman. Except for the skull, the bones are in no way remarkable, and it is possible that the skull does not belong with the bones at all because it is extraordinarily ape-like. The brow ridges are enormous, and it has a low forehead. It resembles very much the present-day gorilla. The teeth are large but of human proportions. The canines are reduced to the level of the other teeth, a human characteristic. The third molars are reduced and degenerate. Keith calls attention to the fact that acromegaly, an endocrine disturbance of the pituitary gland, sometimes causes changes similar to those found in the Rhodesian Skull.[32]

Neanderthal Man

The first group of fossil men of which there are a fair number of skeletons is the Neanderthal Man. The first of the Neanderthal Men

was found in a cave in a valley called the Neanderthal in Germany
near Duesseldorf. The find was made in 1856. Not much was made
of the discovery at this time. Later, in 1864 at a meeting of the Royal
Zoological Society of London, D. Burk showed a human skull that had
been excavated in 1846 in Gibraltar. Then in 1866 the "Man of Spy"
was discovered. It was not until 1908 that the first complete skeleton
of a man similar to these finds was discovered in La Chapelle-Aux-
Saints in France.

The Neanderthal Man is believed to have reached his peak development in Europe from about 200,000 years ago to 115,000 years
ago, and he is supposed to have disappeared completely about 72,000
years ago. Remains of Neanderthal Men have been found in Jersey,
France, Belgium, Germany, Czechoslovakia, Yugoslavia, Spain, Italy,
Russia, Gibraltar, Israel, and Uzbek in the U.S.S.R.[33]

Neanderthal Men were once portrayed as semi-erect, stooped,
ape-like individuals, but it is now known that many of them walked
erect. It is recognized that the stooped and semi-erect position found
in some of them is due to their having suffered from some bone disease.[34]

Wells says that the twin complex of osteoarthritis and osteo-
phytosis was common among the Neanderthal Men. The jaw was especially prone to attack, and since the joint was often affected at an
early age in Neanderthals we can assume that they fed on rough,
perhaps uncooked food and used their jaws vigorously in gnawing
bones, cracking nuts, and champing roots. The La Chappelle skeleton
also had extensive vertebral changes which were the basis for many
of these stooped, semi-erect reconstructions.[35]

It should be pointed out that the Neanderthals survived under
environmental conditions which would quickly wipe out most civilized
men. Kraus says that our Neanderthaloid ancestors would have had
a chuckle over our helplessness under such severe environmental
conditions.[36]

The Neanderthal Man seems to have had a well-developed culture as well as an interest in religion. It is among the Neanderthals
that we find the first real evidence of human burial. Some of the
Neanderthals are found in intentional burials, their skeletons either
flexed or extended, sometimes with the bones of animals arranged
nearby in a way suggesting the modern customs of some primitive
people in providing the dead with food for their journey into the other
world.[37]

Two definite types of Neanderthal Men have been described. The first of these is the so-called conservative type, with a flattened-down brain case, a bun-shaped protuberant occiput, a marked projection of the jaws, and practically no chin. The bones of the post-cranial skeleton in the conservative type show many ape-like features.

The second type is the so-called progressive type. Representatives of this type have a laterally compressed and higher cranial vault. They also show a lower attachment of the neck muscles and a sub-medium to fair development of a bony chin. Other skeletal features are approximately those of primitive but anatomically modern forms of man.

The height of the conservative type is estimated as about 5'1" to about 5'5". The cranial capacity is at least that of Europeans today.

The progressive Neanderthals have skeletons very similar to those of modern man with thin bones in the skull, a moderately high forehead, and a cranial capacity of almost 1500 cc.

Complete skeletons of the Neanderthal Men were found in two adjoining caves in Mount Carmel in 1931—32. The remains of 10 progressive Neanderthals were found in the first of these caves, and the second contained remains of conservative Neanderthals. In the progressive Neanderthals the men were tall and the women short or medium in height. In these the brain was better developed than that of most progressive Neanderthals, and for that reason the Mount Carmel skeletons are sometimes regarded as representing the next step in human evolution after the Neanderthal Man.

There are two opinions as to the significance of this progressive Neanderthal type. Some believe it represents the next step in evolution beyond the conservative Neanderthal type, while others believe that it represents the hybrid between the Neanderthal man and some variety of *Homo sapiens*. Hooton believes that the Neanderthal stock may have been the ancestors of one type of human, such as the Australian aborigines, but he does not believe that the Neanderthal Man is the only ancestor of modern man.[38]

Recently it has been suggested that the Neanderthals who are supposed to have died about 45,000 years ago became extinct because they could not articulate certain sounds necessary for rapidly-spoken, complex language. Several workers constructed a model of the vocal tracts of the Neanderthals by comparing their skulls with those of present-day human adults, human newborns, apes, and chimpanzees. Then they used a computer program to determine which sound could be produced by such vocal tracts. Their analysis suggested that the

Neanderthals could not have had a language that was spoken as rapidly and understood as easily as modern languages. Other early humans could have had such language, they suggest.[39]

Herman Schaafhausen, the first scientist who published on the Neanderthal finds, concluded that they belonged to some unknown "barbarous and savage race." Rudolf Virchow, a leading anatomist of the day, pronounced the bones to be the remains of a recently deceased "pathological idiot." T. H. Huxley said the bones were ape-like but recent, and therefore they represented a reversion to an ancestral form. Others said the specimens were from a Cossack who died in 1814 chasing Napolean back to France. In 1913 Marcellin Boule produced a monograph on the Neanderthal finds which shaped the thinking regarding the Neanderthals as bull-necked, slouching brutes. Today it is recognized that the Neanderthals were not the dim-witted brutes they have been pictured to be. It is also clear that the grisly scenes of cannibalism once suggested are scientifically doubtful. It is clear that the Neanderthals took care of the old and the lame. Discoveries in Iraq showed evidence of burial with flowers as well as long-term care of the disabled. It is rather clear that the Neanderthals were portrayed as brutish in an effort "to place the beast farther from us."[40]

In any case, it should be emphasized that the Neanderthal Man is distinctively human. There is no question that he is *Homo sapiens*. McCown, for instance, says that while the Neanderthal pattern is distinctive, it seems to him to be impossible for anyone to hold any longer to the view of a morphological hiatus between modern man and the Neanderthal population.[41]

The Cro-Magnon Man

Another well-known early human form is the Cro-Magnon Man. The first of these was discovered in the small rock shelter of Cro-Magnon in the village of Les Eyzies in France. The rock shelter was excavated by Lartet. He found human remains in the highest strata of the deposit back underneath the overhanging wall of the cliff. The remains consisted of a skull and some other bones of an old man. A short distance away he found parts of the skeleton of four other individuals. It is believed that this type of man lived in various places in Western Europe during the Old Stone Age.

The "Old Man of Cro-Magnon" is believed to have been about 5'6" tall. His forearms were rather long compared with his upper arms, and his shins were long relative to his size. These are negroid proportions today, and while they do not occur in modern Europeans they are also found in the taller groups of American Indians and in other modern races.

The Cro-Magnon people had massive skulls. The brain case of the old man of Cro-Magnon had a capacity of 1600 cc. The forehead was broad and of moderate height. Most of the Cro-Magnons had larger brains that the average modern man, and this was true of at least some of the Neanderthals.

In any case, it is clear that the Cro-Magnons were definitely *Homo sapiens*.

Evaluating the Fossil Record

It is clear that there are many problems in connection with the human and pre-human fossil record. If any group of fossils has been studied intensely, it is that group which represents man's ancestors. The net effect of these studies has been to reduce the number of forms which are different from modern man. The exotic genus and species names have disappeared, and today it is generally believed that all of the pre-human forms ancestral to man can be classified in the genus *Homo*. It may well be that a similar application of careful study to other fossil forms will reduce the problem which the fossils in general presently make for the creationist.[42]

It is striking that we find relatively few human and pre-human fossils. Most are represented by one or two series of bone remnants and only in the Neanderthal Man do we have fairly complete skeletons. Boyd says that any idea that human pre-history can be reconstructed from an examination of fossil remains is a will-o'-the-wisp. He points out that there are simply not enough bones.[43] Jepson is reported to have said at a 1965 symposium, "What we need are more competent fossils. We have plenty of competent anthropologists, but not enough specimens."[44] Holden speaks of "a pitifully small array of bones from which to construct man's evolutionary history." One anthropologist, she says, has compared the task to that of "reconstructing the plot of *War and Peace* with 13 randomly selected pages."[45]

Another striking thing is the fragmentary character of most of these fossils. There are few complete skulls and even fewer complete skeletons. Often the find is represented by a piece of the skull or by a jaw bone. Certainly any reconstruction based upon such fragmentary remains is extremely precarious. Hooton points out that when we recall the fragmentary condition of most fossil skulls, and when we remember that the faces are usually missing, we can readily see that even the reconstruction of the facial *skeleton* (his emphasis) leaves room for a great deal of doubt as to details. To attempt to reconstruct the soft parts, he points out, is an even more hazardous undertaking. The lips, the eyes, the ears, and the nasal tip leave no clues on the underlying bone parts. Hooton says that you can model on a Neanderthal skull either the features of a chimpanzee or those of a philosopher. He concludes by saying that the alleged restorations of ancient types of man have very little scientific value and are likely only to mislead the public.[46]

Another problem involves the dating of these human remains. There is no doubt that it is difficult to come up with reasonably accurate dates of rock strata. In man the problem is multiplied by the custom man has had of burying his dead. It is quite possible that a human fossil found in a given stratum did not die at the period in which the stratum was laid down. He may have been buried in that stratum much later. Moreover, many of the remains are excavated before a competent geologist has a chance to study them *in situ.*

Still another problem is that of scattered remains. It is rarely possible to be certain that a given skull belongs with a given skeleton. Hooton comments on the habit of many investigators who insist that bones found by them in widely scattered areas belong to the same individual, while they doubt that scattered fragments discovered by someone else can possibily belong to one person.[47]

Another factor to be considered is the precariousness of a classification based on skeleton remains alone. We have pointed out that the skeleton is very easily affected by environmental changes, either external or internal. It is quite possible that some of these fossil men represent human beings whose skeletal structure has in some way or other been altered from the normal. We know that endocrine disorders can alter substantially the skeleton—witness the case of M. Tillet, who wrestled professionally as "The Angel." It has been suggested, too, that acromegaly sometimes causes changes similar to those found in the Rhodesian Man. The Neanderthal Man with his arthritis is another example of this.

Frauds in the Story of Human Evolution

In general, science has been characterized by the high ethical and moral standards of its practitioners. Frauds in science, the faking of observations or results, have been so exceptional that they have attracted attention. Unfortunately, in recent years the number seems to have increased.

In the study of human evolution there seems to have been an unusual lack of objectivity and honesty, ranging from innocent error to some cases of outright fraud. In 1922 Henry Fairfield Osborn of the American Museum of Natural History hailed the unearthing of a tooth in Nebraska as a great discovery of the first American. He postulated a whole man and named him *Hesperopithecus haroldcookii*, considering him to be on the level with other ape men. Later the tooth was more accurately identified as the molar of a peccary (a pig-like animal).

There is also Dubois' peculiar behavior over against the *Pithecantropus* finds. Although he publicized these in 1894, he concealed the fact that at the same time he had also found what later became known as the Wadjak skulls. The latter were kept under the floorboards of his room and were not available to the public until 1920.

Perhaps the best known "form" which seems to have been a complete fraud is the Piltdown Man, known also a *Eoanthropus dawsoni* or the Dawn Man, discovered by Charles Dawson and Sir Arthur Smith-Woodward in 1912. It was found in a gravel pit along the side of the road in a lane leading up to Barkham Manor, an English farmhouse. The age of this fossil was variously estimated at from 200,000 to one million years. It was suggested very early that the remains which were found near the surface may have been moved. The fragments included the large part of the left side of the frontal bone, almost the whole of the left parietal bone, two-thirds of the right parietal, most of the lower part of the occipital bone, almost the entire left temporal bone, the nasal bones, the right half of the mandible, and a lower canine tooth. The bones were very thick, and it has been suggested that this may have been a pathological thickening.

In addition, there was a lower jaw with a second and third molar intact. This was almost indistinguishable from the jaw of a chimpanzee. The chin region did not jut out but fell away as in the apes.

Eoanthropus was the center of controversy from its beginning. Its sex was in dispute. Some suggested that it was male; others insisted that it was female. Another controversy raged over the brain capacity. Smith-Woodward assumed the brain capacity of 1070 cc. Keith in his reconstruction believed that the Dawn Man had a brain capacity of 1500 cc.

The chief problem of the Piltdown Man was that he had a large and noble-browed skull and an almost ape-like jaw. There were those already at the beginning of the controversy who insisted that the jaw was that of a chimpanzee or an orangutan. Others, however, insisted that the two must belong together because there was no evidence of apes in Britain during the Pleistocene epoch, the period from which the cranium was supposed to date.

A few years ago the newly discovered fluorine technique of dating organic remains was applied to *Eoanthropus*. The first studies indicated that the mandible and the skull were contemporaneous if they did not belong together; both appeared to date from the third interglacial period. In evaluating this first fluoride evidence, Dr. Birdsell said that it presented a more embarrassing problem than *Eoanthropus* did in its pre-fluorine chronology.[48]

Since that time further studies have been made by Weiner, Oakley, and Clark. These have led to the conclusion that the lower jaw and canine tooth are those of a modern anthropoid ape deliberately altered so as to resemble a fossil. Weiner was able to demonstrate experimentally that the teeth of a chimpanzee could be altered by a combination of artificial abrasions and proper staining so as to appear similar to the molars and canine teeth of *Eoanthropus*. Careful study of the specimen itself showed that the wear on the teeth was produced by an artificial filing down resulting in surfaces unlike those produced by normal wear. Microscopic examination showed fine scratches such as might be produced by an abrasive. X-ray examination showed that there was no deposit of secondary dentine as would be expected if the teeth were worn down naturally before the individual's death. Refined methods of fluorine analysis indicated that while the cranium was a true fossil, the jaw and teeth were not. It appears that these had been artifically stained to match the cranium.[49]

Further studies indicated that the extent of the hoax was even greater than at first believed. Not only has it become very evident that the teeth were deliberately altered, but Weiner has demonstrated that the chin region of the broken lower jaw resembles that of an orangutan. Clark believes that the fragments of the so-called turbinal bone, one of the bones of the nasal cavity, are actually those of a small limb bone of some animal.

Although the gravel and loam from the site and from the nearby ground water are low in sulfate content, mixtures of apatite and gypsum were found in the Piltdown cranium, and gypsum was found in many of the other Piltdown specimens. Gypsum is a sulfate mineral and is believed to have been produced when the apatite was treated with a weak iron alum in an attempt to produce the full brown color characteristic of a fossil.

The black coating on the teeth is believed to have been paint, identified by Werner and Plesters as probably Van Dyke brown. The organic content of the Piltdown mandible is that of fresh bone; intact collagen fibers characteristic of fresh bone were found in the mandible but not in the brain case.

The associated remains of other organisms also present some problems. The teeth of *Elephas* differ from any British mammalian bones of that period and resemble those of a specimen from Tunisia. The hippopotamus teeth and some of the beaver bones are quite unlike those known from any British or even foreign Tertiary fossil beds. Oakley states that the flint "paleoliths" are all artifically stained. The worked elephant bone could not have been carved while fresh. The hippopotamus molar tooth is low in nitrogen and fluorine and is matched only by cave deposit material which is found, for example, in Malta.

From the total evidence it appears that the Piltdown bones and teeth were assembled from a wide variety of sources, some of them outside Britain itself.[50]

One explanation of the fraud has been that it was a practical joke which got out of hand. It may be that Charles Dawson decided to play a trick on his friend, Sir Arthur Smith-Woodward, and planted these fossils. When Smith-Woodward became excited and publicized the discovery, Dawson found it impossible to disclose the truth for fear of embarrassing his friend.

It is interesting to note that Pere Teilhard de Chardin had some association with the Piltdown fraud. W. R. Thompson does not believe that the fraud involved a practical joke but points out that Smith-Woodward, Dawson, and Teilhard de Chardin were convinced and enthusiastic evolutionists. He implies that they reasoned the end justified the means.[51] Stephen Gould shares the judgment that Teilhard was involved. He suggests that it was a youthful prank on the part of Teilhard.

It might also be noted that Teilhard was involved in the discovery of the Peking Man, the originals of which have disappeared so that we have only casts for study.

Also suggested as a perpetrator of the hoax is Sir Arthur Conan Doyle, the creator of Sherlock Holmes. Doyle believed wholeheartedly in spiritualism, and Dr. John Winslow of the University of California believes that he would have welcomed the opportunity to expose the naivete of scientists who ridiculed his acceptance of spiritualism.

Yet another suggested perpetrator is W. J. Sollas, professor of geology at Oxford. Sollas harbored a bitter dislike for Smith-Woodward, the anthropologist who assisted Dawson in identifying the finds. Smith-Woodward, who frequently annoyed his colleagues by pretending expertise which he did not possess, had the most to lose by being taken in by the hoax. Sollas would have been well positioned to procure the various fossils placed in the gravel pit. One individual remembered sending some mastadons to Sollas from Boliva in 1910; mastodon fragments were discovered at Piltdown by Teilhard de Chardin. Douglas, a British geologist, reports in recently published posthumous memoirs that Sollas had ordered potassium bichromate (found in the 1953 analysis of the skull) prior to the discovery at Piltdown, and that around the same time he had taken the unusual step of borrowing ape teeth from the collection of the Oxford anatomy department.[52]

What is the significance of the Piltdown hoax? Does this mean that all of these supposed pre-human forms are fake? Hardly. The fraud was uncovered by the scientific community itself. What is significant is that the fraud went undetected for such a long time and that for many years the authenticity of the Piltdown Man was vouched for by the most competent scientists of the day. It does suggest that the pronouncements of the experts may sometimes be taken with a grain of salt.

The Mechanism of Evolution

In any discussion of evolution the crux of the problem lies in the mechanism. It may be possible to have a great deal of evidence that change of the magnitude required by the theory of evolution has taken place, but before any theory can be reasonably complete some mechanism whereby such changes can be produced and can be inherited must be suggested. It is obvious that this mechanism must be found in the field of genetics. Any change which is not passed on from generation to generation cannot be of any importance to evolution. It is usually stated that the first reasonably complete theory of evolution was that developed by Lamarck, because Buffon, an earlier evolutionist, did not suggest any mechanism whereby evolution took place. And Lamarckianism is rejected because the changes which he believed took place cannot be passed on from generation to generation. Modern genetics is believed to have disproven the concept of the inheritance of acquired characteristics. DeVries' claim to fame rests upon the fact that he suggested a mechanism whereby evolution could come about. So much importance has been attached to the bearing of inheritance on evolution that the field of genetics has often been regarded as a laboratory experiment in evolution.

In general, it has been suggested that evolution has been possible through a combination of mutations and chromosomal changes. The major emphasis in the synthetic theory, which has been generally accepted until very recently when it was attacked by Gould, has been on mutation as a mechanism which provides for small change. Chromosomal changes are changes of greater magnitude within the chromosomes themselves.

DNA

The most dramatic recent development in genetics and possibly in all biology has been the discovery of the structure and function of deoxyribonucleic acid, DNA, by Watson and Crick and other researchers. This material, found in the chromosomes, directs the synthesis of the various enzymes which in turn make possible the production of specific types of protoplasm and in that way determine whether the individual will be mouse, mustard, or man. Raff describes embryology as "the black box in which genes make organisms."[53] In most organisms DNA carries the genetic code specifying not only the species to which the individual belongs but also the individual traits which characterize him. There are, however, a few organisms in which RNA, ribonucleic acid, carries out this function.

Complex molecules, such as those found in proteins, are made up of one or more chains of smaller units, the sub-units of which are the amino acids. There are just 20 common kinds of amino acids. DNA seems to function by specifying which of the 20 amino acids occupies each site in the structure.

DNA is a double-stranded molecule built much like a ladder twisted around its longitudinal axis, so that its sides form a long double helix. The twist, though of some significance to the physical chemist, seems to be unimportant so far as the genetic code is concerned, so that the biologically important aspects of DNA can be visualized by imagining an ordinary ladder in which the sides are made of a sugar phosphate and the rungs constructed of four nucleotides: adenine, thymine, guanine, and cytosine.

Adenine always hooks up with thymine, and guanine always hooks up with cytosine. Sometimes the sequence is adenine, thymine; sometimes it is thymine, adenine. But the same two must always hook up together. It is as if a 10-inch rung is needed to bridge the distance between the two sides. Instead of being in one piece, each rung is built of two parts; some rungs are built of six and four-inch pieces, while others consist of seven and three-inch pieces. Thus, it does not matter whether you have a six-inch plus four-inch rung, or a seven-inch plus three-inch rung. However, you cannot have a six-inch plus seven-inch rung, or, for that matter, a four-inch plus three-inch rung. Furthermore, it does not matter whether the order is six plus four or four plus six.

The genetic code consists of four "letters," the nucleotides. It appears that these four nucleotides are used by the cells in groups of three along the ladder; these are known as codons. Since any one of the four letters can be in each of the three positions of the codon group, there are 64 varieties of codon, and these are used to spell out the message in the synthesizing of enzymes and proteins. Since there are only 20 amino acids, it is apparent that more than one codon can specify a particular amino acid. It has also been suggested that some of the triplets may initiate the synthesis of a particular substance, and others may terminate it.

Only one strand of the DNA ladder seems to be used in the genetic code, though both strands are replicated when the cell reproduces. This strand, for want of a better term, is known as the "sense strand," and on it the messenger RNA is built. Messenger RNA carries the code to the ribosomes in the cytoplasm, where the enzymes and proteins are built up. Thus, the DNA directs the ribosomes to build up enzymes and proteins from amino acids arranged in a certain sequence, and this determines the growth and development of the organism. It also synthesizes the various substances needed for the proper metabolism of the organism.

RNA is believed to be a long, unbranched, single-stranded molecule. Instead of thymine, it contains uracil. Three kinds of RNA molecules are required for the synthesis of enzymes and proteins: messenger RNA, which transmits the genetic information from the DNA molecule in the nucleus to the ribosomes; ribosomal RNA, which serves in the ribosomes; and transfer RNA, which acts as an adapter to bring amino acids into line in the growing polypeptid chain in the appropriate place.

That DNA should direct the development of the organism is truly remarkable and an indication of the complexity of living things. To suggest that this has developed by chance is incredible, for it is too complex an arrangement. It is believed that the amount of zygote DNA needed to specify all of the world's population would weigh only

1/17th as much as a postage stamp.

It would seem logical that the amount of information developed in the organism could be measured by the amount of DNA in the zygote. Some studies indicate that this is indeed the case. Organisms considered to be simple tend to have smaller amounts of DNA. Among the vertebrates, however, there seems to be a trend toward a reduction of DNA from lower to higher organisms. Mammals have more than birds but not as much as amphibians. The lung-fish has at least 16 times as much DNA as does man. There have been a variety of suggestions by evolutionists as to why this should be the case. Dobzhansky says that we can only conclude that no satisfactory explanation has been reached.[54]

DNA seems to work through enzymes, antigens, organizer substances, and hormones. It acts chiefly by determining which chemical processes take place in embryo and adult, and the rate at which these are to take place. One of the major problems is the problem of inactivation of the DNA. Today it is believed that a particular type of DNA, Z-DNA, is involved in controlling which genes are turned on and which are not.[55]

Apparently every cell has the complex genetic code; yet cells are specialized in what they produce. The DNA code for the production of hemoglobin, for example, is present in every cell of the body, but only the erythroblasts manufacture it. There must be some control which inactivates most of the genes in most cells. On the other hand, there must be some mechanism for reactivating inactive cells when as a result of some injury particular substances are needed or are needed in a larger quantity.

Molecular biologists now believe that the genes of animal viruses and of animals, including man, occur in pieces, spread out along the DNA. In between the gene fragments are long stretches of DNA whose functions are unknown. In man, only slightly more than one percent of the DNA is involved in protein-coding.[56] Bacterial genes, however, are not spread out in pieces. Studies have indicated that the genes of most organisms are in pieces. It appears that a RNA copy is made of the entire length of the DNA containing the fragments of the genes. There is so much of the extra DNA—called intervening sequences— that the RNA copy of the gene and its intervening sequences is often five to 10 times longer than the sum of the length of the gene fragments. Subsequently, it is believed that copies of the extra DNA are snipped out of the long piece of the RNA, and the remaining RNA copies of the gene fragments are sealed together. This shortened piece of RNA, which is now a copy of just the genes, moves from the cell nucleus to the cytoplasm, where the cell reads its genetic message and makes the protein that the genes code for. At the present time, much research is going on in an attempt to explain why the genes are in pieces.[57]

Mutations

One of the interesting problems and one that is very important for the theory of evolution is the origin of the different kinds of genes. Some creationists have suggested that God created some variations in Adam when He formed him out of the dust of the earth. Thus, it is possible that Adam was heterozygous (having one dominant and one recessive gene) for a number of characteristics. At the same time, it is probable that a majority of variations which we see in man, in plants, and in animals are the result of mutation. It was their existence which DeVries assumed. He coined the term "mutation," even though he probably never saw a mutation.

Mutations occur spontaneously at a measurable rate. We have no idea at the present time what the causes of natural mutation are, nor are we able to predict exactly when they occur. However, we do know that they occur spontaneously, and we are able to measure the rate at which they occur.

A good example of a natural mutation is the mutation responsible for the appearance of a breed of sheep known as the Ancon sheep. This breed first appeared in 1791 in the flock of a New England farmer, Seth Wright. He found a male lamb with remarkably short, bowed legs and bred him back to the normal ewes in his flock, some of whom were apparently heterozygous. When the Ancon ram was bred to these, Ancon offspring were produced. Of the 15 lambs produced during this first season, two were of the new type. In succeeding years others were produced, and by breeding these to one another a pure breeding Ancon variety was produced. Sheep of this breed are so short-legged that they are unable to jump over an ordinary stone wall or over a fence. This trait is, of course, an advantage to the farmer. In addition, their short legs limit their ability to run, so that they do not lose weight as readily as other sheep.

It might be pointed out in passing that this mutation, in keeping with our general experience with mutations, was actually a harmful one to the sheep. To the sheep it is a disadvantage not to be able to jump over walls and not to be able to run quickly. Such an animal would probably not survive long in a wild state. Moreover, this particular mutation also affected the reproductive rate. This effect was so pronounced that the breed became extinct in the 19th century. Interestingly enough, the mutation reappeared in the flock of a Norwegian farmer in 1925, and it has been possible to develop another Ancon variety of sheep. This recurrence, too, is characteristic of mutations. Most of them appear several times over a period of years.[58]

What causes mutations? We simply do not know. We do know that they occur naturally, and we also know that in the laboratory we can produce them by a variety of types of mutagenic substances—X-ray, radium and radon, neutrons, ultraviolet rays, high temperatures, and chemical agents. Most of the substances which are mutagenic are also carcinogenic. By far the majority of the mutations produced in the laboratory have been produced by X-rays. Others have been produced by mustard gas and other chemical mutagens.

One explanation for mutation has been advanced by Robert Shapiro at New York University, who found in laboratory experiments that sodium bisulfite—the form which sulphur dioxide takes when absorbed into the body—damages nucleic acids, making them nonfunctional. According to Dr. Shapiro, ultraviolet light has a similar effect on nucleic acids. He reported that when the bisulphite molecule breaks away from the nucleic acid it converts one of the four basic components, cytosine, into another, uracil. This change of one letter of the genetic code may explain what is involved in a mutation.[59]

Our present understanding of the DNA code helps us to understand how mutations occur. Normal hemoglobin has 146 amino acids in a chain. Individuals suffering from sickle-cell anemia have hemoglobin which differs from normal hemoglobin in only one respect. It contains a unit of the amino acid valine in the place of a unit of the amino acid called glutamic acid. The code for glutamic acid is GAA or GAG; the code for valine is GUA or GUG. Thus, a change of one "letter" in the code could result in the substitution of valine for glutamic acid. The code for the two amino acids differs by only one letter. It may well be that the production of sickle-cell hemoglobin arose from a change in which a single nucleotide in the code was changed.

We do not know the cause of mutations which occur spontaneously. Natural radiation has been suggested. We are bombarded constantly by radiation from outer space. Only within the past few years have we learned of the existence of the Van Allen layers, a protective umbrella which God has placed over us to minimize the effect of this bombardment. Some of it, however, does strike the earth. Moreover, there are naturally occurring radioactive substances in the soil. Chemical substances no doubt also contribute to the natural mutation rate.

Still, we do not know the cause of the natural mutation rate. We can determine these rates, but we do not know what factors are bringing them about.

It may well be that being subject to mutagenic substances is one of the penalties of original sin. There is no doubt, as we shall see, that most mutations are harmful and that the number of these accumulating in the human germ plasm increases from age to age. The limited exposure to radiation experienced at the beginning of time may also, according to some, account for the longevity of the patriarchs.

Most Mutations Are Harmful

The question for the evolutionist is whether mutations can bring about the changes in living things that the theory of evolution would require. There is little doubt that mutations occur frequently enough to bring about change. In the fruit fly, *Drosophila*, it is estimated that about one in every 20 germ cells will contain some sort of mutation. The comparable figure in man is between one per individual and one in 10 individuals. Not all agree. Winchester believes that in man the mutation rate is less than 10 percent of the rate in *Drosophila*.[60] In any case, it is apparent that the mutation rate in itself is adequate to bring about a great deal of change.

The chief difficulty in the way of evolution by mutation is the fact that most mutations are either lethal, killing the individual before he is able to reproduce, or semi-lethal, reducing his reproductive rate below the normal rate. Almost all mutations affect the fertility rates; this was the case with the Ancon sheep. Winchester says that over 99 percent of the mutations which have been studied in the various forms of life are harmful in some degree.[61] It is hard to believe that this mechanism can lead to an improvement in living things as the theory of evolution demands. Rather, it would seem that the changes it provides might better be expected to be similar to the changes which the psalmist describes when he says, "they will all wear out like a garment" (Ps. 102:26).

This is to be expected. The living organism is a complex being. And his metabolism is not only complex but also delicately balanced. Any random change is much more likely to upset that delicate balance than it is to improve it. A change in a single amino acid, as we have seen in the case of the sickle-cell gene, can bring out marked and harmful effects.

Favorable Mutations?

Is it possible that evolution works through utilizing helpful mutations? It is generally agreed that there are very few, if any, that are genuinely helpful. Even those which seem to provide some desirable characteristics may in their overall effect, particularly if they reduce the reproductive rate, be harmful. Ford says that it appears highly doubtful that any mutations which have occurred have given rise to changes which could be of survival value in nature.[62] He says that of hundreds of mutations which have been studied in the various *Drosophila* species, scarcely one has been found which does not lower the viability as compared with the wild type.[63] Mutations appear to be concerned, he says, with the production of small superficial differences or with obviously pathological departures from the normal condition, which could not in any event survive in the state of nature.[64]

Cited as examples of favorable mutations and of natural selection in action are the instances of micro-organisms that have developed resistance to antibiotics. It is believed that as a result of consistent overuse of antibiotics in the last 30 years there has been a steady and worldwide increase in the prevalence of antibiotic-resistant pathogens. Novick of the Public Research Institute in New York City believes that antibiotic overuse is a typical case of human shortsightedness because of this result. There are indeed many instances that appear to be examples of change which have resulted in resistance in micro-organisms. However, one question that needs to be determined is whether this is indeed a change in resistance or simply an increase in a resistance already present, similar to the process whereby immunization to disease takes place in man.[65]

Another question that needs to be faced is the likelihood of the survival of a mutation even if it is favorable and has selective value. In general, the smaller the mutation the more likely it is to be favorable; conversely, the larger it is the more likely it is to be harmful. Any mutation that upsets the complex we know as a living thing may in its totality be harmful, even though it may bring about some favorable characteristics.

Nevertheless, geneticists have developed a mathematical formula which has been called a coefficient of selection. It is a measure of the degree to which a given mutation is favorable. There is disagreement as to whether traits with a high coefficient of selection or a low coefficient of selection have been most important to evolution. Wright believes that most mutations which have been important in evolution have had a much smaller selective coefficient than could be demonstrated in the laboratory.[66] Ehrlich and Holm, on the other hand, believe that very large selection coefficients have been the rule rather than the exception in evolution.[67]

Be that as it may, careful mathematical calculations have indicated that the chance of a favorable gene surviving is limited. Fisher calculated that of genes with a one percent coefficient of selection, only 197 out of 10,000 would survive. In other words, the probability is that even if a mutation is slightly favorable it will be eliminated by chance.[68] Boyd refers to calculations which suggest that a gene with the selective advantage of one percent would replace completely its allele in somewhat more than 1,001,741 generations, a fantastically long time.[69] Carter says that the rate is so slow in recessives as long as the mutation is rare that it is doubtful whether it is fast enough to give an effective basis for differentiation even on an evolutionary scale of time. A possible solution he finds in the fact that mutations occur repeatedly, but even this fact, he says, does not remove the whole difficulty. He believes that another possibility is that some recessives may develop into dominants, though almost all mutations tend to be recessive.[70]

As we have pointed out, much has been made of the resistance developed, presumably by mutation, to various antibiotics, etc. This is frequently cited as an example of evolution in progress. It is true that insects have developed a resistance to DDT, and rats have developed a resistance to warfarin. There are instances of what appears to be a resistance to antibiotics and pesticides which have been reported. It is not clear exactly how this resistance develops. Is it a mutation? Or is it the enhancement of resistance already present in the organism such as is brought about by the various immunization techniques in man? Also to be considered is the overall effects of such resistance. Dobzhansky reports that most genotypes resistant to streptomycin are at some disadvantage in the absence of antibiotics, and that natural selection would actually oppose them.[71]

Johnson, Bogart, and Lindquist report that DDT-resistance is a very complex thing. They believe that DDT may stimulate the production of particles necessary for resistance.[72] It has also been suggested that DDT-resistance may be a matter of adaptation. It may be that some stimulus produces hormones or enzymes which protect against DDT.[73]

Is it possible that a number of favorable mutations might occur in one individual, resulting in a sort of "big jump" evolution? Hardly, for it has been calculated mathematically that if the mutation rate were one in 100,000 (the average mutation rate) and if the occurrence of each mutation doubled the chance of another mutation occurring in the same cell, the probability that five simultaneous mutations would occur in one individual would be 1×10^{-22}. This means that if the population averaged 100 million individuals and if the average generation lasted but one day, the appearance of five simultaneously occurring mutations in one individual would be expected once every 274 billion years.[74]

Reverse Mutations

Another fact to be considered in connection with mutations and evolution is the occurrence of reverse mutations. For a time it was thought that evolution moved in only one direction; now it is believed that it may reverse at times. There is no doubt that reverse mutations occur in organisms. Muller goes so far as to say that most mutations in *Drosophila* are reversible in direction and that very often the reverse mutation appears to reconstitute precisely the original gene.[75] Blum reports a study in which the frequency of reverse mutations was as great as the frequency of forward mutations. Even granting that these figures may be high, it is apparent that reverse mutations occur and that their occurrence would slow down rather than speed up the rate of mutation.[76]

Mutation Restrictions

Still another consideration is the restrictions on the direction of mutation. Changes do not occur in all directions but only in a limited number of directions. This is to be expected from what we know about the nature of DNA. The code can only direct the development of certain substances. Other substances, by the very nature of the code, cannot be produced. It is quite possible that the genetic code limits or makes impossible the direction in which evolution can develop, even though that direction might be favorable.

A recent conference on embryological development focused on the limitations on the direction of evolutionary change. Attention was called to the fact that there are no animals with wheels instead of legs, nor animals festooned with a cross between hair and feathers. Antonio Garcia-Bellido, a Spanish geneticist, answered the question of "why" by stating, "because of a failure of the genes to fill" such a gap. Given sufficient time and opportunity, he believes that all physical forms are possible, and he believes that the restrictions are to be found in the genes.[77]

Other biologists have insisted that a major limitation is the limitation imposed by embryonic development. They believe that small differences in the timing of development may generate large shifts in the physical form. Stephen Gould, best known for his theory of punctuated equilibrium, is quoted as saying, "organisms are not pieces of putty, infinitely moldable by infinitesimal degrees in any direction, but are rather complex, resilient structures endowed with numerable constraints and opportunities based upon inheritance and architecture (both molecular and morphological)." Natural selection, he says, "may be the propelling force of change, but the organism participates in the process substantially by restricting the direction that change will take."[78]

Elements of the Synthetic Theory

The modern synthetic theory of evolution depends on changes in the frequency of genes from one generation to another. Advocates of this theory believe that changes in gene frequency are due to four processes: mutation, migration (the movement of organisms from one geographical area to another, which results in an increase or decrease of genes in a particular area), random drift (the idea that by chance the frequency of a given gene increases or decreases), and natural selection. The mechanism for change is, of course, mutation, and random drift and migration are in effect chance processes. Natural selection then works on the result of changes in gene frequency brought about by the other factors.

It is this theory which Gould and Eldredge have attacked. They believe that "the modern synthesis, as an exclusive proposition, has broken down on both of its fundamental claims: extrapolationism (gradual allelic substitution as a model for all evolutionary change), and nearly exclusive reliance on selection leading to adaptation."[79]

Thus, in the synthetic theory mutations are really the ultimate source of variability. Evolutionary change is a process of gradual gene substitution within a population. Genetic variation is raw material only, however. Natural selection directs evolutionary change. Rates and direction of change are controlled by selection, with little constraint exercised by the raw material. All genetic changes are adaptive; selection leads to adaptation aided, of course, by a number of ancillary processes. One of these is genetic drift. But this is believed to occur only in populations so small and so near the brink that their rapid extinction would almost certainly ensue. According to Mayr, "the proponents of the synthetic theory maintain that all evolution is due to the accumulation of small genetic changes by natural selection and that transspecific evolution is nothing but an extrapolation and magnification of the events that take place within populations and species."[80]

Gould says,

> Speciation occurs at too high a level to be observed directly in nature or produced by experiment in most cases. Therefore theories of speciation have been based on analogy, extrapolation and inference. Darwin himself focused on artificial selection and geographic variation. He regarded sub-species as incipient species and viewed their gradual accumulating divergence as the primary mode of origin for new taxa. The modern synthesis continued this tradition of extrapolation from local populations and used the accepted model for adaptive geographic variation as a paradigm for the origin of species.[81]

Gould's judgment is that this synthetic theory as a general proposition "is effectively dead despite its persistence as textbook orthodoxy."[82]

Mutations certainly appear at first glance to supply a very promising mechanism for evolution. But a more careful analysis of this phenomenon shows that there are a great many problems to the suggestion that evolution has taken place with mutations as its mechanism, and this casts serious doubt on the idea that mutations supply the necessary mechanism for changes as great as are demanded by the theory of evolution. There is no doubt that mutations supply a mechanism for change, changes within the "kinds" of Genesis 1. They make possible variations within species, microevolution. But they are hardly an adequate mechanism for the changes that would be required by the theory of evolution. The fact that Gould and his colleagues have developed the theory of punctuated equilibrium is a commentary on the inadequacy of mutations as a mechanism. R. A. Fisher goes so far as to say that the explanatory content of the theory of evolution only reaches its absolute zero with the mutation theory.[83] Harris believes that it is impossible for evolution to have taken place by mutation in the time assigned to it.[84] Goldschmidt is outspoken in his condemnation of the suggestion that mutations are a mechanism for evolution. He believes that at most they can bring about changes in species. The subspecies and varieties formed, he says, are neither incipient species nor models for the origin of species. Rather, he characterizes them as diversified blind alleys.[85] In commenting on Goldschmidt's views, Mayr says that the fact that some geneticists can come to conclusions diametrically opposed to other geneticists is striking evidence of our ignorance of the actual facts. Goldschmidt believes the major factor in evolution is chromosomal change, which he believes results in "hopeful monsters," organisms with entirely new characteristics.[86]

Chromosomal Change

A second genetic mechanism which evolutionists believe has contributed to the changes bringing about evolution is chromosomal change. A number of types of change are possible: changes in the number of chromosomes, and changes in the number and arrangement of genes within the chromosomes. It is believed that the genes are arranged in a linear order on the chromosomes. Generally today the gene is regarded as an area of the chromosome which determines the specific trait. The chromosomal material appears to be present during all stages of mitotic activity but is readily visible as distinct bodies in cells that are actively dividing.

The number of chromosomes is characteristic of the species. However, there appears to be no relationship between the number of chromosomes and the complexity of the species. Man has 23 pairs of chromosomes, for a total of 46. The crayfish, *Cambarus virilis*, has 200, and the Geometrid moth, *Phigalia pedaria*, has 224. In the Diptera (flies) the chromosome numbers are unusually low; in birds, the chromosome numbers tend to be high. Supposedly, closely related species have widely different chromosome numbers. For example, in the Geometrid moths, *Biston hirtaria*, has 14 chromosomes, and *B. zonaria* has 56. Both of these are haploid chromosome numbers. Among the rodents, *Cricetus auratus*, has 19 chromosomes, while *C. griseus* has seven haploid chromosomes.

Changes in the number of chromosomes may involve whole sets or simply an increase or decrease in single chromosomes. For example, each chromosome may be represented only once (monoploidy) instead of twice as usual, or each chromosome may be represented more than twice (polyploidy). Among polyploids, the extra chromosome sets may be derived from a single diploid individual or the polyploid may be derived from a hybrid between two diploids. Similarly, an organism may have lost one chromosome from one set, or it may have gained one or more chromosomes in a set or in several sets.

188 Studies in Creation

Among changes in the number or arrangement of genes within chromosomes there may be deficiencies or deletions, the loss of one or more genes, or duplication, the addition of one or more genes. There may also be changes in the arrangement of the genes which has a marked phenotypic effect referred to as the position effect. There may be a translocation where a piece of one chromosome is transferred to another chromosome, or there may be an inversion in which within a chromosome a block of genes has been rearranged.

Most of these changes are so pronounced that the organism cannot survive. A number of pathological conditions in man are due to chromosomal changes. For instance, trisomy-21, the addition of a third chromosome to the pair that has been numbered 21, results in Down's Syndrome. Other chromosomal changes have marked effects on the organism and are clearly harmful.

Polyploidy

There can be little doubt that polyploidy, and particularly tetraploidy, has been the means of producing what are ordinarily regarded as new species. There are a number of examples in the lab and a number of observations out in the field that suggest the production of new species by this mechanism. Mayr believes that polyploidy is the only proved mechanism of instantaneous speciation in sexually reproducing organisms.[87] Stebbins says that polyploidy is one way and perhaps the only way in which an interspecific barrier can arise in one step.[88]

Darwin believed that the formation of reproductively isolated units by speciation was the fundamental process of evolution. He believed that when he had demonstrated the origin of new species he had proven evolution—thus the importance of a mechanism for instant speciation. Gould believes that the process of speciation is difficult to demonstrate and prove. He says that it "occurs at too high a level to be observed directly in nature and produced by experiment in most cases." He goes on to say, "therefore theories of speciation have been based on analogy, extrapolation and inference." Darwin, he says, focused on artificial selection and geographical variation. Darwin regarded some species as incipient species and viewed their gradual accumulating divergence as the primary mode of origin of new groups. Modern synthetic theory continued this tradition, according to Gould, of extrapolation from local populations, and used "the accepted model for adaptive geographical variation as a paradigm of the origin of species."[89]

Gould points out that according to Darwin natural selection must represent the primary directing force of evolutionary change. Proponents of the synthetic theory believe that natural selection creates fitter phenotypes by differentially preserving generation by generation the best adapted organisms from a pool of random variants that supply raw material only, not the direction itself. Selection operates through the differential reproductive success of individual organisms, the struggle for existence in Darwin's terminology.[90] Gould's own position, punctuated equilibrium, looks for a mechanism for "big jump evolution." Chromosomal changes bring about changes of that magnitude, and polyploidy does indeed result in new species.

Origin of Polyploidy

It appears, though, that most cases of polyploidy result from an abnormal cell division of one sort or another. Instead of germ cells undergoing reduction division so that they have only the haploid number of chromosomes, the germ cells receive the diploid number, usually as a result of both sets of chromosomes going to one cell and the other cell receiving none at all. Such an abnormal germ cell of an egg is then fertilized, or if a sperm it fertilizes an egg. If the other gamete which it fertilizes or by which it is fertilized is a normal haploid gamete, the zygote is triploid. If, however, it meets another diploid gamete, the zygote is tetraploid. Polyploidy may also develop as a result of an irregular mitosis (ordinary cell division). Instead of one set of chromosomes going to each pole, both sets go to one pole.

Various ways have been employed to bring about such abnormal cell division in the laboratory. Sometimes tissues have been irritated to produce abnormal types of cell division. Most cases of chromosomal doubling, however, have taken place as a result of treating a plant with colchicine, a drug derived from the autumn crocus. The drug interferes with the metabolism of the cell in cell division. It is apparent that this procedure is abnormal and pathological.

Effects of Polyploidy

Polyploidy has a number of effects, some of which are certainly quite favorable. In general, polyploidy results in some degree of gigantism. Polyploids are larger than their diploid relatives. Giant fruits and vegetables and giant flowers are often polyploids.

It has also been suggested that polyploids are better able to stand severe climates and that they are especially adapted to unfavorable habitats. Polyploids are also believed to tolerate a greater variety of climatic conditions; they can stand wider ranges of temperature and water supply than can diploids. Polyploidy tends to decrease the osmotic pressure of the plant. This might be an unfavorable characteristic, since a plant with a high osmotic pressure is able to get more water from the soil than a plant with low osmotic pressure. Polyploids also have a lower growth rate and flower later than do diploids. However, they flower over a longer period of time. The amount of branching is reduced, and the leaves are usually thicker. Under some conditions these characteristics might be favorable; under other conditions they would be unfavorable.

In general, polyploids have a lower reproductive rate than do their diploid ancestors. This would certainly be an unfavorable characteristic. It is especially marked in triploids but appears also in tetraploids. This reduction in fertility is believed to be due to the fact that apparently only those gametes are viable which receive one or two complete sets of chromosomes. If one or more chromosomes is missing, or if one or more is duplicated while the others occur singly, the gamete is likely to be inviable. Because of this marked reduction in viability and fertility, it is generally agreed that chromosomal changes can best survive if the individual is capable of perpetuating itself in some way other than by sexual reproduction. Tetraploid plants can survive, for instance, if they reproduce by clones, stolons, rhizomes, bulbs, or winter buds. It should be noted that in some instances polyploids do appear to regain their fertility after several generations. They appear to become stabilized eventually and are able to reproduce at a normal rate.

Polyploids may be derived from a single parent (autopolyploids) or from more than one parent (allopolyploids). Strict autopolyploids, it is believed, are rare in nature.[91]

Another important difficulty in the way of polyploidy as a mechanism for evolution is the fact that it is limited almost exclusively to the flowering plants, and here most cases are found in the perennial herbs. Only a few cases are reported in woody plants. Polyploidy is very rare in multicellular animals. Wallace points out that for an animal polyploid species to survive sucessfully, a complicated combination of rare events—hybridization and doubling of the chromosome number—would have to occur simultaneously in each of two individuals, one male and one female, living in the same neighborhood. Furthermore, these two individuals would have to choose each other as mates in preference to normal individuals of the parental species living in the same region, and their offspring, too, would have to prefer one another and mate as brother and sister for a number of generations. Animal species then could adopt polyploidy, he believes, only as a consequence of the coincidence of four or five or six extremely rare events.[92]

Polyploids and "Kinds"

In any case, polyploids are certainly not new "kinds" in the sense in which the word is used in Genesis. The tomatoes and apples produced by this mechanism are still tomatoes and apples; they have not begun to change into beans and cantaloupes. Stebbins believes that the long-continued evolution needed to differentiate genera, families, orders, and phyla appears to have taken place chiefly on the diploid or at least on the homoploid level in those forms which have had a polyploid origin. The little evidence that exists for evolution by means of polyploids, he feels, is a bit hazardous at present and not too impressive. He says that even with this evidence it does not appear that progressive evolution is furthered by polyploidy.[93] Cameron believes that polyploidy is an evolutionary dead end, and that ultimately polyploids will succumb as a result of their inability to go back to the diploid condition and because genetic variations seem to be hampered by the high numbers of chromosomes.[94]

Other Chromosomal Changes

Chromosomal changes other than polyploidy are actually of little importance so far as evolution is concerned. They are so harmful that they cannot possibly be the means by which evolution has occurred.[95]

Chromosomal Changes as a Mechanism

It is obvious that the evolutionists have not solved the problem of a mechanism for the changes which evolution would require. There is clear evidence of a mechanism for microevolution, but there is no evidence which justifies this as an explanation for and extrapolation to macroevolution. The problem of a mechanism is still a major problem for the theory of evolution.

Medawar says, "The main weakness of modern evolutionary theory is its lack of a fully worked out theory of variations, that is, of candidature for evolution, of the forms in which genetic variants are proffered for selection. We have therefore no convincing account of evolutionary progress, of the otherwise inexplicable tendency of organisms to adopt ever more complicated solutions of the problems of remaining alive."[96] The attacks of Gould and Eldredge on the synthetic theory and their failures to propose a mechanism for punctuated equilibrium is clear evidence that the mechanism for changes of the magnitude required by evolution is still a problem for evolutionists.

Complexity in Creation

It is really all very simple. There are only two choices. One must accept a supreme being, or one must accept the god of chance. If one is unwilling to accept the creation account, which postulates and depends on the supernatural, you must accept chance as the agent that has brought about the created world and the world of life. Either position requires faith, and in many ways to believe that chance has accomplished the complexities we see about us requires more faith than to believe they are the result of the planning and power of a supreme being.[97] Townrow says,

> When the creationist demands time to present his view, it is to present an alternative way of thinking and *not* to present an alternative scientific hypothesis. I cannot help but feel that the request or demand is reasonable in principle. The scientific way of thinking is not the only one there is, and we should not imply by our actions that it is. It is a truism that the same evidence can be interpreted in different ways depending upon our fundamental position.[98]

Azar writes, "If an evolutionist accepts gaps as a prerequisite for his theory is he not arguing from a lack of evidence? If a biologist teaches that between two existing fossils there was a non-existing third (and perhaps there were others), is he not really like the man of religious faith who says, 'I believe, even though there is no evidence' . . . faith is an acceptance where there is no evidence."[99]

Gould speaks of "the creativity of natural selection . . . natural selection is a creator; it builds adaptation step by step." He quotes Lyell as complaining to Darwin that he could understand how selection might operate like two members of the "Hindoo Triad"—Vishnu the preserver and Siva the destroyer—"but not like Brahma the creator."[100]

The Origin of Matter/Energy

A major problem in the theory that the universe has developed by chance is the origin of matter/energy. There are indeed all sorts of theories as to how matter developed in complexity, how non-living matter became alive, and how the variety of living things originated. But there is no suggestion as to how the original matter/energy came into being. There are ideas as to how the 92 naturally occurring elements developed from a single origin of, let us say, hydrogen. But again there is no explanation of how this original matter/energy came into being. To suggest that this is a philosophical rather that a scientific problem is a cop-out, and to suggest that matter/energy is eternal strains credibility. It is interesting to note that a number of the Greeks solved the problem in just this latter way. They could not conceive of how matter/energy could come into being, and so they assumed that matter/energy is eternal. If evolution is to be an explanation, there should be some explanation for the origin of matter/energy. The author of the Epistle to the Hebrews has an answer. He tells us that by faith we understand that the world was created by the Word of God, so that what is seen was made out of things which do not appear (cf. Heb.11:3).

The Fitness of the Earth for Life

The star which we know as the sun is the right size for a planetary system. It has the proper gravitational attraction to hold the planets. Moreover, the earth is placed just the proper distance from the sun. If it were closer to the sun, life would be impossible, for life as we know it can exist only between zero degrees centigrade and 100 degrees centigrade. Indeed, the limitations of life are even more stringent than this because of the fact that proteins and enzymes, which are essential to life processes, break down at even moderately high temperatures. Most of them break down if they are subjected to temperatures in excess of 40 degrees centigrade for any length of time. It is for this reason that most organisms live between zero to 40 degrees centigrade. The earth must, therefore, not be too close to the sun. If, on the other hand, the earth were too far from the sun, temperatures would be so low that life would be impossible.

Moreover, planet earth is the right size to hold an atmosphere. If it were either larger or smaller, the gases which would surround it and make up its atmosphere would not permit the existence of living things.

The earth revolves on its axis. If the earth always presented one face to the sun, as the moon always presents one face to the earth, one hemisphere would be relatively hot and the other relatively cold.

Three minor constituents of our atmosphere—water vapor, carbon dioxide, and ozone—are largely responsible for maintaining a climate which is neither too hot nor too cold. These minor gases screen us from the active ultraviolet rays of the sun. On the daylight side of the earth, they shield us from the heat of the infrared solar rays, and in turn they serve as a blanket to protect the earth from the cosmic cold of space at night. Without these minor constituents the earth would be intolerably warm on the daylight side and inhospitably cold on the nighttime side.

Moreover, temperatures on earth are moderated by the presence of a large quantity of water in a liquid state, This, too, serves to moderate temperatures between day and night.

To suggest that just by chance the right sized planet happened to be the right distance from the right sized star, that it happened to rotate on its axis as well as revolve around that star, and that it happened to have the proper constituents to moderate its temperatures is incredible. It is much easier to believe this is the result of a plan by an all-wise being.

The Fitness of Water

The chemical compound most intimately associated with living things—water—is eminently fitted for its role. It is a common substance, so common that we do not really appreciate its unusual characteristics. Water, which makes up from 80 to 90 percent of all living things, has, first of all, a very high heat-holding capacity. This particular physical property is known as its specific heat. Compared with other substances, a larger quantity of heat is required to bring about a given increase in the temperature of a given quantity of water than to bring about the same increase in the temperature of another substance. An empty pan put on the stove heats up much more rapidly than a pan that is filled with water. The amount of water on the earth's surface, estimated to be enough to form a layer over a mile deep if spread evenly, tends to prevent sudden increases or decreases in temperature, as, for example, between day and night. It is the presence of this large quantity of water that is responsible, too, for the fact that coastal regions are not as warm in summer or as cold in winter as are inland areas. For not only is the temperature of the ocean kept rather constant by the high specific heat of water, but also the atmosphere in its immediate vicinity is affected. This high specific heat of water also prevents the occurrence of catastrophic ocean currents and winds which might result from rapid changes in temperature. The moon lacks water and therefore suffers from marked temperature changes between day and night. During the lunar day the temperatures may be over 200 degrees Fahrenheit; at night they sink to -460 degrees Fahrenheit.

Another important property of water that is significant so far as living things are concerned is its high latent heat of vaporization. In order to change one gram of water from the liquid to the gaseous state of water as vapor, it is necessary to add between 500 and 600 calories of heat, the exact number depending on the temperature at which vaporization occurs. The condensation of the same quantity of water vapor transfers that much heat from the water to its environment. Thus, water in changing to water vapor soaks up a great deal of heat, and when it condenses again it releases that heat into the environment.

This particular property is important in cooling plants and animals. The fact that the vaporization of water removes a large quantity of heat makes perspiration an effective cooling mechanism in animals. Transpiration, the evaporation of water from the leaves, brings about the same results in plants. This cooling effect is extremely important because of the fact that proteins and enzymes tend to break down at temperatures to which plants and animals are frequently exposed.

This property of water also serves to transfer heat from tropical areas to polar areas and to moderate the temperature in both. As water evaporates in the tropics it cools that area; when this same water condenses to rain and snow in the polar areas it releases heat.

Water also possesses a high latent heat of fusion. This means that a relatively large quantity of heat is released when a given quantity of water is changed from the liquid state to the solid state. In freezing, water actually heats up the surrounding atmosphere. Our grandparents took advantage of this property of water to prevent the freezing of vegetables in a root cellar during the winter. When it became extremely cold they would place large tubs of water in the root cellar. The water would freeze at a temperature higher than the freezing point of the vegetables which they were attempting to protect, and in freezing the water would give off enough heat to maintain the temperature of the root cellar above the temperature at which the vegetables would freeze.

Still another property of water and one which is very unusual is the fact that it reaches its greatest density at four degrees centigrade, about 39 degrees Fahrenheit. Most liquids reach their greatest density at their freezing point. This property of water tends to prevent freezing from the bottom up, since water at the freezing point is lighter than water at 39 degrees Fahrenheit and tends to rise to the top. In this way freezing begins at the surface, and the bottom freezes last, if at all, so that organisms living at the bottom of fresh water ponds and lakes are at least somewhat protected.

This property is also important in the melting of water in the spring. Water is a poor conductor of heat, and if streams froze over from the bottom and melted from the top they would melt very slowly. Indeed, in many places they would never melt at all. However, as water melts it becomes heavier and sinks to the bottom, so that the ice is always found at the top where it can absorb the direct rays of the sun.

This property of water is also important in oxygenating the water of ponds and lakes. Water on the surface is relatively well supplied with oxygen; water at the bottom tends to be deficient in oxygen. As the lake or pond cools down in the fall or winter, the oxygen-rich water on the surface tends to sink and to replace the oxygen-deficient water on the bottom. As it freezes, the liquid water now at the bottom moves to the top once more. In the spring when the ice melts, the water produced moves first to the bottom, and then as it becomes warmer it moves to the top once more. Thus, this property of water provides for at least two complete turnovers of water in a pond or lake each year.

Another point to be considered is the "greenhouse effect" brought about by the presence of water vapor in the atmosphere. A greenhouse maintains a higher temperature than the surrounding environment because the glass permits sunlight to pass in freely but absorbs and reflects many of the longer heat rays re-emitted by objects in the greenhouse. Water vapor in the earth's atmosphere does much the same thing. The sunlight is permitted to pass through freely, but many of the longer heat rays re-emitted by the earth are absorbed and reflected back to the earth. This prevents extreme variations in temperature between night and day.

Still another important property of water is that it is the "universal solvent." While not all substances are soluble in water (and it is fortunate that this is the case, since if water were truly a universal solvent we should find nothing in which to keep it), more substances are soluble in water than in any other solvent. Substances in solution react much more readily than substances that are not in solution. Indeed, it seems probable that all the chemical reactions of protoplasm take place between substances in solution or in colloidal suspension. A number of substances which will not dissolve in water form a colloidal suspension with water, and in many ways colloids behave as materials in true solution. Protoplasm itself is a mixture of substances in solution and in colloidal suspension.

The freezing and boiling points of water are unusual. If it were to behave according to the general rule derived from the periodic table it would probably boil at about -80 degrees centigrade, since the heavier compounds of similar pairs invariably have higher boiling and freezing points. Hydrogen sulphide has almost twice the mass as water and should have a higher boiling point. Yet the boiling point of water is 161 degrees centigrade above that of hydrogen sulphide.

Still other properties of water that deserve to be considered are its ability to produce ionization of substances in solution, its high surface tension, and the ability of its molecules to associate or react with one another or with other kinds of molecules.

Water is certainly a unusual substance and in many ways a unique substance. It is preposterous to suggest that this substance by chance happens to have all of these properties which are so necessary for life. It requires less faith and is easier to believe that water is an especially designed substance programmed by an all-wise supreme being to meet the needs of living things as he was designing these living things.

The Origin of Life

Life is an extremely complex substance, both in its chemical makeup and in its physiology. There was a time when people thought it was self-evident that non-living material became alive. They believed that they could observe spontaneous generation, that they could see decaying meat turning into maggots and mud turning into frogs. Today it is believed that spontaneous generation is a myth and that all life comes from life. Consequently, one of the serious problems for evolutionary theory is the origin of life, and this problem is compounded by the complexity of living things.

Modern theories suggest that the origin of life, like evolution itself, was a gradual process. The original atmosphere of the earth is believed to have contained no oxygen at all, nor is it believed to have contained free nitrogen, though there was nitrogen present in the earth's crust. Superheated water vapor is supposed to have been present in the atmosphere, and it is believed that the meeting of this superheated steam with carbides from the earth's crust gave rise to the first hydrocarbons.

The first nitrogen is believed to have existed in the form of metallic nitrides, which when combined with superheated steam produced ammonia, or in combination with the carbides produced cyanamides. These, when combined with the superheated steam, also gave rise to ammonia. Thus, it is believed that ammonia became a part of the earth's early atmosphere.

Most theories of the origin of life today assume that the atmosphere of the primitive earth was a reducing one, that it contained no oxygen whatsoever. Some years ago Urey suggested that the original atmosphere was a mixture of methane, hydrogen, ammonia, and water vapor. He recognized that combining these into amino acids, the building blocks of the proteins, would require substantial amounts of energy. He believed this came from cosmic rays, only a few of which penetrate the earth at present because of the presence of ozone in the upper atmosphere. At Urey's suggestion, S. L. Miller exposed a mixture of these gases to a continuous electric discharge and found that some amino acids were produced. Amino acids must combine into linear chains in the process of polymerization, which requires the loss of water. Ordinarily, this can be accomplished only at relatively high temperatures. However, the chemist S. W. Fox discovered that in the presence of phosphoric acid this reaction would occur at temperatures as low as 70 degrees centigrade. Fox also reported that when he mixed together 18 amino acids common in living systems, these were not distributed in a haphazard fashion but exhibited a considerable number of non-random combinations. It is believed that using energy from the sun and from cosmic rays, organic molecules accumulated in the seas. These formed the primitive living things which began to metabolize in a fermentation process which released carbon dioxide into the primitive atmosphere. Other anaerobic processes followed.

Subsequently, photophosphorylation processes came into existence. These used the energy of light to provide high-energy organic phosphates. This was followed by photosynthesis, which released oxygen as a by-product. Some of the oxygen was changed to ozone, which still serves to screen out most of the cosmic rays. The absence of oxygen prior to this time prevented the oxidation of the relatively simple compounds which could exist in a reducing atmosphere but which would have been destroyed in the present oxidizing atmosphere.

Not to be ignored is the effect of radiation from the sun and from outer space. At present we are shielded by ozone and the Van Allen layers; at least the ozone shield is not believed to have been there from the beginning. Caldwell points out that solar ultraviolet radiation would be a major constraint in the evolution of life exposed to sunlight in the absence of an atmosphere with effective ultraviolet-filtering capacity. He believes that the photochemical "liability" of some bands of ultraviolet "can be very pronounced" and that this is especially true for DNA. There are, to be sure, repair systems, but the repair systems "have their limitations."[101]

In effect, present theories suggest that life originated in a reducing atmosphere which no longer exists and that life by its very presence modified the atmosphere in such a way that life can no longer originate spontaneously.

The work of Miller and Fox did not result in the production of proteins but only of the amino acids, their building blocks. The problem of the origin of the first protein is still a very serious one—and one to which there has been no answer. Proteins are the most complex compounds known, and yet they are fundamental to living protoplasm and characteristic of it.[102] Haldane has suggested that the primal oceans contained reaction systems having the consistency of diluted hot soup. Oparin suggests that these early seas contained colloidal systems called coacervates. Both of these are thought to have brought about the development of proteins.

But Blum does not believe that even this explanation helps solve the problem of the origin of protein. He points out that both heterotrophic and autotrophic metabolism (energy processes which depend upon the release of energy from energy-rich carbohydrates and on the independent capture of energy) are in modern organisms strictly dependent on the assistance of proteins in the form of catalysts. This creates a very real problem, for at a time when life did not exist how did substances come into existence which today are absolutely essential to living systems and yet can be formed only by those systems?[103]

Another difficulty is the mathematical chance of the formation of a compound as complex as a protein. Blum points out that the chance of forming a polypetid of only 10 amino acid units would be something like 10^{-20}. Such a polypeptid is still very small. After the polypeptid stage the proteose stage must be reached, and only after the proteose stage can the protein stage be reached. Blum says that the formation of a polypeptid of the size of the smallest known protein seems beyond all probability.[104]

The amino acids used in protein synthesis are all alpha amino acids (those in which the NH_2 and the COOH groups are attached to the same carbon). With possible rare exceptions, they are all "l" forms (rotating a beam of polarized light to the left) as opposed to "d" forms (those rotating a beam of polarized light to the right). This is the case in spite of the fact that if an optically active substance is synthesized in the laboratory, a mixture of "d" and "l" forms is obtained.

Another question concerns the simplicity and primitiveness of organisms generally regarded as such. Becking discussed the iron bacteria and the sulphur bacteria, which some believe to be models for the origin of living things. He says that they are not simple and primitive. While their outer environment is extremely simple, they need highly complicated internal machinery to translate the simple components into "themselves." Moreover, as far as enzyme systems are concerned, these simple autotrophs represent the highest biochemical complexity. He, therefore, believes that it is most unlikely that organisms similar to these could have been among the earliest.[105]

An additional problem is posed by the complexity of photosynthesis in plants. Steward discusses this. He says that every high school student now professes to know how protein is made because he has learned this in high school and in popular magazines. But Steward asks whether a company set up to make protein in a protein-poor world, on whose board of directors all the recent Nobel prize winners serve, would succeed. He answers, "Perhaps in a century but not in this decade." He goes on to say, "Despite the most glowing scientific brochures I would not buy shares in a company floated to do this." Living cells, he says, have intrinsic properties by virtue of their organization. The subtle way in which they are put together then enables them to do these things. Cells take the biochemically and biophysically feasible events which can be demonstrated *in vitro* to an often infinitesimal degree, and by a subtle sort of biological engineering they render the merely feasible to be practical.[106]

Another example of the complexity of photosynthesis is evident in the studies of Glazer at the University of California. It has been known for many years that photosynthesis consists of a "light" and a "dark" reaction. The former takes place in the light and uses light energy to break up water. The latter is a synthetic reaction building up glucose from the raw materials involved in the process and does not require light.

In the blue-green and red algae there are additional pigments, phycobilins, which harvest the energy of light. These are large multi-protein particles of intricate structure. They are of a variety of colors, such as red, blue, and violet. These colors are ordinarily masked by the green of the chlorophyll. Essentially, the phycobilosomes are batteries which gather the energy of light and distribute it to both chlorophyll-containing photoreaction centers of photosynthesis. The light energy absorbed is transferred to the chlorophyll complexes with an efficiency approaching 100 percent, a truly remarkable efficiency.

Another complexity is evident in the fact that the phycobilin bio-synthesis process is controlled by the wavelength of the light. Phycocyanin synthesis is enhanced in red light, phycoerythrin synthesis is enhanced in green light. Other conditions, too, influence the process. High levels of phycocyanin are obtained under conditions of high temperature, light intensity, and carbon dioxide concentration. On the other hand, nitrogen starvation under high light intensity and carbon dioxide concentration leads to a phycocyanin decrease. All of these contribute to the efficiency of the process.

Once more we ask: could such complexity develop by chance? Is it not easier to explain this complexity on the basis of creation by an all-wise and all-powerful supreme being?

It has been generally believed that living organisms split into two major lines of descent very early in the history of life on earth. The two lines of descent are prokaryotes, organisms such as bacteria and blue-green algae, whose cells do not have a well-defined nucleus, and eukaryotes, more complex organisms whose cells do have a nucleus. Some biologists have proposed a third class whose members superficially resemble bacteria but have genetic and metabolic characteristics that make them unique. These are the methanogens, anaerobic, methane-producing micro-organisms that occur in places as different as the gastrointestinal tract of man and animals, sediments of natural waters, sewage treatment plants, and hot springs. They are involved in the last stages of breaking down organic matter, living on carbon dioxide and hydrogen produced by anaerobic bacteria and converting them to methane. Their cell walls are chemically different from bacterial cell walls, and their metabolism is substantially different from that of bacteria. They also have RNA sequences markedly different from those of other organisms.

It is believed that they have changed very little since they split off from the two other lines of living things. They are ideally suited to the conditions that are thought to have existed very early in the earth's history, particularly in an atmosphere that lacked oxygen and was rich in hydrogen, ammonia, and carbon dioxide. Marvin Bryant of the University of Illinois, however, believes that they should be classified only as an early form of bacteria and not as a class separate from the prokaryotes. He suggests that their similarities to the bacteria are more important than their differences.[107]

In studying the origin of these forms it is recognized that the early fossil record is "sparse and subject to some uncertainty of interpretation." The oldest known bacterium-like structures that could possibly be biogenic are preserved in Swaziland sediments and are believed to be more than 3.1 billion years old. Stromatolitic structures have been dated at nearly three billion years old. These structures are widely assumed to be evidence for the antiquity of blue-green algae but might equally well be interpreted as products of communities of photosynthetic bacteria. The fossil record of micro-organisms believed to be from about two billion years ago clearly shows a great abundance and diversity of morphological types, many resembling present day bacteria and blue-green algae. Geological evidence suggests that free oxygen began to accumulate in the atmosphere at about two billion years ago. Eukaryote cells may have originated as early as 1.4 billion years ago because there is an abrupt increase in cell size and diversity in micro-fossils of this age. The multicellular eukaryote kingdoms—plants, animals, and fungi—are thought to have diverged between one billion and 700 million years ago. Fossils of metazoans believed to be nearly 700 million years old have been found.

It is believed that bacteria very similar to *Clostridium* lived more than 3.1 billion years ago. Bacterial photosynthesis evolved nearly that long ago, and the most ancient stromatolites formed nearly three billion years ago are believed attributable to early photosynthetic bacteria. Blue-green algae appear to have evolved later. There was a great increase in complexity in the fossil record about two billion years ago. Aerobic respiration, it is believed, preceded oxygen-releasing photosynthesis. This suggests that the formation of oxygen from water in the upper atmosphere was important to evolving prokaryotes prior to two billion years ago. Oxygen-releasing photosynthesis arose later and was in a large measure responsible for the final transition to the present oxygen level in the atmosphere. Perhaps 1.1 billion years ago several independent symbioses between protoeukaryotes and various blue-green algae gave rise to photosynthetic eukaryotes. Some of these developed into modern eukaryote algae, whereas a single line, possibly from an ancestral green algae, appears to have evolved into the higher plants.[108]

The origin of life does pose a very real problem for evolutionary theory. Becking says that until advanced chemistry has made the position of biologists untenable he will believe that the living cell is more than a pot full of enzymes.[109] He refers to a symposium held in Moscow in 1957, in which there was general agreement as to the possibility of creating living systems out of inanimate matter, and he goes on to say, "Maybe this confidence is only given to the biochemist. As a biologist I cannot share this optimism (or pessimism)."[110] P. T.

Mora is quoted as saying that understanding of the transition from chemical to life is impossible through modern physics and chemistry.[111]

Recent studies of plant defense mechanisms suggest that plants are also more complex than once thought. Plant biologists once believed that plants were generally helpless, in that they lacked defenses against the various organisms that attack them— infectious fungi, bacteria, and viruses as well as insects. It was believed that plant survival under attack depended on factors beyond its control. Now, however, studies have indicated that plants have defense systems, chemical responses as active and precisely targeted as those of animal immune systems, which protect them against predation and disease. Once more a wide variety of field evidences exists for such defense mechanisms. Already in 1940 K. O. Mueller, an Austrian plant pathologist, suggested that plants were capable of active response to attacks. He worked with the fungus responsible for late-blight rot. In the early 1970s Peter Albersheim and his colleagues realized that plant response to pathogens was triggered by something in the pest, that a message was conveyed from microbe to the plant indicating that the plant was under attack. Since that time a wide variety of instances have been reported.[112] Recently it was suggested that these toxic chemicals are synthesized as a defense against hordes of bacterial, fungal, insect, and other animal predators. Many of these substances, which appear then also in the human diet, are natural mutagens, teratogens, and carcinogens.[113]

Once more it is evident that living things are much more complex than they were believed to be. It is hardly responsible to suggest that these protective mechanisms developed by chance. It is much easier to believe that they were created by an all-wise and all-powerful supreme being.

Biologists accept uniformitarianism in theory but, according to Azar, "inevitably renege in its application." He quotes Claude Villee, who states, "One of the fundamental tenets of biology is that 'all life comes only from living things.' The classic experiment disproving the spontaneous generation of life was performed by an Italian, Francesco Redi, about 1680 . . . . Louis Pasteur about 300 years later showed that bacteria do not arise by spontaneous generation but only from existing bacteria." Nevertheless, Azar says, Villee added, "it is likely that billions of years ago when chemical and physical conditions on the earth's surface were quite different from those at present, the first living things *did* actually arise from non-living material." Villee is quoted as saying, "The spontaneous origin of living things at the present time is believed to be extremely improbable, yet that this same event occurred in the past is quite probable. The difference lies in the conditions existing on the earth."[114]

The Fitness of Carbon

One of the very important elements and the element on which the compounds making up living things are based is carbon. The number of compounds which it forms is second only to the number of hydrogen compounds. Carbon occupies the central position in the periodic table. Consequently, it can achieve a stable configuration either by losing or gaining four electrons. Usually it does this by sharing electrons. Furthemore, it has the ability to form strong carbon-to-carbon linkages, a rather unique quality which only it and silicon possess. Silicon, moreover, shows this ability only to a limited degree. Because of this ability to form strong carbon-to-carbon linkages, long chains, side chains, and rings are possible. This makes possible the wide variety of compounds required for the chemistry of living things.

Another important property of carbon is that its stable oxide, carbon dioxide, is a gas. Silicon has some of the properties of carbon, but its oxide is gaseous only at temperatures of several thousand degrees centigrade. Carbon dioxide is quite soluble in water. This is a unique property, since most gases show only a limited solubility in liquids. Carbon dioxide actually forms a compound with water. This compound, carbonic acid, is the source of the bicarbonate ion. The bicarbonate ion is an amphoteric substance, behaving as an acid in the presence of a base and as a base in the presence of an acid. Substances acting in this way are known as "buffers," and they are important in maintaining the hydrogen-ion concentration of a solution. Living organisms are quite sensitive to changes in the hydrogen-ion concentration, and most of them are killed if it moves very far from neutrality.

The bicarbonate ion is, moreover, an effective buffer. There are a great many weak acids which will buffer near neutrality, and in some living organisms phosphates and proteins act as buffers. But the buffer system built up by carbon dioxide has a particular advantage in that carbon dioxide is a gas which can easily be gotten rid of, and also in that carbon dioxide is a by-product of the organism's metabolism and is therefore constantly renewable. Thus, if an acid is introduced the bicarbonate ion reacts with it to keep the hydrogen-ion concentration near neutrality, and at the same time carbon dioxide tends to form more of the bicarbonate ion. If an excess base is introduced, the carbonic acid tends to neutralize it, once more buffering it near neutrality.

This solubility of carbon dioxide and water is also important from another angle. At ordinary temperatures a given volume of water dissolves almost an equal volume of carbon dioxide (0.9 volumes at 20 degrees centigrade). Under the same conditions only about 0.03 volumes of oxygen dissolves. This is significant in the process of photosynthesis, since it makes available to water plants a relatively large quantity of carbon dioxide.

It requires a great deal of faith to believe that carbon by chance has those properties which fit it for its role in living things. It is far easier to believe that the Supreme Being gave it those properties which He knew were needed for the living things He planned to create.

Obligate Relationships

There are a number of obligate relationships in nature in which there is an interrelationship of organisms difficult to explain on the basis of the evolutionary theory. One of the best known of these is the relationship between the Yucca moth and the Yucca plant, or Spanish Bayonet (*Yucca glauca*). The Yucca flowers hang down, and the pistil or female part of the flower is lower than the stamens or male parts. However, it is impossible for the pollen to fall from the anthers or pollens sacs to the stigma, the part of the pistil which receives the pollen, because the stigma is cup-shaped, and the section receptive to the pollen is on the innermost surface of the cup. The female of the Yucca Moth (*Pronuba*) begins activity shortly after sundown. She collects a quantity of pollen from the anthers of the Yucca plant and holds it in her specially-constructed mouth parts. She then usually flies to another Yucca flower, pierces the ovary with her ovipositor, and after laying one or more eggs creeps down the stalk of the pistil and stuffs a ball of pollen into the stigma. The plant produces a large number of seeds. Some of these are eaten by the larvae of the moth, and some mature to perpetuate the species.

It is difficult to imagine what would cause a moth to collect pollen and stuff it into a stigma. It is hard to believe that the female knows what the result will be; this is generally assumed to be an example of instinctive behavior. Yet this is an obligate relationship, for in the absence of the moth the Yucca plant produces no seeds while without the Yucca plant the moth cannot complete its life cycle. The moth larvae can feed only on the seeds of the Yucca plant. Thus, if the moth should fail to pollinate the Yucca the result will be the eventual extinction of both plant and insect.

How can this phenomenon be explained on the basis of evolutionary development? At the present time the moth cannot live very long without the Yucca plant, for it needs the plant to complete its life cycle. The plant cannot live for more than a few years without the moth, for it would not be able to produce seeds, and with the death of those plants now alive the species would become extinct. It is incredible that both the Yucca moth and the Yucca plant should have reached their present stage of development within a period of just a few years. Yet to assume that at one time both had different methods of completing their life cycles does not solve the problem. Then the question arises as to why they gave up these other methods of reproduction. For instance, if the Yucca plant at one time was capable of being fertilized by several species of insects, why should it evolve in such a way as to be dependent on a single species at the present time? And if the Yucca moth larvae at one time were able to feed on several kinds of food, why did they evolve in such a way as to restrict their diets to a single food?

It takes a great deal of faith to believe that this developed through the process of evolution. It is much easier to believe that God established this relationship at creation.

The Commercial Fig

A similar situation is to be found in the relationship between the commercial fig and the wasp of the genus *Blastophaga* which pollinates it. The fig has a very complicated reproductive cycle. Its flowers are produced in structures called syconia. Each consists of a hollow, fleshy receptacle with a very small opening at the upper end. There are numerous small flowers which line the inside of this hollow receptacle. Two kinds of syconia are produced. One contains both male and female flowers and is called a carpifig. It is not eaten. The other, which produces edible figs, has only female flowers.

Pollination of both kinds of syconia is accomplished by female wasps. The openings of the syconia are so nearly closed by overlapping scales that the wasps have great difficulty in getting in, and they usually tear off their wings in the process. After the female wasp has entered a syconium with both male and female flowers, she lays her eggs and dies. Her eggs hatch, and the young wasps feed on the tissues of the flowers. When the male wasps mature, they eat their way out of the flowers in which they have been hatched and into those occupied by females. Here they mate, and shortly thereafter the males die without leaving the syconium. The females are dusted with pollen from the male flowers, make their way to the outside, and fly to another syconium. If this is a syconium with both male and female flowers the process is repeated. If, however, it is a syconium with female flowers only, the wasp dies without laying her eggs, for the flowers in this case are so long that the female cannot get to the base of them to lay her eggs. In her attempts to do so, however, she dusts the flowers with pollen. These female flowers develop into mature figs which may be eaten.

Once more it is difficult to believe that such an arrangement could have developed by evolution. It is incredible that these two should reach the present stage of development within a relatively short time. If at one time, on the other hand, they had several methods of completing their life cycles, it is difficult to see why they should have given up these additional methods. McDougall says that the course of evolution that has brought about such a strange relationship can scarcely be imagined.[115]

Environmental Problems

There is probably no better illustration of the complexities of the living world and the limitations of the human mind than that demonstrated by our environmental problems. We have learned that natural processes can cope with a limited amount of pollution, but that overloading such systems can only result in disaster. Pollution is always with us and has always been with us. The bacteria of decay and the fungi take care of a great deal of it. Particulate matter in the air, smoke, is actually necessary for the formation of raindrops.

Many of our pollution problems have been due to synthetics. For a time non-biodegradable detergents were the focus of considerable attention. Calling them "non-biodegradable" meant that there were no substances in the environment which broke them down. Many of the harmful carcinogenic substances in our environment, such as DDT and dioxin, are synthetic substances, stable chemicals which do not break down readily and for the breakdown of which there are no substances in the environment.

We live in a complex world which has been provided with mechanisms for the breakdown of waste substances. Our problems arise when we overload the system, or when we introduce into it substances which do not occur naturally in the environment.

Upsetting the Balance of Nature

Many other problems in the natural world are the result of the introduction of exotic species, that is, of species which are not native to the area into which they are introduced. Some of these introductions have been deliberate; others have been accidental. When the early settlers came to Australia, they found there no placental mammals except the dingo or wild dog and a few species of rodents. Coming from Europe as they did, they remembered the fine hunting provided by the rabbit there. So, in an attempt to improve on nature, Thomas Austin imported some 24 European rabbits in 1859. Unfortunately, the European rabbit had no natural enemies to keep it in check. The rabbits multiplied beyond all expectation and did serious damage, destroying the grass upon which the sheep fed.

At first an attempt was made to control the rabbits by building a rabbit-proof fence across the continent in Queensland, but this proved useless, for either the rabbits were already beyond the fence or it was not truly rabbit-proof. Then an attempt was made to reduce their numbers by a system of bounties, but this again proved unsuccessful because of the greedy nature of some who kept a few rabbits around so that they might breed and provide a source of future bounty payments. Only in recent years has a solution been found, and this is the introduction of a virus disease which kills the rabbits and keeps the numbers in check.

Rabbits were introduced in the Macquarie Islands to improve the food resources there. Soon they began to destroy the crops. To repair this damage cats were released. For a time this was successful, as the cats preyed on the rabbits. But once the rabbits had been disposed of the cats attacked the seabirds, whose eggs the natives greatly prized. Once more man intervened. This time he released dogs to keep the cats in check. But the dogs preferred the seals, which were important in supplementing the natives' food supply, and so at the present time attempts are being made to destroy the dogs that man introduced to destroy the cats that man introduced to destroy the rabbits that man introduced!

Nor have we in the United States been immune from such practices. The ranchers of the Toponas District in Colorado, wishing to save their sheep and cattle, carried out a campaign to exterminate the coyotes that were attacking their lambs and young calves. The coyotes disappeared, but the ranchers noticed that their pasture land was no longer able to support as many animals as before. The reason was that with nothing to prey on them, rabbits, gophers, prairie dogs, and other rodents began to attack the meadows. Now the Colorado ranchers are encouraging coyotes to breed.

In the 1870s the German carp was introduced into the streams and lakes of the midwest. This fish is a valuable food fish in Europe, and when first introduced carp sold for as high as $80 a pair. Their introduction was actually promoted by the Bureau of Fisheries. The streams in which they live in Europe are clear, but in the United States they found streams and lakes with muddy bottoms. In feeding off the vegetation of their new homes, the carp swallowed muck with their food, and their flesh took on an unpleasant muddy taste. In the spring great schools of carp came up the streams to spawn, rooting up the bottoms. The result was the destruction of much of the vegetation. Because of this vegetation destruction the water became muddy, and most of the native game fish disappeared from the streams in which the carp were abundant.

An example of the accidental introduction of an import was that of the Gypsy Moth, which reached the United States in 1886. It was hoped that by using the moth a native silk industry could be established. The moth escaped accidentally and has proven to be serious pest.

The state of Florida is involved in an intensive control program to destroy thousands of fist-sized snails, *Achatina fulica*. The origin of the snails is unknown, but the Department of Agriculture believes that several of the snails were brought from Hawaii some years ago by a child as a gift for his grandmother. The snails multiply hermaphroditically—each individual has both male and female sex organs—and reach adulthood in about 30 days.[116]

Such examples could be multiplied. Man is simply not wise enough to anticipate the results of altering his environment. Living things are extremely complex, and any change is likely to cause harm or even to prove disastrous.

Complexity and Evolution

It is simply unbelievable to suggest that all of these complexities have arisen by chance and that there is no purpose in the universe. Some scientists ridicule creationists because they postulate the existence of a supernatural being. Their claim is that they work only with natural, cause-and-effect relationships. But they, too, have a god, the god of chance. It requires more faith to believe that their god could have brought about the complexities of the living world than it does to believe in creation by an all-wise, omnipotent being. Chance changes are far more likely to be harmful than they are to effect improvement. To suggest that the present complexities have resulted from chance developments would require an eternity of time. Perhaps the ancient Greeks and their modern counterparts who suggest that matter/energy is eternal have found the only possible suggestion which would make evolution at all credible.

Does It Matter?

But does it matter?

> To practical men and women in this work-a-day world, do these questions of origin of the universe, the earth's environment, and mankind make any real difference? Cannot such abstract disputations be resigned to preachers and professors?
>
> No, they cannot. For upon the questions about origins depend the answers to the questions of whether life is worth living—and how life is to be lived. . . . The bent condition of human existence in these closing decades of the 20th century is an affliction resulting principally from the decay of belief in an ordered universe and in a purpose for human existence.

So writes Russell Kirk.

Kirk quotes Dr. Stanley L. Jaki, a Hungarian-born priest, as saying, "Darwinism is a creed not only with scientists committed to document the all-purpose role of natural selection. It is a creed with masses of people who have at best a vague notion of the mechanism of evolution as proposed by Darwin, let alone as further complicated by his successors. Clearly, the appeal cannot be that of a scientific truth but of a philosophical belief which is not difficult to identify. Darwinism is a belief in the meaninglessness of existence."[117]

Notes

1. George Gaylord Simpson, *This View of Life* (New York: Harcourt, Brace & World, 1964), p. 12.
2. Roger Lewin, "Adaption Can Be a Problem for Evolutionists," *Science* 216 (1982):1213.
3. Bozo Sklerj, "Comments," *Cold Spring Harbor Symposia on Quantitative Biology* XXIV (1959):215.
4. Ernst Mayr, "Taxonomic Categories in Fossil Hominids," *Cold Spring Harbor Symposia on Quantitative Biology* XV (1950):116.

5. Edward L. Bennett, Marian C. Diamond, David Krech, and Mark R. Rosenzweig, "Chemical and Anatomical Plasticity of the Brain," *Science* 146 (1964):610.
6. Theodosius Dobzhansky, "Changing Man," *Science* 155 (1967): 410.
7. Earnest Albert Hooten, *Up From the Ape* (New York: Macmillan, 1946), p. 278.
8. Mary-Claire King and A. C. Wilson, "Evolution at Two Levels in Humans and Chimpanzees," *Science* 188 (1975):315.
9. Jorge J. Yunis. Jeffrey R. Sawyer, and Kelly Dunham, "The Striking Resemblance of High-Resolution G-Banded Chromosomes of Man and Chimpanzee," *Science* 208 (1980):1145—48.
10. Adolph H. Schultz, "Characters Common to Higher Primates and Characters Specific for Man," *Quarterly Review of Biology* II (1936):449.
11. George Gaylord Simpson, "The Biological Nature of Man," *Science* 152 (1966):473.
12. Dorothy A. Miller, "Evolution of Primate Chromosomes," *Science* 198 (1977):1116—24.
13. H. S. Terrace, L. A. Petitto, R. J. Sanders, and T. G. Bever, "Can An Ape Create a Sentence?" *Science* 206 (1979):891—902. Jean L. Marx, "Ape Language Controversy Flares Up," *Science* 207 (1980):1330—34.
14. Nicholas Wade, "Does Man Alone Have Language? Apes Reply in Riddles and a Horse Says Neigh," *Science* 208 (1980):1349—51.
15. Leslie Roberts, "Insights Into the Animal Mind," *BioScience* 33 (1983):362—64.
16. Ibid.
17. Gina Bari Kolata, "The Demise of the Neanderthals: Was Language a Factor?" *Science* 186 (1974):618f.
18. Gina Bari Kolata, "Human Evolution: Hominoids of the Miocene," *Science* 197 (1977):244—45, 294.
19. Eugene Dubois, "On the Gibbonlike Appearance of *Pithecanthropus erectus*," *Koninklijke Akademie van Wetenschappen te Amsterdam* XXXVIII (1935):578—85.
20. Wilbert H. Rusch, Sr., "Human Fossils," *Rock Strata and the Bible Record*, ed. Paul A. Zimmerman (St Louis: Concordia, 1970), p. 134.
21. Carleton Coon, *The Story of Man* (New York: Knopf, 1954), pp. 399f.
22. G. Von Koenigswald, *Meeting Prehistoric Man* (New York: Harper & Row, 1956), p. 114.
23. Harry L. Shapiro, *Peking Man* (New York: Simon & Schuster, 1974), pp. 21-24.
24. Charles E. Oxnard, "Human Fossils: New Views of Old Bones," *The American Biology Teacher* 41 (1979):274.
25. Roger Lewin, "Were Lucy's Feet Made for Walking?" *Science* 220 (1983):700—02.

26. R. E. F. Leaky and A. Walker, "On the Status of *Australopithecus afarensis,*" *Science* 207 (1980):1103.
27. Roger Lewin, "Studying Humans as Animals," *Science* 220 (1983):1141.
28. John W. Klotz, *Genes, Genesis and Evolution* (St. Louis: Concordia, 1970), pp. 356f.
29. T. D. Stewart, "The Problem of the Earliest Claimed Representatives of *Homo sapiens,*" *Cold Spring Harbor Symposia on Quantitative Biology* XV (1950):101.
30. Hooton, p. 363.
31. Klotz, p. 356.
32. Hooton, pp. 339—46.
33. Rusch, pp. 155—60.
34. W. L. Straus, Jr., "Review of L. S. Palmer's 'Man's Journey Through Time,' " *Science* 131 (1960):220.
35. Calvin Wells, *Bones, Bodies, and Disease* (New York: Praeger, 1964), p. 62.
36. Bertram S. Kraus, *The Basis of Human Evolution* (New York: Harper & Row, 1964), p. 279.
37. Kraus, p. 273.
38. Hooton, p. 338.
39. Kolata, "The Demise of the Neanderthals," pp. 618f.
40. Boyce Rensberger, "Facing the Past," *Science 81* (October 1981):41—50.
41. Theodore D. McCown, "The Genus *Palaeoanthropus* and the Problems of Superspecific Differentiation Among the Hominidae," *Cold Spring Harbor Symposia on Quantitative Biology* XV (1950):92.
42. Klotz, p. 375. Wilbert H. Rusch, Sr., "Analysis of So-Called Evidences of Evolution," *Creation, Evolution and God's Word*, ed. Paul A. Zimmerman (St. Louis: Concordia, 1972), pp. 63f.
43. William C. Boyd, *Genetics and the Races of Man* (Boston: Little, Brown, 1950), p. 324.
44. "Problems of Evolution," *Christianity Today*, X, 8 (January 21, 1966):411.
45. Constance Holden, "The Politics of Paleontology," *Science* 213 (1981):737.
46. Hooton, p. 329.
47. Ibid, p. 303.
48. Joseph B. Birdsell, "Discussion," *Cold Spring Harbor Symposia on Quantitative Biology* XV (1950):107.
49. William L. Straus, Jr., "The Great Piltdown Hoax," *Science* 119 (1954):266—68.
50. *Science* 120 (1954):366f.
51. Vincent E. Smith, ed., *Philosophical Problems in Biology* (Jamaica, New York: St. John's University Press, 1966), pp. 119f.

52. Nicholas Wade, "Voice from the Dead Names New Suspect for Piltdown Hoax," *Science* 202 (1978):1062.

53. Roger Lewin, "Molecules Come to Darwin's Aid," *Science* 216 (1982):1092.

54. Theodosius Dobzhansky, "Evolution of Genes and Genes in Evolution," *Cold Springs Harbor Symposia on Quantitative Biology* XXIV (1959):16.

55. Gina Kolata, "Z-DNA Moves Toward 'Real Biology'", *Science* 222 (1983):495.

56. Roger Lewin, "Do Jumping Genes Make Evolutionary Leaps?" *Science* 213 (1981):634.

57. Gina Kolata, "Genes in Pieces," *Science* 207 (1980): 392f.

58. Klotz, pp. 256—58.

59. "In Brief—In Biology," *BioScience* 20 (1970):240.

60. A. M. Winchester, *Genetics* (Boston: Houghton Mifflin, 1951), p. 228.

61. Ibid., p. 290.

62. E. B. Ford, *Mendelism and Evolution* (London: Methuen and Co., 1949), p. 44.

63. Ibid., p. 37.

64. Ibid., pp. 43f.

65. Nancy K. Eskridge, "Are Antibiotics Endangered Resources?" *BioScience* 28 (1978):249—52.

66. Sewall Wright, "The Statistical Consequences of Mendelian Heredity in Relation to Speciation," *The New Systematics*, ed. Julian Huxley (Oxford: Oxford University Press, 1940), p. 178.

67. Paul R. Ehrlich and Richard Holm, *The Process of Evolution* (New York: McGraw-Hill, 1963), p. 310.

68. R. A. Fisher, *The Genetical Theory of Natural Selection* (Oxford: Clarendon Press, 1930), p. 76.

69. Boyd, p. 146.

70. G. S. Carter, *Animal Evolution* (London: Sidgwick and Jackson, 1951), p. 217.

71. Th. Dobzhansky, *Mankind Evolving* (New Haven: Yale University Press, 1962), p. 142.

72. E. F. Johnston, Ralph Bogart, and A. W. Lindquist, "The Resistance to DDT by Houseflies: Some Genetic and Evironmental Factors," *Journal of Heredity* XLV (1954):177—82.

73. R. W. Gerad, "Experiments in Micro-evolution," *Science* 120 (1954):728—30.

74. George Gaylord Simpson, *Tempo and Mode in Evolution* (New York: Columbia University Press, 1944), pp. 54f.

75. H. J. Muller, "Reversibility in Evolution Considered From the Standpoint of Genetics," *Biological Reviews* XIV (1939): 276.

76. Harold F. Blum, *Time's Arrow and Evolution* (Princeton: Princeton University Press, 1951), p. 148.

77. Roger Lewin, "Seeds of Change in Embryonic Development," *Science* 214 (1981):42.
78. Ibid, pp. 42—44.
79. Stephen Jay Gould, "Is a New and General Theory of Evolution Emerging?" *Paleobiology*, 6 (1980):119.
80. Ernst Mayr, *Animal Species and Evolution* (Cambridge: Harvard University Press, 1962), p. 586.
81. Gould, p. 122.
82. Ibid, p. 120.
83. R. A. Fisher, "The Measurement of Selective Intensity," *Proceedings of the Royal Society of London*, B, CXXI (820) (1936), p. 59.
84. Errol E. Harris, *The Foundations of Metaphysics in Science* (London: George Allen and Unwin, 1965), pp. 232—35.
85. Richard Goldschmidt, *The Material Basis of Evolution* (New Haven: Yale University Press, 1940), pp. 183, 205f.
86. Ernst Mayr, *Systematics and the Origin of Species* (New York: Columbia University Press, 1942), p. 65.
87. Ernst Mayr, "Speciation and Systematics," *Genetics, Paleontology, and Evolution*, ed. Gleen Jepsen, Ernst Mayr, and George Gaylord Simpson (Princeton: Princeton University Press, 1949), p. 285.
88. G. Ledyard Stebbins, *Variation and Evolution in Plants* (New York: Columbia University Press, 1950), p. 308.
89. Gould, p. 122.
90. Stephen J. Gould, "Darwinism and the Expansion of Evolutionary Theory," *Science* 216 (1982):380f.
91. Ehrlich and Holm, p. 190.
92. Bruce Wallace, *Chromosomes, Giant Molecules, and Evolution* (New York: Norton, 1966), p. 42.
93. Stebbins, pp. 359—66.
94. Thomas W. M. Cameron, ed., *Evolution: Its Science and Doctrine* (Toronto: University of Toronto Press, 1960), p. 121.
95. Klotz, pp. 305—12.
96. Sir Peter Medwar, "A Biological Retrospect," *BioScience* 16 (1966):94.
97. Paul A. Zimmerman, "The Evidence for Creation," *Darwin, Evolution and Creation*, pp. 85—92.
98. John Townrow, "Misinterpretation," *BioScience* 33 (1983): 154.
99. Larry Azar, "Biologists, Help!" *BioScience* 28 (1978):714.
100. Gould, "Darwinism and the Expansion of Evolutionary Theory," pp. 380f.
101. Martyn M. Caldwell, "Plant Life and Ultraviolet Radiation: Some Perspective in the History of the Earth's UV Climate," *BioScience* 29 (1979):520—25.
102. Rusch, "Evidences of Evolution," pp. 52—54.
103. Blum, p. 170.
104. Ibid., p. 163.

105. L. G. M. Baas Becking, "On the Origin of Life," *The Evolution of Living Organisms*, ed. G. W. Leeper (Victoria: Melbourne University Press, 1962), p. 34.

106. F. C. Steward, "Botany in the Biology Curriculum," *BioScience* XVII, 2 (February, 1967):88.

107. Thomas H. Maugh, II, "Phylogeny: Are Methanogens a Third Class of Life?" *Science* 198 (1977):812.

108. Robert M. Schwartz and Margaret O. Dayoff, "Origins of Prokaryotes, Eukaryotes, Mitochondia and Chloroplasts," *Science* 199 (1978):395—403.

109. Becking, *On the Origins of Life*, p. 39.

110. Ibid. p. 38.

111. Richard S. Young and Cyril Ponnamperuma, "Life: Origin and Evolution," *Science* 193 (1964):384.

112. Ben Patrusky, "Plants in Their Own Behalf," *Mosaic* March/April (1983):33.

113. Bruce N. Ames, "Dietary Carcinogens and Anticarcinogens," *Science* 221 (1983):1256.

114. Claude Villee, *Biology* (Philadelphia: W. B. Saunders, 1963), pp. 18—20, 521. Quoted by Larry Azar, "Biologists, Help!" p. 714.

115. W. B. McDougall, *Plant Ecology* (Philadelphia: Lea and Febiger, 1941), p. 87.

116. John W. Klotz, *Ecology Crisis* (St. Louis: Concordia, 1971), pp. 44—58.

117. Russell Kirk, "The Rediscovery of Creation," *National Review*, May 27, 1983, 626—41.

Appendix

Specific References to Genesis 1—3
in the Lutheran Confessions

Genesis 1:11—Ap XXIII 8, Tappert, p. 240.
Genesis 1:27f.—AC XXIII 5, Tappert, p. 52.
Genesis 1:27—Ap II 18, Tappert, p. 102.
Genesis 1:28—Ap XXIII 8, Tappert, p. 240; FC SD vii 76, p. 583.
Genesis 2:3—LC I 80, Tappert, p. 375.
Genesis 2:16—FC Ep VI 2, Tappert, p. 480.
Genesis 2:18—AC XXVII 20, Tappert, p. 74.
Genesis 3—FC SD ii 62, Tappert, p. 519.
Genesis 3:3—FC Ep VI 2, Tappert, p. 480.
Genesis 3:6ff—SA Part 3 I 3, Tappert, p. 302.
Genesis 3:15—Ap IV 46, Tappert, p. 106; FC SD vi 23, p. 562.